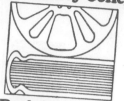

Quality and Pleasure in Latin Poetry

Quality and Pleasure in Latin Poetry

EDITED BY

TONY WOODMAN &
DAVID WEST

THE UNIVERSITY OF NEWCASTLE UPON TYNE

CAMBRIDGE UNIVERSITY PRESS

Published by the Syndics of the Cambridge University Press
Bentley House, 200 Euston Road, London NW1 2DB
American Branch: 32 East 57th Street, New York, N.Y.10022

© Cambridge University Press 1974

ISBN: 0 521 20532 8

First published 1974

Printed in Great Britain
at the University Printing House, Cambridge
(Brooke Crutchley, University Printer)

CONTENTS

CONTRIBUTORS

FRANCIS CAIRNS. Professor of Latin in the University of Liverpool and author of *Generic Composition in Greek and Roman Poetry* (1972)

E. J. KENNEY, F.B.A. Kennedy Professor of Latin in the University of Cambridge; editor of Ovid, *Amores, Ars Amatoria* and *Remedia Amoris* (1961), and of Lucretius Book 3 (1971), and with Mrs P. E. Easterling of *Ovidiana Graeca* (1965)

GORDON WILLIAMS. Senior Professor of Classics at Yale University; author of *Tradition and Originality in Roman Poetry* (1968), and *Horace* (1972), and editor of Horace, *Odes* Book 3 (1969)

R. O. A. M. LYNE. Fellow and Tutor of Balliol College, Oxford, and author of a forthcoming commentary on the *Ciris*

DAVID WEST. Professor of Latin in the University of Newcastle upon Tyne; author of *Reading Horace* (1967) and *The Imagery and Poetry of Lucretius* (1969)

JOHN BRAMBLE. Tutor in Classics at Corpus Christi College, Oxford, and author of *Persius and the Programmatic Satire* (1974)

GUY LEE. Fellow of St John's College, Cambridge; editor of Ovid, *Metamorphoses* Book 1 (1953), and translator of Ovid, *Amores* (1968), at present working on a new edition of Tibullus for the Loeb series.

TONY WOODMAN. Lecturer in Classics in the University of Newcastle upon Tyne, at present working on an edition, with commentary, of Velleius Paterculus

The editors wish to thank everyone at the Cambridge University Press for their kindness, and the care they have spent on this book.

PROLOGUE

Horace prophesied that his fame would increase as long as the silent Vestal Virgin continued to climb the Capitol. Two millennia have passed. Silent virgins have long since disappeared from the Campidoglio. But the ancient poets are being studied today as intensely as ever. This book gathers under a single cover some specimens of what working Latinists in the 1970s produce when they tackle a poetic text some two thousand years old.

A book of this nature is inevitably diverse. The work of six different poets appears here, and several different types of poetry. There are eight different contributors, and therefore eight different approaches. (Some, for instance, have relied on translations as a critical aid, others have decided that their poetic text defies helpful translation.) Similarly the questions raised by these essays are wide-ranging and involve the relationship of contemporary Latin scholarship to modern literary criticism.

As editors we believe such variety to be a decisive advantage. There is everything to be said for showing that one cannot and should not approach every poem in the same way, and that the 'answer' to a poem cannot pop out like so many inches of computer print-out. At the same time contributors have been united in trying to make these essays as wide as possible in their appeal, useful to both students and scholars alike. Technical terms, except the most common, have been explained; and, for both comparative and protreptic purposes, contributors have freely referred to other critiques and discussions where appropriate. In the epilogue the editors have tried to sketch the actual state of literary criticism in Latin poetry as it is represented by this selection of contributors.

Finally there is of course a sense in which these very different essays do belong together. They are all attempting (in A. E. Housman's phrase) to say something both true and new about literature which was written during the late Republic and early Empire – a period of little more than thirty years which produced poetry of a quality which has given pleasure for twenty centuries.

A.J.W., D.A.W.

I

Francis Cairns

VENVSTA SIRMIO
Catullus 31

Paeneinsularum, Sirmio, insularumque
ocelle, quascumque in liquentibus stagnis
marique uasto fert uterque Neptunus,
quam te libenter quamque laetus inuiso,
uix mi ipse credens Thuniam atque Bithunos   5
liquisse campos et uidere te in tuto.
o quid solutis est beatius curis,
cum mens onus reponit, ac peregrino
labore fessi uenimus larem ad nostrum,
desideratoque acquiescimus lecto?   10
hoc est quod unum est pro laboribus tantis.
salue, o uenusta Sirmio, atque ero gaude
gaudente; uosque, o Lydiae lacus undae,
ridete quidquid est domi cachinnorum.

13 *gaudente* Bergk: *gaude* O: *gaudete* X

THE EMOTIONS OF POET AND READER

Catullus' homecoming poem addressed to his villa at Sirmio is one of
his most attractive lyrics. Its effusive representation of that universal
human sentiment, love for home, shows us clearly why Catullus is
reckoned to be outstanding among Latin poets as a creator of the
illusion of spontaneity.

    A superficial reader might happily be deceived by this illusion. He
would have some justification: the 'deceptive' power of poetry is one
of its most basic characteristics. Hesiod, who obviously disapproved,
made the Muses say to him on Helicon: 'we know how to tell many
untrue things, making them appear true' (*Theogony* 27). But the
scholarly critic is more exacting: he is not so much interested in his own
feelings about the poem. Rather he wants to know the intentions of the
poem and the ways in which these intentions have been carried out;

and this involves a stringent effort to discover the meaning of the poem on all its levels.

In these terms Catullus' own feelings are irrelevant to poem 31. We can well believe – although we cannot know – that Catullus felt warmly towards his home at Sirmio. But the poem is not a simple expression of love for home; it is a complex effort to convey this emotion to a reader. The process of conveyance forms an impermeable barrier between us and any questions we might ask about Catullus' own emotions. To us as critical readers, it does not matter whether Catullus really felt the emotion conveyed by a poem or not; the poem can stand by itself as a medium of expression. Of course its seemingly artless simplicity is the principal means whereby the emotion is conveyed.

When we investigate and expound 31 we are not attempting to dissect the reader's experience of the poem. We are investigating the poem itself as objectively as possible. The situation has physical parallels: we can for example investigate the chemical properties of sodium chloride and study their physiological interaction with the human tastebuds; but we cannot with any success describe or analyse the taste of salt. The investigation of poetry differs however in one important respect from the investigation of salt. No amount of scientific erudition will help us taste salt better or more intensely. But the scholarly investigation of poetry, especially poetry of other ages and cultures than our own, does help us towards a truer and deeper experience of the poem. It does so partly by clearing from our minds irrelevant and prejudiced attitudes, which could generate in us false reactions; and partly by informing us about the intellectual content of poetry. So while we cannot compel the 'romantic' to read commentaries on Catullus, we can advise him to do so. Our grounds are that if he does not, he is in danger of splashing in a bath of ignorant and self-generated sentimentality which has nothing to do with Catullus. The application of scholarship to Catullus 31 ought then to produce a deeper and more objective appreciation of it and enable it to be read with a more mature and reasoned pleasure.

POETIC CRAFTSMANSHIP

Catullus was one of a group of Roman poets who adopted the ideals of the Greek 'Alexandrian' literary movement.[1] In his prologue poem (1) he claimed as the hallmarks of his poetry the Alexandrian virtues: fine finish and sophistication in the laboured treatment of small scale work, learning and originality.[2] Technical expertise and careful composition are of course characteristic of all good poetry in antiquity, non-Alexandrian as well as Alexandrian. But in his conscious proclamation and intensive practice of them Catullus is typically Alexandrian. Some of Catullus' craftsmanship in 31 can easily be detected. Something as simple as the relative lengths of individual words demonstrates it well. The first three lines are particularly interesting in this respect. The word-lengths (with *in liquentibus* in line 2 taken as one word-unit) are:

line 1   5, 3, 5
line 2   3, 3, 5, 2
line 3   3, 2, 1, 3, 3

Here Catullus is employing a traditional device which goes back to remote antiquity. J. D. Denniston describes the opening sentence of Herodotus' history in these words:

> 'The power of the sentence is heightened by the relative word-lengths, the four sweeping polysyllables with which it opens being followed by a series of short words (a rhythmic effect which we can observe also in the openings of the *De Rerum Natura* and Sappho's ode to Aphrodite).'[3]

Catullus is doing something similar. The longer words of the first line are followed by the run of shorter words in lines 2–3, broken only by *in liquentibus* in line 2. We can see the effect which Catullus achieves by this device: the praise of Sirmio, a place making its first appearance in literature (see below, pp. 8–9), is made to sound more impressive. Catullus' use of similar patterns of word-lengths to obtain an effect of anticlimax and parody can be seen at the beginning of poem 3.

The remainder of Catullus 31 also shows a delicate sense of balance in word-lengths. Notable is line 10 standing in contrast to line 9 and line 11. It is unlikely that every detail of the word-length patterning is Catullus' conscious creation. But an easy and partly unconscious achievement of balance and alternation between long and short words characterizes the fully trained, competent and careful craftsman-poet. It makes for a flowing, pleasing and natural-sounding diction.

Another very basic and easily observable aspect of poetic craftsmanship is the poet's care to vary the positions of pauses within his lines. This usually involves variation in the use of end-stopped and enjambed lines (for which see below, p. 19 and n. 2). Catullus' care for this in 31 is easy to see. If stopped lines are symbolized by *S* and enjambed lines by *E*, we observe the following pattern:

E E S S E S S E S S S E E S

3

Besides illustrating Catullus' poetic technique this analysis helps with the textual problem in line 13. One of our manuscripts gives us the reading *gaude* which is unmetrical and does not make sense. Another offers *gaudete*. With the latter reading the line has meaning. But if this reading were correct then both lines 12 and 13 would be end-stopped. This would mean that six successive lines (9–14), with no significant internal pauses to break them up, would be end-stopped. Such wooden regularity is not normal Catullan practice. Bergk's emendation *gaudente*, as well as its other advantages (see below, p. 5), turns lines 12 and 13 into enjambed lines. This affords the desired variety in pause-structure; and the fact that it does so favours *gaudente*.

Besides noting whether a line is enjambed or end-stopped, we can distinguish various strengths of enjambment or end-stopping. The end-stop at 10, for example, is stronger than at 3; the enjambment at 1 carries the reader over to 2 with greater force than he is carried from 5 to 6. Further variety is introduced into enjambment when different cases run on to pauses at different points in the next lines. *ocelle* (line 2) and *gaudente* (line 13) take us three syllables into the next line to a pause; but the enjambment from lines 2 and 5 take us to the end of lines 3 and 6 respectively. All these variations prevent the poem becoming monotonous or rhythmically repetitive at any place. The metrical regularity of the iambic scazon is subtly counterpointed by the studied irregularity of the poet's speaking voice.

The details of technique so far observed are accessible on the surface, although they are no less interesting for this. We could add to them, if we wished, some account of the sounds of the words chosen by Catullus and their relation to the meaning of the poem. But this is something every reader can do for himself. It is more interesting to go on to less obvious aspects of poetic technique. One is grammatical variation. For example there are considerable differences in the grammatical status of verbs: lines 1–6 are a statement in the indicative; 7–10 are still in the indicative but are a 'rhetorical' question; 11 returns to statement and 12–14 are in the imperative mood of command. Similarly descriptions of Sirmio (1–3, 12–14) are mingled with reflections on Catullus' travels (4–6, 8–10) and with generalizations (7, 11). These variations overlap. The effect is one of alert liveliness; the poem is never regular or capable of being anticipated.

A fair number of figures of speech and of thought are found in Catullus 31. In line 1 there is assonance and homoeoteleuton[4] in the repeated *insularum*. Catullus prevented this sound-play from becoming trite by placing *que* at the end of the second *insularum*. Another assonance combined with polyptoton (for which see below, p. 70) appears in *gaude gaudente* (12–13). This may be an elegant imitation of a Greek turn of phrase like χαίροντι . . . χαίρων ('you rejoicing to me rejoicing', Homer, *Odyssey* 17. 83) (see below, pp. 11–12). Line 4 employs anaphora (the repetition of a word at the beginning of successive clauses, phrases or verses) in *quam . . . quamque*. In lines 8–10 three clauses describe the joy of homecoming. In lines 12–14, three commands constitute an 'ascending tricolon'⁵ climaxing in the last line. In each case the three clauses are deliberately varied to avoid any suggestion of the prosaic or monotonous. Lines 8–10 show differences in clause length, with the longest clause in the centre. This prevents the final clause of the three becoming so weighty that the poem comes to a halt at line 10. The positions of the verb differ in the three clauses; and there is a deliberate and obvious grammatical variation. In lines 12–14 the first two clauses are short, the third longer than the first two put together. The weight of length is given to the final clause because the poem ends at this point. The positions and grammar of the verbs are again varied.

All these figures and especially the two tricola are meant to convey the plenitude of Catullus' emotions and to give the impression of a man carried away by his feelings. The same joy and pleasure is expressed in other kinds of fullness of language throughout the poem. So in the first few lines we have a style almost reminiscent of Ciceronian rotundity:

paeneinsularum ∼ insularumque	(1)
liquentibus stagnis ∼ marique uasto	(2–3)
libenter ∼ laetus	(4)
Thuniam ∼ Bithunos	(5)

Note however that three times out of four he places one of the pair at the end of a line, at the point where the 'limping' trochaic rhythm is found. Thus one of each pair is contrasted rhythmically with its complement, which occurs in the earlier iambic part of a line. We also find this expansive tendency in the indefinite clauses (*quascumque* . . . , 2; *quidquid* . . . , 14) (*te*, 4, 6; *mi ipse*, 5; *nostrum*, 9; *uosque*, 13), in the phrase *hoc est quod unum est* (11) and in the uses of the emotional *o* (7, 12, 13).

But Catullus, although aiming at effusiveness in poem 31, never lapses into the fault of looseness of composition. Tautness is achieved by his habit of constantly setting words in tension with, opposition to, or concordance with each other. These little touches sharpen the intellectual edge of the poem. So *liquentibus stagnis* (2), designating lakes, is answered by *uasto mari* (3), the sea. *inuiso* (4) is picked up by *uidere* (6). The central section contains multiple contrast and complementation: *solutis curis* (7) corresponding to *onus reponit* (8), *peregrino* (8) contrasting with *larem nostrum* (9), *fessi* (9) contrasting with *acquiescimus* (10), *labore* (9) contrasting with *lecto* (10). Framing the whole section is *curis* (7) corresponding to *laboribus* (11).

These then are some of the detailed resources of Catullus' poetic technique. A more general technical problem faced by Catullus is one of the most difficult faced by all professional lyric poets. This is the problem of how to give the audience in brief all the information it needs to understand the poem while avoiding a tedious statement of facts. In poem 31 Catullus must convey to his audience the following information: 'I have just returned from Bithynia to my beloved home at Sirmio. I did not enjoy being abroad and I am glad to be back.' At the beginning of the poem Catullus deliberately postpones giving hard information. He launches straight away into three lines of colourful praise of Sirmio. These three lines tell the reader little, although there is some informational content. The reader who has begun not even knowing what Sirmio is now knows that Catullus likes Sirmio very much and that Sirmio is either an island or a peninsula. But the main point of these lines is not to give information. They are meant to intrigue the reader and awaken his interest in Sirmio and in the poet's attachment to it.

It is because the reader's curiosity is aroused and his imagination stimulated in the first three lines that Catullus is able to slip most of the information necessary for understanding of the poem into lines 5 and 6: he has left Bithynia behind and is now safely at Sirmio. These two informative lines are strategically placed between 4, in which Catullus tells us something we already know from 1–3 (that he likes Sirmio), and 7, in which Catullus does some general philosophizing. Lines 4 and 7 are deliberately non-informative: they are meant to disguise and palliate the informativeness of 5–6. Catullus' skill extends even to an indirect presentation of the facts of 5–6. We are not told them as plain facts but as something Catullus can 'hardly believe'. The calculated interplay of personality and fact in this presentation is typical of the best kind of writer.

Catullus has reserved one very important fact until line 8 – that Sirmio is his home. The effect of not revealing his relationship to Sirmio for so long is to keep the reader in suspense and so retain his attention. In lines 8–10 Catullus finally reveals his relationship to Sirmio. As in lines 5–6, this fact is expressed indirectly. The general reflection begun by Catullus in line 7 is continued in lines 8–10:

'What is nicer than coming home after wearying foreign travel?' Since Catullus has already told us in 5–6 that he has been abroad, we naturally assume that Sirmio is the home to which he has returned. The poet shows his skill by allowing us to draw a conclusion here rather than simply giving us a fact. The general reflection also implies a second fact about Catullus' stay abroad; it was wearisome. This fact is cleverly represented as an additional reason for Catullus' joy at being home. The first informative section (5–6) was framed between the generalities of 4 and 7; 7 is a centrepiece in the poem and combines with 11 to form a generalizing frame for 8–10. By 11, therefore, we know all the facts we need to know; and Catullus uses a second non-informative address to Sirmio to complete the poem.

This analysis reveals an interesting structure of information conveyance. The poem is constructed like a double sandwich. The first section (1–4), third section (7) and fifth section (11–14) are repetitive, non-informative expressions of Catullus' love for Sirmio and of his pleasure at returning there. The hard core of factual information is sandwiched between these relatively non-factual expressions of feeling; it forms the second and fourth sections of the poem (5–6, 8–10). The particular artistic technique found here is also used, for example, in poem 9, the *prosphonetikon* (welcome-home poem) for Veranius' return from Spain.[6]

We can usefully analyse Catullus 31 also in terms of another kind of structure – that of thematic content. The themes of the poem are arranged in the commonest pattern found in ancient poetry – a 'ring'. The description 'ring-composition' is sometimes applied to poems which end with a repetition and further development of their initial concept. But in the case of Catullus 31 I am using the term to mean a structure in which not one but all the themes recur. The central point is sometimes a unique and non-repeated theme (as e.g. in the form *A B C D C B A*); but sometimes, as in Catullus 31, the central theme is yet another expression of one of the surrounding themes. A ring-structure provided a convenient framework upon which ancient poets could arrange their material. In addition it had the advantages of artistic symmetry and of allowing the poet to achieve subtle contrasts between his two treatments of a single theme. Finally, an ancient poet's audience anticipated that he might employ this device. Their expectation therefore eased the problem of communication between writer and reader.

In Catullus 31 the ring-structure is easy to detect. Sirmio is named and apostrophized at 1 and 12; and the subject of both 1–3 and 12–14 is praise of Sirmio and its lake. The body of the lyric lies between two general expressions of Catullus' pleasure at coming home – lines 4 and 11. Line 7, another such expression, is the centre-piece of the poem. The two informational passages (5–6 and 8–10) are parallel in function and content, the second being a development upon and addition to the first. So we can schematize the poem roughly as follows:

A^1	1–3	Praise of Sirmio
B^1	4	C.'s pleasure in seeing Sirmio (his home)
C^1	5–6	C.'s journey and return
B^2	7	The pleasure of freedom from care
C^2	8–10	Homecoming after work abroad
B^3	11	The pleasure of homecoming and freedom from care
A^2	12–14	Praise of Sirmio and requests to it and the lake to share C.'s pleasure

LEARNING

Another Alexandrian literary catchphrase – the one which is nowadays thought to be most characteristic of the movement – was learning. Catullus in his first poem also claimed this virtue for his work. It used to be thought that this Catullan learning was shown in his longer poems rather than in his short lyrics. But in fact his short lyrics are just as learned in every way as the longer poems.

The learning of poem 31 is seen first in Catullus' choice of Sirmio as its addressee. Sirmio is a small peninsula in the northern Italian Lake Garda. To our knowledge no previous writer had given Sirmio literary or any other kind of fame. It was Catullus who first decided to dignify his unknown Italian home with a literary accolade. In doing so he is in the great tradition of Alexandrian learning. Alexandrian poets did sometimes write about hackneyed myths and places, although always in an original manner. But, as Catullus does here, they often treated unusual or even seemingly insignificant subjects untouched by previous literature (compare Horace on *his* local territory, below, p. 123). This is part of what the greatest of Alexandrian poets, Callimachus, meant when he described how Apollo, in metaphorical language, gave him the following advice about writing poetry:

> I also tell you this: walk a path
> untrodden by chariots; do not drive your carriage

on the common prints of others, or on a wide road,
but on unworn ways, though your track be narrower.

Aetia fr. 1. 25–8 Pfeiffer

The format of Catullus' description of Sirmio further demonstrates his learning. He gives Sirmio encomiastic treatment of a kind familiar to us not only from Alexandrian but also from earlier Greek literature. The eulogistic method is to dignify the unusual and previously unsung deity or hero or place or whatever in two ways: by association with more celebrated deities, heroes, places; and by employing formulaic language of a kind usually employed in association with important deities etc.[7] Catullus says that Sirmio is the gem of all the peninsulas and islands in all the lakes and seas under Neptune's control (1–3). The little lake of Garda is thus associated with the awe-inspiring concept of the three divisions of the universe, under its tutelary deity, the great god Neptune, brother of Jupiter and Pluto. This encomiastic formula strengthens the praise of Sirmio in another way too: it is one familiarly used of great themes for praise – a sweeping favourable comparison of the object lauded with all other things of the same type. It takes the form: 'best of (all) the . . . s in the . . .'. We may compare for example:

πάντων ἄριστον ἄνδρα τῶν ἐπὶ χθονί
the best man of all men in the world

Sophocles, *Trachiniae* 811

optima caelicolum Saturnia magna dearum.

Ennius, *Annales* 491 Vahlen

A use of this formula somewhat similar to Catullus' use can be found, interestingly enough, in Callimachus:

. . . surely all
the Cyclades, most sacred of islands that lie in the sea,
are worthy of song. . .   *Hymn* 4. 2–4

Two further touches in lines 1–3 reveal the flavour of scholarship sought after by Alexandrian poets like Catullus. The extended reference to all the lakes and seas in the world is reminiscent of the encyclopaedic prose works which Greek Alexandrian scholar-poets composed. In particular Callimachus' work, 'On the Rivers of the World', a different but related study, comes to mind (frr. 457–9 Pfeiffer). Such prose catalogues provided raw material for Alexandrian poetry. The 'On the Rivers' is reflected in Callimachus' *Hymn to Zeus* (lines 16ff.); and a similar interest in islands can be detected in Callimachus' *Hymn to*

Delos (lines 13ff., 48ff., 153ff.). The second touch of scholarship in lines 1–3 is the phrase *uterque Neptunus*. Alexandrian poets were deeply concerned with local cults and with the odd characteristics which deities were given in different localities. Mythographers sometimes spoke as though the various attributes meant that there was not one god with a particular name but several. The end result can be seen for example in Cicero, *De Natura Deorum* 3. 53–9 and in Clement of Alexandria, *Protreptikos* 24P with their lists of 'three Jupiters and several Vulcans' and so on.

This interest is connected not only with antiquarianism but with religious syncretism and philosophic scepticism about the more literal side of polytheism. In Greek Alexandrian literature however it is the antiquarian interest which predominates, along with the passion for obscure cult-practices and local history. We can see this from a fragment of Callimachus:

> The Aphrodites – for the goddess is not one –
> are excelled in wisdom by Aphrodite of Castnion,
> all of them...
> for she alone allows the sacrifice of swine.
> > Callimachus, *Iambi* 10. 1–4 Pfeiffer

In Catullus the concept of 'two Neptunes' is just literary ornament, possibly with a humorous overtone (see below, p. 17). But it sets him firmly in the Alexandrian tradition.

Lines 5–6 contain a varied and precise reference to the Thuni and Bithuni, the two tribes inhabiting Bithynia. Ancient poets, including Alexandrian poets, were usually, by our criteria, very ignorant of geography and tend to confuse and misplace localities. But Alexandrian poets tried to give the impression of having accurate and detailed geographical and ethnographical information; and in his reference to the Thuni and Bithuni Catullus is following in their footsteps. He has recently been in the area himself and so has precise knowledge which he can, in Alexandrian fashion, show off to his literary friends back home. There is also some kind of word-play here: Bithuni with its prefix *bi* brings to mind the notion 'second Thuni'. Part of the intention of this word-play may be etymological to show how the Bithuni came to have this name. Etymology, much of it inaccurate, was a favourite occupation of Alexandrian poets, although it is also found in earlier Greek poetry. Another jocular etymological word-play may possibly occur in the final section of Catullus 31. Catullus describes Lake Garda's waves as 'Lydian' (line 13). He may be hinting that *Lydius* is connected with *ludere* and so underlining the aptness of the word to describe the playful waves. If so the proximity of *gaude, gaudente, ridete* and *cachinnorum* would help the reader to guess that this was what Catullus had in mind.[8]

Whether this suggestion is correct or not the adjective *Lydiae* is certainly learned in another way. The Etruscans were supposed to have originated in Lydia and so were called Lydians. To call Garda's waves Lydian is therefore an allusion to the Etruscan settlers who had once occupied the Garda region. This reference recalls the great interest of Alexandrian poets in the foundations of cities and in foundation legends. As well as many poetic treatments of these themes Greek Alexandrian interest expressed itself in Callimachus' prose work 'On the Foundations of Islands and Cities and their Changes of Name' (see Pfeiffer (1949), 339).

IMAGERY

Catullus 31 contains a sustained personification of Sirmio.[9] Catullus is the owner of Sirmio so that Sirmio stands in an inferior social position to him. But it is an exaggeration to suggest, as a recent commentator has done, that Catullus is thinking of his estate as a slave.[10] The arguments advanced for this view were that *ero* (12) is 'the slave's word for his master' and that the notion is continued in the 'ambiguity' of *domi* (14) so that 'Catullus' Sirmio property and its lake setting are spoken of as his household of slaves'. Neither argument is valid. The word *erus* used in line 12 is a substitute for *dominus*. It may be used because the three short syllables of *dominus* are hard to fit into the iambic metre. *Erus* may have overtones of 'common' speech; but it is not specifically and solely 'a slave's word for his master'. It is used in poetry on three other occasions also of the 'owner of a place' – Horace, *Satires* 2. 1. 12; *Epistles* 1. 16. 2; *Catalepta* 2. 4. In no instance is there a notion of slavery. Similarly *domi* does not suggest slavery. The whole phrase *quidquid est domi* is common and colloquial[11] and means '(laugh) all the laughs you have'. In any case a slave household in Latin is *familia* not *domus*.

Catullus then is just the master of Sirmio asking his property to welcome him and personifying his property in his request. The highly personalized quality of Catullus' command to Sirmio and to the lake is achieved by Catullus' exploitation of the Greek greeting χαῖρε, which he has in mind. Roman poets often render Greek terms, sometimes as learned ornament, sometimes also, as here, because they convey a useful shade of meaning. The greeting χαῖρε means both 'hello' and 'show your joy' and so conveys more than the Latin *salue*. Catullus translates it by both *salue* and *gaude*, so that the pair together make up a full equivalent of χαῖρε. Catullus' contemporary Cicero explains the principle behind this type of multiple translation: 'equidem soleo etiam, quod uno Graeci, si aliter non possum, idem pluribus uerbis exponere' (*De Finibus* 3. 15).

By moving from *salue* to *gaude* Catullus strikes a direct and personal note. This is continued in his command to the waters of the lake. From *gaude* he graduates to a more specific instruction to joy – 'laugh'. Waves in antiquity were often said to 'laugh', so that the notion is in no way odd.[12] Yet it forms an apt climax to the personification.

LANGUAGE

Lyric poets in all literatures have the same problem. They must use language not too different from that of ordinary life and at the same time elevate it with an infusion of 'poetic' vocabulary. Or in alternative terms, they must revivify traditional 'poetic' diction without debasing it by blending into it hitherto common or even vulgar vocabulary. This process in Latin poetry is difficult to discuss. Our limited knowledge of the Latin language often leaves us uncertain whether a word is prosaic, vulgar, refined or whatever. The difficulty is particularly acute in Catullus, because one source of his 'non-poetic' vocabulary is clearly the smart clichés and elegant social idiom of the Roman upper classes. Such diction tends to contain an admixture of former vulgarisms purged of their vulgarity by use in unvulgar contexts. A further complication is that old vulgar or common words may in time become 'archaic' and hence 'poetic' through sheer hoariness.

Our pronouncements therefore are highly fallible; but in spite of the danger of error, it is worth trying to glimpse Catullus' intentions. Lines 1–3 contain much elevated language. *paeneinsula*, although perhaps not a distinguished word in itself, gains distinction from its context. The diminutive *ocelle* (line 2) stands in contrast. It is at once urbane and tender. Lines 4–6 are more relaxed; the use of *quam... quamque* is emotive and familiar, as is the phrase *uix mi ipse credens*. But the jingle *Thuniam atque Bithunos campos* provides weight and contrast in these lines. Lines 7–11 begin with the emotional *o* and the rhetorical question of 7. This leads into four lines of familiar but not common language followed by the emotional and prolix summary of 11. At the end of the poem, a formulaic, exalted setting is filled out with a combination of familiar, affectionate expressions (*salue . . . ero . . . est domi*) and of urbane touches (*gaude, gaudente, uenusta*).

GENRE

Catullus 31 is an *epibaterion* – 'the speech of a man who wishes to address his native land on arrival from abroad, or to address another city at which he has arrived . . .' (Menander 377. 32–378. 2).[13] Examples of this genre are found throughout antiquity. It became one of the epideictic speeches taught in rhetorical schools and practised by professional orators; and it is not only defined but exemplified by Menander the Rhetor in his work 'On Epideictic Genres'.

A complete study of the genre would be long and detailed. Present purposes allow only a rough placement of Catullus 31 in its generic context. The *epibaterion*, like many other genres, is in origin Homeric, in the sense that the actions, feelings and circumstances described in the genre were first set down in permanent literary form by Homer. There are several scenes of arrival in Homer;[14] but no single passage is detailed enough to have been considered by late antiquity as the proto-type of the genre. In this respect the *epibaterion* differs, for example, from the *syntaktikon* (the speech of farewell), where Menander specifies the speeches of farewell by Odysseus to Alcinous, Arete and the Phaeacians as the Homeric prototype.[15] Although the arrival scenes in the *Odyssey* taken in combination supplied antiquity with enough basic material for the genre, the lack of a single exemplar was probably felt. This may be one reason why a much later writer made up his own example of the *epibaterion* Odysseus 'should' have given on returning home to Ithaca. This takes the form of a prosopopoeia – a rhetorical exercise in which words appropriate to a mythical or historical character in a particular recorded situation were invented:

> Ithaca, hail! After my labours, after the bitter woes
> of the sea, with joy I come to your soil, hoping to see
> Laertes and my wife and my glorious only son.
> Love of you enticed my heart; I have learnt for myself that
> 'Nothing is sweeter than a man's country and his parents.'
> Anon., *Anthologia Palatina* 9. 458

Here we can see some basic elements of the *epibaterion* in simple forms: the greeting to the land; the toils and the miseries of abroad and of the journey; the man's joy at returning; mention of his loved ones; more expressions of love for his country and family.

13

This is a basic 'personal' *epibaterion*. The other extreme to which the genre could go is shown by Menander's prescription. This is a recipe for the elaborate, formal, public *epibaterion* of a professional rhetor returning to his native city. According to Menander, the rhetor's *epibaterion* could include:

(i) The returner's affection for his native city expressed in some heightened, elaborated form.
(ii) Praise of the founder of the city.
(iii) An encomiastic description of the city's physical features.
(iv) An account of the city's development (?).
(v) A laudatory rendering of the character of the inhabitants.
(vi) A eulogy of the actions of the inhabitants in terms of the four virtues division,[16] embroidered by comparisons.
(vii) A general comparison of the city with others to the city's benefit.
(viii) An epilogue dealing with the city and its buildings.

The place of Catullus 31 between these two extremes can now be seen. It is a personal, not a public *epibaterion*. It consists mainly in expressions of Catullus' affection for Sirmio and of his joy at his return (*ocelle* (2), *quam* etc. (4), 7–11). Various other topoi (i.e. motifs of the genre) stress the personal nature of Catullus' *epibaterion*. The first is mention of the private difficulties which Catullus has surmounted – *solutis curis* (7), *labore fessi* (9) (compare Aeschylus, *Agamemnon* 511; Horace, *Odes* 1. 7. 16–21; 2. 6. 7–8). The second is the topos that the returner had lost, or almost lost, hope of return. Catullus cleverly varies the topos in lines 5–6 by saying that, even now that he is back, he can hardly believe he is back. This topos first appears in the Homeric Odysseus' address to the Nymphs of Ithaca on his return home: 'Naiad Nymphs, daughters of Zeus, I never thought I would see you (again)!' (*Odyssey* 13. 356). It is later found again in *epibateria*.[17] A third personal topos is mention of Catullus' safety (line 6).[18]

Catullus does of course praise his home Sirmio (lines 1–3) and describes its character in laudatory terms (lines 12–14); and in these respects his *epibaterion* is nearer the formal prescription of Menander. Catullus also alludes to another formal topos in *Lydiae* (line 13). Here he is touching on the topos of 'praise of the city's founder' (Menander 382. 24ff.; 383. 9f.) in a reference to the Etruscan 'founders' of the Lake Garda region. But Catullus is mainly concerned to expand personal topoi, to contract others and to blend topoi with artful simplicity so as to produce an illusion of unthinking emotional spontaneity. In this respect also Catullus 31 is comparable with Catullus 9.

THE BLEND OF GREEK AND ROMAN

By Catullus' time educated Roman society and thought were already heavily Hellenized. Roman poetry was influenced through and through by its Greek forebears; and we have already spent some time on an examination of the Greek side of Catullus 31. But at the same time Romans were always conscious that they were different from Greeks; and Roman poets often express their Roman character by additions, omissions or emphases which give a new turn to a Greek genre. In Catullus 31 the Roman side is subtle and not at first obvious.

We can best approach it by considering the difference between Greek and Roman attitudes to the home. For a Greek his native land was sacred: a Greek homecomer would kiss the soil on returning to it; and he would treat the gods of his homeland and household with awe and reverence. This was because the principal gods of localities were wild gods of the open air, owned by no man, potentially dangerous and requiring placation. Even the Greeks' θεοὶ πατρῷοι (family gods) were not possessions of the family but protectors of it. In contrast the principal deity of a Roman homestead was the *lar familiaris* – the household god – a domesticated spirit associated with the farm and its buildings and with human beings, 'owned' by the farmer and worshipped indoors. Other rustic deities of localities were usually amenable to summary and simple dealing. When Catullus returns to Sirmio he does not kiss the earth or show any other reverence to the gods of Sirmio. He simply mentions in passing his Roman *lar* (line 9). We may compare Cato's instructions for the Roman farmer's visit to his *uilla*: 'pater familias, ubi ad uillam uenit, ubi larem familiarem salutauit, fundum eodem die, si potest, circumeat' (*De Agri Cultura* 2. 1). The business-like attitude of Catullus to the religious side of his homecoming is just as typically Roman.

The passage of Cato quoted illustrates also the second Roman factor in the poem. It continues with the Roman farmer surveying his property, asking questions and giving orders. It is imbued with the proprietorial attitude. This too pervades Catullus 31. Such an attitude is not in itself any more Roman than Greek; but in the generic context of the *epibaterion* it contributes to the Roman side of the poem. The standard Greek *epibaterion* is addressed either to an individual or a *polis*, a collection of men. Thus the addressee will tend to be superior or at least equal to the speaker; and such distinctions are important in ancient generic examples.[19] In Catullus 31 however the addressee

Sirmio is a place, Catullus' property, and so inferior, to whom he can give orders like a typical *Romanus paterfamilias*.

ORIGINALITY

Catullus also claimed in his prologue the Alexandrian virtue of originality. This quality is difficult to discuss because the loss of much ancient literature means that we cannot be sure what is really new in the surviving portion. But something can be done; and the concept is a useful peg for a summary of what precedes, since originality is manifest in all the aspects of Catullus 31 which have been treated.

The choice and arrangement of words and rhythms, the grammatical variations, the figures of speech, the information conveyance, the thematic structure, all these evidences of craftsmanship also show Catullus' originality. Little earlier Roman lyric poetry survives with which Catullan lyrics can be compared. But the ease and control which allow Catullus to appear so simple and straightforward are an advance on the laboured quality of the lyric fragments of Laevius and of the elegiac epigrams of the early first century B.C. Catullus' own contemporaries and fellow Alexandrians appear from the remains of their lyric poetry to have written in a manner fairly close to his. But Catullus was the leader of the school so that in this style we should probably see the predominant influence of his originality.

We can also discern Catullan originality in the content of 31. The learned allusions and literary devices are part of Catullus' individual contribution; so too are the word-plays and his poetic diction with its ingenious use of material from several levels of the Latin language. But it is in his use of genre that Catullus shows his greatest originality. Our knowledge of the traditional content of the genre *epibaterion* allows us to detect the alterations made by Catullus to the generic material. As we saw above, Catullus 31 is notable for original and apt selection of topoi, compression of some and elaboration of others. Lyric poets above all others must select among the available topoi because their small scale work cannot usually convey a large number – except in allusive form. They must differentiate their handling of the chosen topoi to produce the genuine flavour of lyric by elaborating personal topoi and compressing others. So Catullus elaborates those topoi which convey a personal relationship between himself, the Roman master, and his home Sirmio. Catullus also provides satisfactory transitions between the topoi and as we saw above, subtly alters the form of some topoi in an original and engaging manner. Finally he combines in his *epibaterion* the commonplace joy of homecoming with a new emotion – the pride of home-ownership – by making his addressee an inferior. At the same time Catullus innovates on general generic practice by expressing also in 31 the emotions characteristic of the other two status relationships – encomium and affection.

The overall tone of the poem is also worth mentioning. It is serious in the sense that it conveys genuine joy at homecoming, and love of home. But the word-plays and jingles, the application of great learning to a small subject, the flippant handling of the learning and the mock heroic beginning and ending, all these combine with the other side of the poem to produce a tone which is humorous without being mocking and serious without being dull.

Catullus 31 is therefore a miniature masterpiece in every way. To appreciate it fully, it is necessary to understand how Catullus created it.

2

E. J. Kenney
VIVIDA VIS
Polemic and Pathos in Lucretius 1. 62–101

Humana ante oculos foede cum uita iaceret
in terris oppressa graui sub religione,
quae caput a caeli regionibus ostendebat
horribili super aspectu mortalibus instans,   65
primum Graius homo mortalis tendere contra
est oculos ausus primusque obsistere contra,
quem neque fama deum nec fulmina nec minitanti
murmure compressit caelum, sed eo magis acrem
irritat animi uirtutem, effringere ut arta   70
naturae primus portarum claustra cupiret.
ergo uiuida uis animi peruicit, et extra
processit longe flammantia moenia mundi
atque omne immensum peragrauit mente animoque,
unde refert nobis uictor quid possit oriri,   75
quid nequeat, finita potestas denique cuique
quanam sit ratione atque alte terminus haerens.
quare religio pedibus subiecta uicissim
obteritur, nos exaequat uictoria caelo.

Illud in his rebus uereor, ne forte rearis   80
impia te rationis inire elementa uiamque
indugredi sceleris; quod contra saepius illa
religio peperit scelerosa atque impia facta.
Aulide quo pacto Triuiai uirginis aram
Iphianassai turparunt sanguine foede   85
ductores Danaum delecti, prima uirorum.
cui simul infula uirgineos circumdata comptus
ex utraque pari malarum parte profusast,
et maestum simul ante aras adstare parentem
sensit et hunc propter ferrum celare ministros   90
aspectuque suo lacrimas effundere ciuis,

muta metu terram genibus summissa petebat.
nec miserae prodesse in tali tempore quibat
quod patrio princeps donarat nomine regem:
nam sublata uirum manibus tremibundaque ad aras   95
deductast, non ut sollemni more sacrorum
perfecto posset claro comitari Hymenaeo,
sed casta inceste nubendi tempore in ipso
hostia concideret mactatu maesta parentis,
exitus ut classi felix faustusque daretur.   100
tantum religio potuit suadere malorum.

66 *tendere* Nonius Marcellus, *De compendiosa doctrina*, ed. W. M. Lindsay (1903), p. 662: *tollere* the MSS of Lucretius.
68 *fana* Bentley.
70 *effringere* Priscian, *Institutiones grammaticae* 10. 6 (*G.L.* 2. 499 K), some late MSS of Lucretius: *perfringere* Nonius, p. 815: *confringere* the chief MSS of Lucretius (*frangere* the first hand of the Oblongus).

62–79 THE ACHIEVEMENT OF EPICURUS

62–71 form a single sentence: (*a*) a dependent section of four verses (62–5) leads up to (*b*) a main section of six verses (66–71). These two sections are parallel in structure: in (*a*) the *cum*-clause occupies two verses and is followed by a descriptive expansion in the form of a relative clause; in (*b*) the main clause similarly occupies two verses, but the relative clause that follows is both longer and structurally more complex than its counterpart in (*a*), having itself a final clause dependent on it. As usual in the more elaborately written parts of the poem, the formal grammatical structure is contrived so as to contribute to the development of the sense. (i) Down to v. 65 each grammatical clause occupies two verses, so that the reader is constrained to pause (where the modern editor duly places a comma), after vv. 63, 65 and 67. Within the first two distichs the writing is 'linear',[1] that is to say the grammatical structure does not transgress the boundaries of the verse: the first verse of each pair forms a grammatically complete sentence, which is expanded in the second verse by a participial phrase, the tense and positioning of the participle (63 *oppressa*, 65 *instans*) being varied. In the third distich the grammatical structure is divided between the two verses by enjambment:[2]

    mortalis **tendere** contra | **est** *oculos* **ausus**,

constraining the reader not to pause at the end of v. 66 but to read on. The effect is therefore one of acceleration of tempo in the last two verses, an acceleration sustained in vv. 68–71, which are all heavily enjambed: *minitanti | murmure, acrem | . . . uirtutem, arta | . . . claustra.* It should be noted that in every case where a noun–adjective phrase is enjambed, it is the adjective that precedes and the noun that follows. This is the usual way of securing one of the distinctive qualities of the best Latin writing in prose and verse, what may be called suspense or 'tension': it may also be seen operating *within* the verse at e.g. 62 *humana. . .uita,* 63 *graui. . .religione,* 65 *horribili. . .aspectu,* etc. The epithet, being incomplete without the noun that it qualifies, engenders expectation and induces the reader to look forward; if the noun, which in sense is autonomous, were to precede, the epithet would be no more than an afterthought.[3] Thus the whole sentence is engineered by Lucretius as a crescendo. (ii) The grammatical structure is 'periodic', though not in the extreme sense that a series of subordinate clauses prepares the way for a final main clause to which the point and climax of the sentence are reserved. The power of vv. 70–1 resides in the imagery and the sound of the words; the effect is not impaired by the circumstance that the clause *effringere. . .cupiret* is subordinate to a clause (*quem. . .uirtutem*) which is itself subordinate to the main clause. In fact Lucretius has deliberately constructed the sentence to bring Epicurus and his achievement into its exact centre, the *sedes maiestatis*:[4] the structure is 4+2+4, the middle pair of verses being both the grammatical main clause and the emotional and rhetorical pivot of the argument. They are formally bracketed together, so to say, by the correspondence of the verse-endings: *tendere contra ∼ (ob)sistere contra.* The whole sentence exemplifies a combination of formal symmetry and dynamic movement that is characteristic of the *De Rerum Natura* both as a whole and in its parts.[5]

62–65 The imagery[6] is, as usual with Lucretius, consistently vivid and physical. The life of man – meaning all humanity – *lay crushed* under the *weight* of superstition *for all to see: ante oculos* is not a semi-formulaic filler, but represents the usual Epicurean appeal to the evidence of the senses; when Epicurus exposed *religio* for what it was he was able to do so precisely because he used his eyes on the visible universe. *tendere contra est oculos ausus,* that is, connotes not only defiance but observation. The domination of man by superstition was and is self-evidently (for those that have eyes to see) shocking and evil – and unnecessary. The framing of v. 62 by the words *humana. . .iaceret* emphasizes a paradox. Man is the one animal who walks upright: Cicero, *De Legibus* 1.26 *nam cum* [sc. *natura*] *ceteras animantis abiecisset ad pastum, solum hominem erexit et ad caeli quasi cognationis domiciliique pristini*[7] *conspectum excitauit*; Ovid, *Metamorphoses* 1. 84–6 *pronaque cum spectant animalia cetera terram,* | *os homini sublime dedit caelumque uidere* | *iussit et erectos ad sidera tollere uultus* – and here he is figured as grovelling before the heavens that he should contemplate unafraid, before a monster of his own creation (for that is to be the implication of the argument). Similarly the picture of *religio* as a lowering presence menacing the world from above (*in terris* picked up by *a caeli regionibus*) is given point and definition by the phrasing of v. 65: *horribili...aspectu...instans*. As West has pointed out, the image springs immediately from a play on words: *religio* = *superstitio* = *quod super (in)stat*.[8] Paronomasia[9] was a standard device in the ancient rhetorical and poetical repertory, and poets did not shrink from it even in solemn and pathetic contexts.[10] It is interesting that the point of this passage appears to have been grasped by Servius (or his source), for in his note on Virgil, *Aeneid* 8. 187 he remarked 'secundum Lucretium superstitio est superstantium rerum, id est caelestium et diuinarum, quae super nos stant, inanis et superfluus timor'. Lachmann (1882) dismissed this with the single word 'ineptissime'; Ernout–Robin (1962) quote it without comment. But Lucretius has not contented himself with a rhetorical figure: he has invested this abstraction with physical characteristics, with a head and an expression. This is a fine imaginative stroke, which he embellishes and develops later in the poem, in the remarkable phrase at 4. 172–3 *usque adeo taetra nimborum nocte coorta* | *impendent atrae formidinis ora superne*; and, most important of all, in his explanation of the origins of *religio* in Book 5. Fear of the gods, he there explains, was born of men's misunderstanding of celestial phenomena: they looked up at the sky and, overawed and frightened by the regular motions and inexorable majesty of sun, moon and stars, they ascribed all to the operation of supernatural – i.e. divine – power:

> tunc aliis *oppressa* malis in pectora cura
> illa quoque expergefactum *caput* erigere infit. (5. 1207–8)

This *cura* is the *religio* of 1. 63, and it is man's own creation, for it rears its head *in pectora e pectoribus*, from within; there is nowhere else for it to come from. It is only when one has reached this passage in a continuous reading of the poem that one can appreciate to the full both the originality and the irony of Lucretius' magnificent image. It is clearly due to his own inspiration – at least the commentators quote no Epicurean source (and *a priori* none is likely): what suggested it to him? Again the clue may be offered by Book 5, this time by the prooemium (vv. 1–54), in which Epicurus is specifically compared, to their disadvantage, with such mythological benefactors of the human race as Ceres and Bacchus and, especially, the demi-god and Stoic hero Hercules.[11] What Lucretius stresses and, as the inflated language makes clear, derides, is the traditional role of Hercules as dragon-killer, destroyer of monsters: he lists the Nemean lion, the Arcadian boar, the Hydra, Geryon, the Stymphalian birds, the man-eating mares of Diomede, and, finally and most elaborately, the dragon of the Hesperides:

> asper, acerba tuens, immani corpore serpens (5. 33).

The real destroyer of monsters, he goes on to say, was Epicurus, who purged the human heart of its passions (5. 43–51). It is, I suggest, possible that the idea of figuring *religio–superstitio* in this concrete guise was put into Lucretius' mind by the complementary image of Epicurus as ἀλεξίκακος, banisher of banes.[12] If this suggestion seems plausible, it is worth remarking also that Lucretius refrains from actually figuring *religio* as a dragon or equipping it with any more specific attributes than a head and a threatening expression. In what follows, as will be seen, it is a rather different image that predominates.

66–71 With the advent of Epicurus the image changes. Humanity now has its first (real) champion. There is strong emphasis on the fact that he was a man: the solemn phrase *Graius homo*, accentuated by the archaic scansion,[13] the juxtaposition *homo mortalis*, and the picking up by *mortalis* of *mortalibus* from the preceding verse, all combine to make the point. A man, *not a god*; in the traditional mythology, as has been remarked, the defenders of mankind were all gods or demi-gods. In the main (and spatially central) clause of this long first sentence Epicurus is seen, as it were, preparing for the assault: he gazes steadfastly back[14] at the enemy, in itself a specifically epic and martial trait[15] and not merely an act of defiance,[16] he takes up his stance, and he refuses to be intimidated by a show of force; rather his courage is stimulated by the opposition, until he longs (*cupiret*) to be leading the charge (*primus*). From the context it seems clear that he breaks *out*[17] and not in: mankind is under siege, confined within the *arta naturae claustra* by its own incomprehension, cowed by nothing more than threatening propaganda and long-range artillery fire. The phrasing and alliteration convey contempt for these empty menaces:

> quem neque *f*ama[18] deum nec *f*ulmina nec *m*initanti
> *m*urmure *c*ompressit *c*aelum.

'The stories and thunderbolts of the gods' almost amounts to a hendiadys[19] meaning 'the thunderbolts which men vainly say are

aimed at them', a belief on which Lucretius later in the poem predict-
ably pours scorn (6. 87–9, 379–422); and the accompanying thunder is
implied to be a loud noise which may so und dangerous but is in fact
quite harmless.

72–77 form a sentence of six verses which falls into two equal halves.
The first half is constructed round a sequence of three main verbs in
the past tense, *peruicit...processit...peragrauit*; the second half,
which is grammatically dependent on the first, has a single main verb
with a triple indirect question dependent on it. Within this fundamentally simple structure Lucretius achieves a number of effects that are
essential to his purpose. In v. 72 the sortie, so to say, takes off; force
and speed are imparted by the rhythm, with diaeresis[20] after both first
and second feet and consequent coincidence of verse ictus and word-
accent, reinforced by repeated *ī*-sounds and alliteration of consonantal
u:

$$\text{érgo } u\acute{\text{u}}\text{ida } u\acute{\text{i}}\text{s animī per-}u\acute{\text{i}}\text{cit}\dots$$

The *uis animi* of Epicurus, thus launched on its course (enjambment of
vv. 72–3 *extra | processit*), escapes 'the flaming ramparts of the world',
the fiery envelope that according to the Epicurean cosmology sur-
rounds the world (5. 457–70); it transcends, that is to say, the physical
limits of our own *mundus* and wanders unchecked through the entire
universe. The sequence of verbs *peruicit...processit...peragrauit*,
with their alliterative prefixes, leads up to the climactic oxymoron[21] of
immensum peragrauit, which connotes the magnitude of Epicurus'
achievement – he has in fact performed the impossible; and the emphatic
(not tautologous: so, rightly, Giussani (1921) and Bailey (1947))
mente animoque repeats and reinforces the idea of *uiuida uis animi* from
which the sentence began. There follows the triumphant return from
campaign, with Epicurus' new status as conqueror brought out by the
central positioning in the verse of the word *uictor*:

$$\text{unde refert nobis} \parallel \text{uictor} \parallel \text{quid possit oriri}\dots;$$

but the spoils of war are, like the victorious sally and the triumphant
progress over the conquered territory,[22] intangible: this is the empire of
the mind. For what Epicurus brought back was his theory of the universe as subject to the operation of inflexible natural laws and the
revelation that there was no place in the scheme of things for the super-
natural, for the intervention of the traditional gods and their caprices.
Everything has its defined properties and sphere of action, its *potestas*,
and the properties of one thing can no more be the properties of another
than this field can be that field. The triple indirect question is an exercise

in theme and variation, with the grammatical structure tied in to the verse-structure by the positioning of the second and third interrogative pronouns at the beginnings of the verses, with anaphora playing the part of connexion:[23]

> *quid* possit oriri,
> *quid* nequeat, finita potestas denique cuique
> *quanam* sit ratione atque alte terminus haerens.

Once again the point is made by the use of highly concrete imagery, in this case with a specifically Roman cast (cf. also the phrase *finita potestas*). Terminus was a Roman god, with a festival of his own, the Terminalia; the last three words of the sentence are emphasized, as were the first three, by diaeresis (with consequent coincidence of verse ictus and word-accent) and assonance:

> atque álte términus haeréns.

78–79 sum up the argument of the 'paragraph'[24] and return us to the point of departure by the device known as 'ring-composition'.[25] *quare*, with a foot to itself, like *ergo* at v. 72, summarizes and dignifies Epicurus' achievement.[26] The roles of mankind and *religio* are now reversed (*uicissim*): now it is *religio* that is down and man who stands erect and triumphant. Once again the imagery is hard and physical (*pedibus subiecta...obteritur*), perhaps with a renewed and slightly more positive suggestion of trampling upon a noxious beast, but still with the metaphor of military conquest and domination uppermost. The final phrase, *nos exaequat uictoria caelo*, is full of power and irony: Epicurus' victory makes man master of the heavens in two senses. Following his lead, human beings can themselves traverse the skies *mente animoque*; but the words also connote a victory over the false gods spawned by *religio*: *caelum* = both the heavens and their (mythical) inhabitants, the conventional pantheon.[27] These phantasms have been annihilated by Epicurus – indeed in Epicurean theory they *were* nothing, having sprung from nothing – and their old empire is claimed by the rightful heir: man.

80–101 THE SACRIFICE OF IPHIGENIA

Lucretius now counters a possible objection to his teaching, that it leads to wickedness. His response, though logically presented,[28] is essentially emotional, a *tu quoque*: it is *religio* and what, against their natural instincts, it induces men to do, that is wicked and impious. To exemplify his thesis he chooses the story of the sacrifice of Iphigenia to appease the anger of the goddess Artemis and so to secure the Greek fleet its passage to Troy. That his example is taken from what we call legend rather than history does not weaken it. For Lucretius and his contemporaries the Trojan War was a real historical event (cf. 1. 471–7); and the cycle of stories connected with it, like the other great mythological cycles, had (and to some extent for the conventionally educated person still has) authoritative and archetypal status. The story of the sacrifice was familiar in both art and literature, especially in a great chorus of Aeschylus' *Agamemnon*, which it seems almost certain that Lucretius had in mind when writing this passage.[29] But by describing the scene as he does Lucretius strips from it the tragic nobility with which Aeschylus had invested it, and presents it as sheerly evil: the murder of a daughter – innocent, virgin, beautiful – by her own father, to placate a god. Worse, a god that did not exist, except in men's minds: the wretched girl was killed for reasons of state, and the real murderers were priests and kings (see below on vv. 99–100).

80–83 constitute a fast-moving period, designed to carry the reader on to the episode proper. All the verses are enjambed and the lines are appreciably more dactylic than the Lucretian average: d s d s, d d d d, d d s s, d d d s.[30] The words *impia* and *sceleris* are picked up and repeated in reverse (chiastic[31]) order in the phrase *scelerosa atque impia*: the charge of wickedness that (by a common rhetorical figure) Lucretius anticipates from the defenders of conventional religion is thrown back at them in the same words. *illa* is contemptuous: 'that religion', sc. which the misguided think good. The metaphor in *inire* and *indugredi*,[32] emphasized by the repeated prefix after *impia*, is more than formal: Memmius (the addressee of the poem) and Lucretius' readers are expected to follow in Epicurus' footsteps in the free exploration of time and space: cf. 3. 3–4 *te sequor, o Graiae gentis decus, inque tuis nunc | ficta pedum pono pressis uestigia signis*. Similarly the metaphor in *peperit* is 'live': the monster *religio* has hatched a dragon's brood of crime and misery.

84–86 The structure and the metre change; the tempo of the verse becomes solemn and dignified. Whereas the preceding four verses were enjambed, in this period the grammatical elements of the sentence are kept within the verses:

> Aulide quo pacto (connecting phrase) Triuiai uirginis aram (object)
> Iphianassai turparunt sanguine foede (verb and adverbial phrase)
> ductores Danaum delecti, prima uirorum (subject).

This is what was described above as 'linear' writing; note however that in the middle verse there is grammatical interlocking, the effect of which is to bring *Iphianassai* and *foede* to the ends of the line (cf. above on 62 *humana...iaceret*). As with vv. 62–71, though the scale is much smaller, there is a duality of structure and effect. On the one hand the sentence is contrived so that the identification of the murderers in the last verse comes as a climax, reinforced by the language and the alliteration. On the other hand the protagonist, Iphigenia herself, occupies the middle position: v. 85 consists of four words only, *decreasing* (unusually) in length and metrical 'weight', with the proper name occupying the entire first half of the verse. The language is elevated, using devices appropriate to the epic such as the periphrasis *Triuiai uirginis* for Artemis, the cliché *ductores Danaum*, the Grecism *prima uirorum*,[33] and the archaic termination of the genitive in *-ai*. All this, in the context, is bitterly ironical; only in the words in which the killing is described is there no irony but plain statement: *turparunt sanguine foede*. The altar is foully stained, literally and metaphorically, with the girl's blood (a fine contrast between the brutal reality and the empty glory of her heroic name): the sacrifice was an act of pollution. Since in ancient religious usage anyone approaching the altar of a god in a state of impurity committed a sin, this equation of the sacrifice itself with defilement implies a strong and conscious irony. Here, as throughout, Lucretius seems to have had Aeschylus in mind: cf. *Agamemnon* 209–11 μιαίνων παρθενοσφάγοισιν ῥείθροις πατρῴους χέρας πέλας βωμοῦ, 'defiling a father's hands with a virgin's blood at the altar'.[34] There is however an important difference: whereas in Aeschylus it is Agamemnon who speaks, condemning himself, a truly tragic situation (see Fraenkel (1950) on v. 206), Lucretius assails the society and the state of belief that made such things possible.

87–92 The sentence is constructed simply but artfully. First comes a subordinate clause dependent on *simul* (*ac*); it occupies five verses, first two lines of apparently 'editorial' description, then three lines describing the scene as it presented itself to the eyes of the terrified girl. The main clause describing her action occupies one verse. There is little or no enjambment: though the construction of vv. 87–8 is continuous, none of the constituents of the sentence is divided between the verses (87 = subject, 88 = predicate). The description in vv. 87–8 is only in appearance 'objective': the placing of the sacrificial fillet on Iphigenia's head is presented as she must have sensed it; the physical details are what she would have felt and so convey through her apprehensions the first shock of revelation of what was to happen to her.

The word *infula* is emphasized by diaeresis (cf. above on v. 72):
Iphigenia had come to the assembly thinking that it was for her wedding,[35] and found herself arrayed for the slaughter. Instead of the
bridal *uittae* it is the sacrificial *infula* that is placed on her head. The
phrase *uirgineos...comptus* suggests that her hair had been carefully
dressed as for a ceremony, and there may be in v. 88 a yet more specific
reference to marriage.[36] Then in vv. 89–91 her eyes take in the scene in
a flash, as she would naturally have seen it: first her mourning father
(*maestum*, when he should have been happy at her marriage), next
the sacrificial attendants, uneasy at what they must do, and finally the
weeping crowd. The treatment is extremely formal. The elements of the
description are presented in a simple enumeration connected by
et...et...-que, each self-contained in a verse; the persons and actions
described are placed in an identical construction at the ends of the
verses:

> adstare parentem
> celare ministros
> effundere ciuis.

The verb on which these infinitives depend is placed symmetrically at
the beginning of the middle verse. More than one commentator has
suggested that Lucretius has a painting of the scene in mind; this is
by no means improbable, but the systematic management of description
formed part of the standard rhetorical training and can be detected in
descriptions of a purely 'literary' character, as for instance in Virgil's
depiction of the Trojan landfall in Africa at *Aeneid* 1. 159–69, where the
mind's eye of the reader is, as here, carefully led from point to point
according to a determined plan. Taking all this in, Iphigenia falls to her
knees in terror (92). The language is simple,[37] but reinforced by
alliteration and paronomasia:

> *m*uta *m*etu terram genibus sum-*m*issa petebat.

Why *petebat*, imperfect? It so happens that the perfect form *petiuit*,
which scans identically, is not attested in Lucretius or otherwise before
Cicero. The explanation of metrical necessity, however, should not be
too readily accepted in this elaborately written passage. Lucretius
must have intended an antithesis between the tenses of *sensit* 'suddenly
she caught sight' (Latham (1951)) and *petebat* 'she began to kneel'. If
the grim ritual was to be completed according to plan and without
provoking a mutiny in the army, she could not be allowed to perform
the act of supplication (which would have automatically entitled her
to the protection of a god), and she is hustled to the altar (the tenses of

27

sublata...deductast again antithetical to *petebat*) before she has time to reach the ground. Thus the terse comment of Munro (1873), that the imperfect is 'more graphic than the perf.', is essentially correct.[38]

93–100 There follow, first a pathetic interjection in the epic manner,[39] then the sacrifice. It is best with Lachmann to place a colon after v. 94, for these two verses look forward to and are explained by the *nam* of v. 95; a full stop spoils the flow of the narrative. Now the tempo again accelerates: after the 'self-contained' structure of vv. 93–4 (93 = main, 94 = subordinate clause) there is enjambment at vv. 95–6, 96–7, 98–9. The unenjambed verses, 97–8, 99–100, are those which carry the weight of Lucretius' message, the enormity of the crime and the reason for it: *non ut...sed*; the self-contained v. 100 provides a muted but bitterly ironical conclusion.

93–94 The language of v. 93 is simple, that of v. 94 both stately and unusual: *nomine donare* for the more ordinary *nomen dare* enhances the value to Agamemnon of what he wantonly destroys, and *patrium nomen* is more poetic and literary than *nomen patris*. Restrained alliteration contributes to the sad and mordantly reflective tone; it is interesting and striking that the metrical structure of these two verses is all but identical:

> nec |miserae | *pro*dess(e) | in *t*ali | *t*empore | *qu*ibat
> *qu*od | *p*atrio | *p*rinceps | donarat | nomine | regem.

The measured effect seems to contribute to the pathos.

95–100 The image first broached allusively at vv. 87–8 is now developed: Iphigenia is lifted to the altar in a sort of cruel parody of the ceremonies used at a Roman wedding. The words *sublata*[40]... *tremibunda...deductast* are equally appropriate to the ritual of mock-abduction, and *deducere* is a technical term of law in this connexion. In what follows the image is made explicit: she was not carried to the altar to be married with the usual forms, including sacrifice (*sollemni more sacrorum | perfecto*), and then escorted to her new home with hymns and rejoicing:

> *p*erfecto *p*osset *c*laro *c*omitari Hymenaeo;

Iphigenia is herself the sacrifice. The hideous paradox is relentlessly enforced by the paronomasia and alliteration of the following verses:

> sed *cas*ta in*ces*te nubendi tempore in ipso
> hostia *c*oncideret *m*actatu *m*aesta parentis.

The adverb *inceste* is separated from its verb and juxtaposed with *casta* to heighten the pathos and horror. *mactatus* occurs nowhere else in Latin and is probably a coinage of Lucretius' own, to fit this context. *maesta* looks back to *maestum* at v. 89; but whereas the word there agreed with *parentem* it is here juxtaposed with *parentis*, a fact which should be recognized in translating. The version of Latham (1951), 'slaughtered to her greater grief by a father's hand', is on the right lines. Finally in v. 100 we are told the object of the murder, a fair wind for the fleet. Here too Lucretius uses specifically Roman terminology, *felix faustusque* being a sacral formula. The use of this phrase is a brilliant device to suggest the wickedness of priestly statecraft, which cloaks inhuman brutality under an impersonal and official form of words. So the Nazis used the term 'final solution (*endgültige Lösung*) of the Jewish question' to mean the murder of six million human beings. All Lucretius' contempt for human stupidity and perversity is expressed in these two words.

101 'Perhaps the most famous line in Lucretius', as Bailey (1947) observes. Its effectiveness stems from the spanning of the verse by the phrase *tantum...malorum* and the reservation of the point to the final word, with which we are once again brought back to the beginning of the paragraph. The word *suadere* also merits attention. Superstition does not force men to do these things, it persuades them. It is on the plane of reason and argument that its evil challenge must be met and crushed:

> hunc igitur terrorem animi tenebrasque necesse est
> non radii solis neque lucida tela diei
> discutiant, sed naturae species ratioque.　(1. 146–8)

APPENDIX

METRE

The passage exemplifies Lucretius' 'pathetic', as opposed to his expository, style (for the distinction see Kenney (1971), 26–9). Thus, while the grammatical and rhetorical structures are relatively elaborate, the metre is relatively regular. The post-Ciceronian norm (to which modern composers of Latin verse are generally required to conform) broadly speaking allowed division between words at the end of the hexameter only in two places: $-\cup\cup\,|-\times$ or $-\cup\,|\cup-\times$. By this standard there are in the passage only a handful of 'irregular' verse-endings: 63 *sub religione* (the possibilities for fitting this essential word into the verse are in any case limited); 64 *ostendebat* (descriptive effect); 68 *nec minitanti* (+enjambment for descriptive effect); 69 *sed eo magis acrem* (speed and vigour); 74 *mente animoque* (emphatic); 97 *Hymenaeo* (the only example in the Iphigenia-episode and a conscious Greek poeticism accompanying a rare elision). Similarly there are relatively few irregularities in the treatment of the caesura; more or less unobtrusive variations from the norm occur at:

> 65 horribili super a|spectu[41] mortalibus instans (2s(trong)[42]+ 4s only; effect emphatic and descriptive)
>
> 76 quid nequeat, finita potestas denique cuique (2s+3w(eak)[42] only)
>
> 79 obteritur, nos ex|aequat uictoria caelo (= 65)
>
> 81 impia te rationis inire elementa uiamque (2s+3w+4(w))
>
> 87 cui simul infula uirgineos circumdata comptus (4s only).

3

Gordon Williams

A VERSION OF PASTORAL

Virgil, *Eclogue* 4

Sicelides Musae, paulo maiora canamus:
non omnis arbusta iuuant humilesque myricae –
si canimus siluas, siluae sint consule dignae.

Vltima Cumaei uenit iam carminis aetas:
magnus ab integro saeclorum nascitur ordo.   5
iam redit et uirgo, redeunt Saturnia regna:
iam noua progenies caelo demittitur alto.
tu modo nascenti puero, quo ferrea primum
desinet ac toto surget gens aurea mundo,
casta faue Lucina: tuus iam regnat Apollo.   10

(teque adeo decus hoc aeui, te consule, inibit,
Pollio, et incipient magni procedere menses;
te duce, si qua manent sceleris uestigia nostri,
inrita perpetua soluent formidine terras.)

ille deum uitam accipiet diuisque uidebit   15
permixtos heroas et ipse uidebitur illis,
pacatumque reget patriis uirtutibus orbem.

at tibi prima, puer, nullo munuscula cultu
errantis hederas passim cum baccare tellus
mixtaque ridenti colocasia fundet acantho.   20
ipsae lacte domum referent distenta capellae
ubera, nec magnos metuent armenta leones.
ipsa tibi blandos fundent cunabula flores.
occidet et serpens, et fallax herba ueneni
occidet; Assyrium uulgo nascetur amomum.   25

at simul heroum laudes et facta parentis
iam legere et quae sit poteris cognoscere uirtus,
molli paulatim flauescet campus arista

31

incultisque rubens pendebit sentibus uua
et durae quercus sudabunt roscida mella.   30
pauca tamen suberunt priscae uestigia fraudis,
quae temptare Thetim ratibus, quae cingere muris
oppida, quae iubeant telluri infindere sulcos;
alter erit tum Tiphys et altera quae uehat Argo
delectos heroas, erunt etiam altera bella   35
atque iterum ad Troiam magnus mittetur Achilles.

hinc, ubi iam firmata uirum te fecerit aetas,
cedet et ipse mari uector, nec nautica pinus
mutabit merces; omnis feret omnia tellus –
non rastros patietur humus, non uinea falcem,   40
robustus quoque iam tauris iuga soluet arator.
nec uarios discet mentiri lana colores,
ipse sed in pratis aries iam suaue rubenti
murice, iam croceo mutabit uellera luto;
sponte sua sandyx pascentis uestiet agnos.   45

'Talia saecla' suis dixerunt 'currite' fusis
concordes stabili fatorum numine Parcae.
adgredere o magnos (aderit iam tempus) honores,
cara deum suboles, magnum Iouis incrementum!
aspice conuexo nutantem pondere mundum,   50
terrasque tractusque maris caelumque profundum;
aspice, uenturo laetentur ut omnia saeclo!

(o mihi tum longae maneat pars ultima uitae,
spiritus et quantum sat erit tua dicere facta!
non me carminibus uincet nec Thracius Orpheus   55
nec Linus, huic mater quamuis atque huic pater adsit,
Orphei Calliopea, Lino formosus Apollo.
Pan etiam, Arcadia mecum si iudice certet,
Pan etiam Arcadia dicat se iudice uictum.)

incipe, parue puer, risu cognoscere matrem   60
(matri longa decem tulerunt fastidia menses),
incipe, parue puer: qui non risere parenti,
nec deus hunc mensa, dea nec dignata cubili est.

1–3 The poet begins with a prayer for inspiration to the Muses whom he deliberately calls 'Sicilian' to designate Theocritus[1] as his model; this emphasis is expanded in the next three words – the theme is to be grander than any normal pastoral theme. This elevation is further explained in the next two lines by symbolizing pastoral poetry in a common feature of its landscape as described by Theocritus, *myricae* 'tamarisks'.[2] The word *humiles* here not only describes the shrub but also suggests that pastoral themes normally lack elevation.[3] The climax of the opening is reached with *consule*: the poet intends to address a Roman consul, therefore the subject-matter (*siluae*) must be grander than usual. The tone is not apologetic, but excited.

4–7 The tone deepens as the poet utters a solemn prophecy. This is marked by the parallelism of each of two pairs of line-long sentences. In the first (4–5), each line is framed by adjective and noun in agreement (*ultima...aetas*; *magnus...ordo*),[4] and the second line (5) expands and explains the first. 'The last age of the Sibylline prophecy has come' is portentous (with precise symmetry) and riddling; the poet says nothing more of this Sibylline prophecy, but his words refer it to the famous Italian Sibyl[5] and assume the reader's understanding of that reference.[6] When the poet says the age 'has come', he is, as will become clear, slightly anticipating: the age will actually begin with the birth of the child, to be mentioned in lines 8–9. The phrase *magnus saeclorum ordo* is ambiguous since there is no definite article in Latin, and it could mean either 'the great cycle of ages' or 'a great series of centuries';[7] the former interpretation is ruled out by line 4 since the 'last age' is clearly identical with the 'Golden Age' of the poem.[8] This means that the common interpretation of *magnus ordo* as referring to the Stoic concept of a *Magnus Annus*[9] is mistaken: that would involve a repetition of the series of 'Ages',[10] and contradict the sense of *ultima aetas*. The Sibyl's prediction is of a final age that will be ideal and will last for ever; *magnus* (5) is used in an emotive, not a descriptive, way.[11] So the lines (4–5) mean: 'The final age of the Sibyl's prophecy has come; a grand succession of centuries is beginning from a completely new start.'

The second pair of lines (6–7) is linked by anaphora of *iam* and makes precise what was meant by (5) *ab integro*. The Virgin is returning to earth: this is Justice, called Virgin because she was identified with the constellation Virgo (Παρθένος), having been placed there when she left degenerate men in the Age of Bronze.[12] Also the age of Saturn is returning: by this was meant the original Golden Age, identified as the age of Saturn by Virgil.[13] This line has a particularly artistic shape, since the repetition of the verb (*redit...redeunt*) can function as a repetition of *et*, and the structure is equivalent to the prose sentence *et Virgo et Saturnia regna redeunt*.[14] The prophecy reaches its climax and becomes most specific in line 7. Here *nova progenies* means 'new race of men', a meaning which becomes obvious if the reader thinks of the Ages of Men as described by Hesiod and Aratus, since the ages were treated by both poets in terms of the men who lived in them, and since Hesiod spoke specifically of each age of men being successively created and destroyed by Zeus. The language reflects the traditional account of the Ages of Men. There is now a pause and change of direction.

8–10 The poet turns aside into a prayer. This break comes after the momentous words *caelo demittitur alto*, and allows the poet not only to give an oblique explanation of *nova progenies*, but also to introduce an astonishing new assertion. A boy is being born and the disappearance of 'iron' men and the rise of 'golden' men are directly[15] related to his birth. The future tenses here are simple and absolutely authoritative. So the poet calls on the goddess of child birth (who is Diana – or Artemis – in one of her aspects) to assist at the birth, and adds, by way of encouragement, that her brother Apollo 'is in control' (*regnat*). The form of the words need not imply an ascendancy of Apollo at the expense of other deities;[16] they can express a fact relative only to the immediate situation.[17] There are several sides to this. In one way the assertion refers to the Sibylline oracle, for which Apollo (as god of prophecy and especially the god who controlled the Sibyl) was the ultimate authority. But the confident future tenses of the poet suggest superior knowledge. Here it is relevant that the break and change of direction between lines 7 and 8 show that the birth of the child was not part of the original oracle but is being added by the poet. This is underlined by the mention of Apollo here since the poet is unlikely to be imagining that there was any reference to Apollo in the oracle which Apollo had himself inspired and, as it were, dictated to the Sibyl.[18] The implication is rather that Apollo has revealed something to the poet that was not mentioned in the oracle,[19] and that the poet suddenly realizes, with Apollo's help, that not only was the oracle true but that the birth of the child is intimately connected with the fulfilment of the oracle. It is because of this that he can assure Diana 'your brother now is in control'; he means by this both that the oracle is coming true and also that the poet is himself personally being inspired by Apollo. For the birth of the child (as will become clear) is associated with the recent Peace of Brundisium[20] (its effects are treated as still in the future) which the poet goes on now to mention in the following parenthesis (11–14); and, beyond the parenthesis, the poet expounds further miracles connected with the child which can only have come to him by Apollo's revelation. So (10) *tuus iam regnat*

Apollo functions dramatically (as it were) as an encouragement to Diana, but poetically to the reader as an indication of the poet's source for his assertions here. That is, the 'control' of Apollo is evidenced by the conception of the child, by the Peace of Brundisium and by Apollo's further revelations to the poet. The control of Apollo may also express the important concept that, civil war being now over, the arts of civilization (which were Apollo's concern) will now be practised without hindrance.

Something of Virgil's meaning here can be illustrated by a poem which was clearly influenced by *Eclogue* 4, that is Tibullus 2. 5. There Apollo is asked to attend at his temple on the Palatine, where Augustus had deposited the Sibylline books, for the installation of the new *quindecimuir*, Messalinus. Apollo is invoked as wearing laurels of triumph (5); this refers to the battle of Actium and points to the idea that Apollo not only foretells the future but also, in some degree, sees that his predictions are carried out. His control of the future is emphasized (11–16) and especially (15–16) *te duce Romanos numquam frustrata Sibylla | abdita quae senis fata canit pedibus*. At a later stage in the poem (71–8) Tibullus lists the portents connected with the murder of Julius Caesar and the last stages of the civil war; then (79) he says that all these were in the past, and calls on Apollo who is now *mitis* to sink prodigies in the sea and to produce an omen for a new age (80–2). Here, quite clearly, the prodigies and the events portended by them are treated as interchangeable and Apollo's actions will be effective not only in foreshadowing the future but also in actually bringing it to realization. It is this way of thinking, by which Apollo is regarded as responsible for the future which he foresees, that Virgil expresses in saying *tuus iam regnat Apollo*; and *regnat* expresses the same idea as Tibullus in (15) *te duce*.

11–14 A parenthesis[21] here adds a further address and connects the miracle with concrete events on earth. This glorious age[22] will begin in Pollio's consulship and the great months will commence their course. Here (12) *magnus* has the same emotive function as in line 5 and it likewise has no hint of the Stoic Great Year about it. The phrase *magni menses* can only naturally refer to the period of a pregnancy and the line is taken up at the end of the poem by (61) *matri longa decem tulerunt fastidia menses*. The implication of these two lines (11–12), as a parenthesis following on the mention of the child and of the child's connexion with the coming of (9) *gens aurea*, is that a child has been conceived in Pollio's consulship and that future generations will date the beginning of the glorious age by saying *consule Pollione*. But the next two lines assign a much more active role to Pollio and culminate in an impressive prophecy (14): Pollio will lead the Roman people in rendering harmless (*inrita*) all traces of sin[23] and so relieve the world from its never-ending fear. Both Horace and Virgil constantly refer to the civil war which tore Rome and Italy apart almost continuously for over half a century from about 90 B.C. as 'sin' (*scelus*).[24] Here there is a clear reference to the part which Pollio played in bringing about the Peace of Brundisium in September 40 B.C.[25] This address to a mere individual human being (after a goddess) is cleverly managed in a parenthesis, as the poet turns aside for a moment from his grand theme, motivated by the mention of the child's birth; these four lines also serve to establish the entire historical setting for the poem.

15–17 The poet prophesies that the child will live as if he were a god on earth[26] and will meet with gods and heroes face to face on earth – thus bringing back a feature of the Golden Age whose loss was explicitly regretted by Catullus (64. 384ff.).[27] Finally, the child will rule with inherited virtues a world made peaceful.[28] This prophecy connects with the poet's words to Lucina (8–10), and, just as it is implied that the poet's prophetic authority is there derived from Lucina's brother Apollo, so here in 15–17 the poet relies on the same prophetic source.[29] This section reaches its climax and end with an impressive line (17) framed between adjective and noun in agreement.[30]

18–45 The next section of the poem (18–45) is divided into three parts. Here the poet switches direction again and apostrophizes the still unborn infant. The contrast in (18) *at tibi prima* means that what has just been said (15–17) was looking further into the future, under Apollo's guidance, than what is now to be said. The poet here describes the Golden Age in nature.

(i) 18–25 The earth will, without cultivation (a traditional feature of the Golden Age), produce gifts for the child[31] – a series of plants with medicinal or cosmetic functions (18–20); pastoral poetry is particularly fond of the names of plants; their sound and strangeness here create one of the specific effects of pastoral poetry[32] and mark the move away from the elevated prophetic style of the last section. Of their own accord (*ipsae*) goats will bring back udders distended with milk: this detail mirrors two features of the Golden Age, its plenty and the absence of work (a goatherd is not needed). A detail follows (22) which belongs to another feature of the Golden Age: men were vegetarians then. This is a widespread feature of descriptions of the Golden Age;[33] only Plato in *Politicus* 271d–e adds the further, logically related, concept that men and animals lived together in harmony so that there was 'no savagery nor eatings of one another, nor was there war nor dissension at all'. It is not that lions did not exist then, but that they were not carnivores. The next detail (23) is introduced by a sense of *ipsa* which differs from that of (21) *ipsae*:[34] 'his very cradle will produce sweet flowers' – this detail is unparalleled in literature before Virgil's time.[35] There follow (24–5) the deaths of snakes and poisonous plants and the growing of the scented Assyrian balsam everywhere. No writer before Virgil says that snakes did not exist in the Golden Age, but in *Georgics* 1. 129 he asserts that god put poison into snakes at a later stage. To destroy them (and poisonous plants) is the one act of violence in the production of the new Golden Age.[36] This section ends (25) with a clause framed between adjective and noun,[37] and notable for its musical sounds.

(ii) 26–36 The child is now depicted as of an age to read, and he reads the favourite themes of Romans, their own great past history;[38] from this he will learn what *uirtus* is. This child has another advantage: he can read of his own father's great deeds (26 *facta parentis*). Once he reaches this age, further features of the Golden Age will appear: (28) corn will grow of its own accord[39] (another 'framed' line); grapes (29) will grow, without cultivation, on thorn-bushes (a 'golden' line);[40] and (30) honey will sweat from oaks.[41] These three lines (28–30) are remarkable for their variation of a basic two nouns with adjectives and a verb (28 has an adverb instead of one adjective) into three different patterns. Now (31–3) comes a warning, a chilling of enthusiasm and a slowing down of the tempo of change, in the form of a tricolon crescendo (see above, p. 5 and n. 5) with anaphora of *quae*. Traces of the old sin (*priscae vestigia fraudis*)[42] will however remain, and these will prolong habits of seafaring,[43] of walling cities (for protection) and of ploughing. All of these were characteristic features of the Iron Age. Then, in another tricolon crescendo (with *alter...et altera...*; *erunt etiam altera...*) the leading characteristic of the Iron Age is exemplified – war; but here, with mention of the Argo and its helmsman Tiphys and the Argonauts and finally with mention of Achilles and the expedition to Troy, war appears in its heroic form against external enemies (*iusta bella* as Romans would have said) and not as the shameful civil war of line 31. Here, in the mention of the Argonauts, there is another recall of Catullus 64, and, of course, most of all in the prominence given to Achilles in the expedition to Troy.[44]

(iii) 37–45 Now (37) the child is pictured as a full-grown man, and the poet foresees that not only will sailing cease (38), but all seaborne commerce (38–9). The reason is (39) that the earth will everywhere produce everything (that man needs), so that exchange of products will be unnecessary. Then two lines (40–1) specify that this will involve man in no labour: no violence will be done to soil or trees or ploughing-oxen.[45] Line 40 is chiastic in form, and 41 concludes the thought with another 'framed' line. These two lines (40–1) also form a tricolon crescendo, with the negatives taken up by the positive *soluet* in 41. Here again is another distinct reminiscence of Catullus 64.[46] There follows a fantastic idea, expressed in complex and difficult language (42–5): dyeing, a deceitful and laborious process, will no longer be necessary – sheep in the fields will grow purple and yellow and scarlet fleeces. The unusual words and the ornate expression of the three colours attempt to achieve something of the same exotic effect in pastoral poetry as the naming of rare plants,[47] but the idea is extrava-gant, even silly, and it is not surprising that it is found nowhere else in Classical literature. The shaping of the lines is particularly artistic: first (42) a line-long general statement, which is a 'framed' line;[48] then the subject of the next clause is stated (43) *ipse sed in pratis aries* and the sentence is executed in the form of a dicolon with anaphora of *iam* and the verb postponed to the second colon;[49] then the whole section is closed (45) with a solemn statement in asyndeton (i.e. without a co-ordinating word such as *et*), commencing with the authoritative *sponte sua* and a notable triple alliteration,[50] and conveying the sense of an unanswerable assertion. Virgil has here lavished his art on an idea which he perhaps sensed would not carry poetic conviction.

46–47 There is a pause and the poet records that 'the Fates, who speak in concord the fixed will of Destiny, said to their spindles "May times like that arrive quickly"'. The word *talis* is often used in Latin poetry to look back over, and sum up, a section of poetic com-position.[51] Here there would be no point in making the Fates say this to their spindles unless they had themselves at some time spoken the prophecy in 18–45. This is simply the poet's way of expressing the idea that in 18–45 he has merely been repeating the prophecy of the Fates. In fact, were it not for the introductory particle (18) *at*, it would be possible to print 18–45 in inverted commas as being the actual speech of the Fates. The purpose of the poet's taking over the exposition of the prophecy was to enable him to dominate the poem in the form of an address to the unborn child from line 18 to the end, since the Fates (as in Catullus 64) would only deliver the prophecy to the parents (not to the child who *ex hypothesi* was not yet conceived). Here is another obvious reference to Catullus 64. Catullus seems to have invented the idea that the Parcae spoke the prophecy about Achilles at the wedding of Peleus and Thetis.[52] Their prophecy there is lengthy (323–81) and is marked by the recurrent refrain *currite ducentes subtegmina, currite, fusi*. The fact that in Virgil the prophecy concerns the birth and growth to maturity of a child (as in Catullus) together with the fact of Virgil's constant reference to Catullus 64 can only mean that the reader is to understand for himself that in Virgil too the prophecy of the Fates was made on the occasion of a wedding. This is underlined by the tense of (46) *dixerunt* which is the only true aorist in the poem (in 4 *uenit* is a true perfect) and which consequently refers to a specific occasion in the past. The contrast between the prophecies in Catullus and Virgil could not be more extreme; that of Catullus is extremely pessimistic, that of Virgil wildly optimistic.

THE MEANING AND STRUCTURE OF 18–47

In other writers Golden Ages were magical times: they existed, they ceased to exist, but one could not possibly imagine a Golden Age gradually coming into being, growing little by little, and no writer before Virgil conceived such a picture. But Virgil has divided the Golden Age into three instalments, as it were, to be handed out at the birth of the child, at his reaching the age of education, and finally at his coming of age as a man. He had the further idea that there should be an intimate connexion between the child's birth and the beginning of the Golden Age. There were two serious difficulties here: (i) the actual establishment of a sympathetic connexion between the child and the New Age; (ii) the devising of some mechanism for slowing down the coming of the Golden Age. Both aims were realized by incorporating among the traditional elements of Golden Ages elements that were quite novel. In 18–25 the novel element is the poet's capacity to address the boy and assert that the new Age would do certain things specifically for him. One of these is the otherwise unheard of flowering of his cradle, and this line (23) is placed in such a position that it breaks up a series of traditional features which could not be linked intimately with the child. The other – the concept of the earth rejoicing at this birth and giving him presents *nullo cultu*, of its own accord (18–20) – has two important analogies in earlier literature. In *Idyll* 17. 64ff. Theocritus (Virgil's pastoral model) describes how the personified island of Cos rejoiced at the birth of Ptolemy and invoked blessings on him. In this, however, Theocritus was inspired by a more significant predecessor: in the *Homeric Hymn to Apollo* (61ff.) Delos takes an active interest in the birth of Apollo, prophesies about him and hopes for future honours from him. This motif was taken up by Callimachus in his hymn to Delos (4. 260–74). This connexion with Apollo is significant in view of the part that Apollo plays in this *Eclogue*. This god was firmly in the forefront of the poet's mind.

In 26–36, the novel element is the mechanism for slowing down the Golden Age, (31) *pauca tamen suberunt priscae vestigia fraudis*, and allowing specific elements of the Iron Age to remain, particularly that of war – but the wars to come are symbolized in terms of the great heroic wars of the past. To anyone looking round the world in 40 B.C. it was clear that war could not immediately end – to look no further the shameful and dangerous defeat of the Roman army under Crassus in 53 B.C. was still unavenged – but it would no longer be disgraceful civil war. The slowing down also allows the elements of ploughing and seafaring to last on and be negated in the third instalment. But there (37–45) it was not sufficient for the poet simply to negate elements that had already been mentioned, and so he invented the fantastic idea of the sheep grazing varicoloured in the fields as a new and positive element.

This whole section of the poem is clearly the real basis to its claim to be pastoral in genre, and it is also the point where Virgil devoted his whole art to combine the details of the Sibylline oracle (the traditional concept of a Golden Age) and his own new inspiration (the theme of the birth of a politically significant child); in this grand conception he tried to weld these themes into a unity, without complete success.

48–63[53] That this should probably be regarded as a single paragraph is indicated by the related imperatives (48) *adgredere* and (60) *incipe*. The address to the child in 48–9 is solemn and high-flown: this is shown not only by the honorific titles that fill line 49, but also by the use of *o* with the imperative in 48, which is always elevated and emotional.[54] The time indication (to become in 60ff. the subject of the poet's impatience), which looks forward over the three periods of the child's growth, is neatly subordinated in a parenthesis. The *magnos honores* which the child is urged to enter upon are those which the poet has described particularly in the three stages of 18–45. On the other hand, the vocative phrases in 49 refer particularly to the poet's revelation (derived from Apollo) in 15–17; the child is *cara deum suboles* 'a cherished descendant of gods', and this phrase is then expanded with the extraordinary *magnum Iouis incrementum*. The meaning here must be that the child is an 'ally', or a 'reinforcement' of Iuppiter,[55] somewhat as Thucydides uses the corresponding Greek word αὔξησις in 1. 69. 4 καὶ μόνοι οὐκ ἀρχομένην τὴν αὔξησιν τῶν ἐχθρῶν, διπλασιουμένην δὲ καταλύοντες ('alone failing to stop the reinforcement of your enemies as it is just beginning but only when it is on the point of doubling'). Virgil's use of *incrementum* here is without real parallel in Latin, but Cicero *De Finibus* 2. 88 (*qui bonum omne in uirtute ponit, is potest dicere perfici beatam uitam perfectione uirtutis; negat summo bono afferre incrementum diem*) and Juvenal 14. 259 (*incrementa domus*) come close to it. It anticipates ideas that Horace and Virgil were later to express about Augustus:[56] for example, Horace, *Odes* 1. 12. 49–52:

> gentis humanae pater atque custos
> orte Saturno, tibi cura magni
> Caesaris fatis data: tu secundo
>   Caesare regnes.

Augustus is there regarded as Iuppiter's right-hand man, his vice-gerent on earth. The child in *Ecl.* 4. 49 is Iuppiter's *incrementum* in that sense.

Now (50–2), by way of encouragement, the poet calls on the child to see how the whole universe anticipates his coming.[57] 'The whole universe, with its arched weight (*conuexo...pondere* i.e. the sky), is trembling.' Then the poet expands the word *mundus* into its constituent parts: the land, the tracts of the sea and the depth of heaven. The trembling of the world (*nutare*) here does not signify imminent collapse, but mirrors the traditional reaction of nature to the epiphany of a god[58] – for example, the phenomena which Callimachus describes (*Hymn to Apollo* 2. 1–8) as Apollo is about to appear in his temple: 'How the laurel branch of Apollo quivers! How the whole shrine trembles! Away, away all sinful persons. Now indeed Phoebus knocks at the door with his fair foot. Look: don't you see? The Delian palm-tree suddenly swayed (ἐπένευσεν = *nutauit*) gently; the swan in the sky sings sweetly. Of their own accord now let the bolts of the gates swing back, now too the locks. The god is now not far off. Young men, prepare for the song and for the dance.' Virgil makes the whole universe move in anticipation, and then (52) calls on the child to see 'how everything is rejoicing at the prospect of the age to come'. Here the 'framed' sentence *uenturo...saeclo* brings the idea to an impressive conclusion.

Now (53–9), with a slight pause (signified by asyndeton and change of direction), the poet in parenthesis muses – mostly to himself, though still formally addressing his thoughts to the child (indicated only in 54 *tua*). He thinks what a wonderful subject for poetry will be the child's life and deeds; and he wishes (53) that 'the final part of a long life may last out' for him – he means, may his life be long and its last part (when the child has grown up) be long enough[59] – and that he may have enough *spiritus*[60] (which means both poetic inspiration and also the capacity to express it) to sing of the child's deeds. When Virgil mentions *tua dicere facta* he is thinking of a different genre of poetry, as when he says to Pollio in *Ecl.* 8. 7–8 en erit umquam | ille dies mihi cum liceat tua dicere facta? and at the beginning of *Ecl.* 6 he regrets that Apollo stopped him (3) *cum canerem reges et proelia* and then consoles Varus with the words (6–7) *namque super tibi erunt qui dicere laudes,* | *Vare, tuas cupiant et tristia condere bella*. In using such language Virgil is always thinking of epic poetry, and it may well be that in such passages he was expressing a real personal ambition. But caution is needed, since these passages are related to the form of *recusatio* which Augustan poets used as an oblique way of expressing such praises, while at the same time declaring themselves incapable, or else postponing them (as in *Ecl.* 4. 54) to an indefinite future.[61] This possibility is underlined by the highly formalized series of comparisons into which the poet now launches himself. The first (55–7) amounts to saying that neither Orpheus nor Linus will outdo him; and the second (58–9) to saying that he will defeat even Pan. The poets or musicians (the concepts were conventionally interchangeable) which the poet thinks of are partly pastoral – Linus appears as a shepherd in *Ecl.* 6. 67 and Pan is the god of the pan-pipes and of the region which Virgil was the first to use as a setting for pastoral poetry;[62] but Orpheus is not particularly pastoral. Antiquity and distinction were the real reasons for choosing Orpheus and Linus; and Pan was chosen not just for his relevance to this pastoral poet, but because he gave ground for an utterance of a particularly Theocritean pattern at a point where Virgil's pastoral model was being left far behind. In fact, it looks as if Virgil in lines 55–9 deliberately employed some characteristic conventions of pastoral poetry. Patterned phrases, with symmetrical elements of repetition are a characteristic feature of Theocritus' poetry.[63] Virgil also uses these patterns in his *Eclogues*, but in a much more restrained way. The structure of 55–7, where *non me carminibus uincet* is followed by three parallel clauses in which the subject is successively expanded, has some similarity in literary motivation to Theocritus, *Idyll* 16. 3–4:

Μοῖσαι μὲν θεαὶ ἐντί, θεοὺς θεαὶ ἀείδοντι·
ἄμμες δὲ βροτοὶ οἵδε, βροτοὺς βροτοὶ ἀείδωμεν.

The Muses are goddesses and, as goddesses, they sing of gods; but we are mortals here and, as mortals, let us sing of mortals.

The Virgilian structure is more sophisticated, but what both have in common is the interest in giving the patterning of verbal structures priority over the actual thought which has to be expressed. This motive can be seen in various passages of the *Eclogues*: for instance, 6. 9–12; 7. 1–5; 8. 22–4; 8. 47–50; 8. 52–6. It can be no coincidence that this motive operates in Virgil most strongly at the beginnings of poems and in particularly formal passages of song. The motive reaches a climax, however, in *Eclogue* 4. 58–9, and to this there are clear Theocritean analogies:[64] for example *Idyll* 1. 120–1:

> Δάφνις ἐγὼν ὅδε τῆνος ὁ τὰς βόας ὧδε νομεύων,
> Δάφνις ὁ τὼς ταύρως καὶ πόρτιας ὧδε ποτίσδων.

> *I am that Daphnis who here herded his cows; the Daphnis who here watered his bulls and heifers.*

or *Idyll* 11. 22–3:

> φοιτῇς δ’ αὖθ’ οὕτως ὅκκα γλυκὺς ὕπνος ἔχῃ με,
> οἴχῃ δ’ εὐθὺς ἰοῖσ’ ὅκκα γλυκὺς ὕπνος ἀνῇ με.

> *You come right near to me whenever sweet sleep subdues me and you go straight away whenever sweet sleep releases me.*

The only real analogy in the *Eclogues* to *Ecl.* 4. 58–9 is 6. 29–30:

> nec tantum Phoebo gaudet Parnasia rupes,
> nec tantum Rhodope miratur et Ismarus Orphea.

The stylistic motive in *Eclogue* 4. 55–9 must be that, at this point, where the poet looks forward to a different form of poetic composition and a new subject-matter, he casts his thought in the most characteristically pastoral style – a feature which also serves to underline the element of *recusatio* here (i.e. this really is a pastoral poet who is expressing this wish and one who is still imprisoned within the pastoral form). The reader is not unjustified in feeling that the poet is here anxious to assert his pastoral identity in a poem which has risen so far above the traditional genre.

Now (60–4) the poet appeals again to the child really to hurry up and be born, though he puts this in the form of a request to recognize his mother with a smile and discreetly expresses in a parenthesis the idea that his mother has carried him long enough (the line directly recalls line 12). He urgently repeats the request, and adds (62–3) the warning that if a child does not smile on his mother,[65] then no god will invite him to his table nor goddess to her bed. In this he thinks mainly of Hercules, the hero who was reckoned among the great benefactors of mankind and who was admitted to heaven and given Hebe in marriage.[66] But the second element of the warning (which ends the poem) also recalls Anchises who was considered by Venus worthy of her bed and who thereby founded the Julian line (which issued most recently in Julius Caesar and Octavian). The patterning of the language in the last sentence conceals a lightness of touch that is at the opposite extreme from the solemnity of the poem's opening (in 3ff.).

THE 'MEANING' OF THE POEM

The clue lies in the historical background. After the battle of Philippi in 42 B.C.,[67] Antony, the senior partner, sent Octavian back with the veterans due for retirement to Italy, while he himself went to the Near East. Octavian's task was the highly dangerous one of pensioning off the veterans in the only way then known to the Romans, i.e. by confiscating land and settling them on it.[68] This led – as no doubt Antony anticipated – to fierce civil war in Italy. A key figure in all this was Gaius Asinius Pollio who had been a close friend of Julius Caesar, but who had no taste for civil war and had only joined Caesar out of friendship (see Cicero, *Ad Fam.* 10. 31). After the murder of Caesar in 44 B.C., his natural allegiance lay with Antony. He had in 43 B.C. been designated to the consulship for 40 B.C., but during the civil wars over Octavian's resettlement of veterans in 41/40 B.C. he played a very ambiguous part (he was, and remained all his life, a foe to Octavian). However, when Antony came to Italy in September 40 B.C. and there seemed a strong likelihood of civil war breaking out again on a large scale between Antony and Octavian, Pollio was instrumental in bringing both men to the conference table in October 40 B.C. at which they arranged the Peace of Brundisium, agreeing to divide the Roman empire virtually between them, with Octavian taking Italy and the West, and Antony the East – and at the same time marrying Octavian's sister, Octavia.

This was the point at which *Eclogue* 4 was composed: peace in the Roman world – i.e. the cessation of civil war – seemed assured and Virgil felt inspired to interpret this as the beginning of a new age. No doubt the Sibylline oracle, declaring this to be the beginning of a new Golden Age, was a reality. But the additional concept of a child whose birth was to mark the beginning of the age was Virgil's. The only real analogy which Virgil had for a poem of this sort in a pastoral collection was Theocritus, *Idyll* 17. There the centre of the poem (53–120) is occupied with the praises of the son of Ptolemy and Berenice; the happiness of the couple occupies the poet and is led up to by the portrait of Ptolemy Soter in heaven, carousing with Alexander the Great and Herakles; then Herakles' happiness with Hebe leads to the marital bliss of Ptolemy and Berenice. The poem finally ends with the marriage of Ptolemy Philadelphus to his sister. Virgil owed to this poem the themes of the birth of a child of great promise, the feasting in the presence of the gods, and the happiness of Herakles.

What is remarkable in Virgil's poem is that there is no indication of the child's identity. There are however two themes which converge on this. (i) There is a great series of references to Catullus 64, culminating in the mention of the *Parcae* (46–7). Catullus' poem is about the marriage of Peleus and Thetis, and a large proportion of it concentrates on the prophecy of the *Parcae* about the child of the wedding, Achilles: it is a most pessimistic prophecy and culminates in that break between divine and human which meant the gods no longer appeared on earth. Virgil's poem moves in the opposite direction: it is highly optimistic and it foresees a new intermingling of gods and men (15–17). At the same time, the clear references to Catullus 64, and particularly the entrance of the *Parcae*, imply a wedding. (ii) The number of references which Virgil makes to the child clearly suggest a divine origin and relationship (15–16, 49, 62–3), and also nominate him as a future ruler of the Roman world (17). Only one family in Rome at the time could be designated in these terms (especially in view of the hint at Anchises in 63): that was the Julian, whose most recent representative, Julius Caesar, had been officially deified in January 42 B.C.

Now it would have been grossly tactless for Virgil, in the context of the Peace of Brundisium, to designate Antony's putative son (he would be the son of Octavia, sister of Octavian, and a member of the Julian family) as the future – and favoured – ruler of the world. But, by an odd coincidence, probably only weeks before the Peace of Brundisium, Octavian himself had married Scribonia, the sister-in-law of Sextus Pompeius, an adherent of Antony, and a desperate enemy of Octavian.[69] Virgil seems to have made use of this unique situation to concentrate his poetic attention on the child of a marriage which had Julian (and so divine) connexions in such a way that he said nothing of the marriage itself, much less of the actual parents. Either marriage could be meant,[70] and in the atmosphere of peace and concord decision was unnecessary. The reminiscences of Catullus 64 were enough for the imaginative reader – so Virgil hoped.[71]

The poem is astonishingly ambitious, and in its imaginative grasp it

4

R. O. A. M. Lyne
SCILICET ET TEMPVS VENIET...
Virgil, *Georgics* 1. 463–514

THE WORLD OF THE 'GEORGICS'

Virgil's *Georgics* is scarcely simply a didactic poem to aid the cultivator. To miss any of its sheer descriptive beauty is surely a pity. Yet too much concentration on this can obscure a greater literary worth.[1] It is also a poetical expression of morals and values. It is an emotional response to a datable historical situation, to a time largely dominated by the threat or actuality of civil war; though of course the poem is as timeless as the essence of the historical situation. Only towards the end of the period of composition (36 B.C., or possibly earlier – 29 B.C.)[2] was the cycle of civil war, it might be assumed, concluded. The poem argues piety, order, peace, productiveness, *life* – in reaction to chaos, destruction and war. It does so through the metaphor of the Farmer.

'Metaphor' is slightly to overstate; or to oversimplify. The strength of the poetic potential of 'the Farmer' lay in his nearness, or his emotional nearness, to all Roman citizens of Italy. The poem is ultimately about and for man. But it is based as a poem of Italy;[3] and Italy was still largely rural. If, according to the realities of agriculture, the self-sufficient *colonus* of the *Georgics* was increasingly a myth, the myth was not distant[4] – and was highly emotive. It tapped a traditional Roman feeling that the rural and the *moral* life were synonymous. Thus we find a practical man like Varro, in fact a main source for the realities of contemporary agriculture, enthusing over the *dignitas* of the *pastoricia res* and maintaining the essential and moral superiority of the country and its life. More, he even alludes to another tradition which contributed to the Farmer's poetic potential, the affinity of rural life to a Golden Age.[5] Here then was an area where, for the Italian consciousness, reality merged with idealizing. Virgil, searching for a poetical obverse to civil war, its causes and concomitants, found a natural and malleable symbol in the *colonus*. Out of his world he created the World of the *Georgics*.

47

That the *Georgics* upholds and argues in symbolic form the essential values mentioned above becomes obvious in the course of reading Book 1. But I mention some salient points. A basic stance of religious piety is set by the opening invocation to the Gods and maintained throughout: it is Jupiter who has willed and shaped man's present existence (see the famous summary 121ff.); if a storm is, or images, the anger of Jupiter (328ff.) we have our answer: *in primis uenerare deos . . .* (338ff.). And the Gods *care* for man, it seems: Jupiter is responsible for all those helpful signs, the *prognostica* (352ff.) whose potential importance we scarcely at first guess.[6] The *Georgics* is a continual and obvious proclamation of 'peace': I single out for mention the military metaphor commonly used of the Farmer's task: see e.g. 145ff. which lead into the account of the farmer's *arma*.[7] The Farmer's 'war' is with nature. His existence is a perpetual embodiment of the idea of 'swords into ploughshares'. The poem's commitment to *life* is symbolized in the continual personification involved in description of nature;[8] we should note particularly the use of suggestive words like *fetus* (55, etc.), *fecunda* (67, etc.), *grauidus* (111, 319, etc.) whose basic sense of 'pregnant' is never dead in good poets, and the recurrent *laetus* (1, 69, etc.) which contributes its full significance of human joy.[9] These words also adequately indicate the ideal of 'productiveness' that infuses the poem – for which however, in the World of the *Georgics*, hard relentless work is essential. But by work we live – and live not only honourably but happily. The necessity of *labor* is stressed in Book 1: see again particularly 121ff. But in the *Georgics* work *is* productive (as well as perhaps a moral virtue in itself) – this is the point.[10]

Thus the *Georgics*, though it as it were remembers the traditional Golden Age,[11] does not image or try to advocate such a Utopia – where work is unheard of and man is innocent (125–8). It recognizes that man is *not* now innocent. By Jupiter's will he must be inventive to live; *ars*, indeed guile, is required of him. Jupiter, it seems, wants no race of slothful dumbwits: cf. 121–4

> pater ipse colendi
> haud facilem esse uiam uoluit, primusque per artem
> mouit agros, curis acuens mortalia corda
> nec torpere graui passus sua regna ueterno.

Cf. too e.g. 139f. *tum laqueis captare feras et fallere uisco* | *inuentum*, 271 *insidias auibus moliri*. But the sharp wits gained *are* at the expense of innocence. Consequently it is imperative that those artful talents remain in defined pursuits. The *Georgics* realizes this acutely, as soon transpires. The poem recognizes and warns of the dangers attending the ambivalent *durum genus* man, and prescribes for them. We think again of the military metaphor. It in one way is also a warning, ever-present. In such 'war' man should confine his inescapable warlike instincts – the *labor* of the Country must occupy his energies. His violence is only dormant, or channelled. A picture, touched upon, vividly reminds us of the fact. Earth itself, *terra*, the basis of the World of the *Georgics* (see below, p. 56) can become *Terra*, giving birth to the monstrous Titans, symbols of uncivilized violence (278–9 *tum partu Terra nefando* | *Coeumque Iapetumque creat saeuumque Typhoea*;[12] the present tense bears reflecting on).[13] The World of the *Georgics*, because of the nature of man, is only precariously maintained.

Order in fact is supremely necessary – to prevent (for example) the military metaphor spilling over into reality. 'Order' is a theme of the poem. Cf. e.g. 6of. *continuo has leges aeternaque foedera certis* | *imposuit natura locis...*; and if, though the earth produced *liberius* before the present Age (128), this still implies a measure of 'freedom' in Nature now, the Roman mind knows that *libertas* is inseparable from *lex*.[14]

Such emotional and philosophical significance to the *Georgics* becomes evident gradually in the course of Book 1. But the peroration at the end, which I examine in detail, makes the whole thing plain; it is a vital part of the book and the poem as a whole – a fact which Macrobius and others have not fully grasped.[15] For it highlights the positive values implicit in the poem by an horrific display of their total negation in the world of actuality.

THE CONCLUSION TO BOOK I ANALYSED

solem quis dicere falsum

audeat? ille etiam caecos instare tumultus
saepe monet fraudemque et operta tumescere bella;   465
ille etiam exstincto miseratus Caesare Romam,
cum caput obscura nitidum ferrugine texit
impiaque aeternam timuerunt saecula noctem.
tempore quamquam illo tellus quoque et aequora ponti,
obscenaeque canes importunaeque uolucres   470
signa dabant. quotiens Cyclopum efferuere in agros
uidimus undantem ruptis fornacibus Aetnam,
flammarumque globos liquefactaque uoluere saxa!
armorum sonitum toto Germania caelo

audiit, insolitis tremuerunt motibus Alpes.   475
uox quoque per lucos uulgo exaudita silentis
ingens, et simulacra modis pallentia miris
uisa sub obscurum noctis, pecudesque locutae
(infandum!); sistunt amnes terraeque dehiscunt,
et maestum inlacrimat templis ebur aeraque sudant.   480
proluit insano contorquens uertice siluas
fluuiorum rex Eridanus camposque per omnis
cum stabulis armenta tulit. nec tempore eodem
tristibus aut extis fibrae apparere minaces
aut puteis manare cruor cessauit, et altae   485
per noctem resonare lupis ululantibus urbes.
non alias caelo ceciderunt plura sereno
fulgura nec diri totiens arsere cometae.
ergo inter sese paribus concurrere telis
Romanas acies iterum uidere Philippi;   490
nec fuit indignum superis bis sanguine nostro
Emathiam et latos Haemi pinguescere campos.
scilicet et tempus ueniet, cum finibus illis
agricola incuruo terram molitus aratro
exesa inueniet scabra robigine pila,   495
aut grauibus rastris galeas pulsabit inanis
grandiaque effossis mirabitur ossa sepulcris.
di patrii Indigetes et Romule Vestaque mater,
quae Tuscum Tiberim et Romana Palatia seruas,
hunc saltem euerso iuuenem succurrere saeclo   500
ne prohibete. satis iam pridem sanguine nostro
Laomedonteae luimus periuria Troiae;
iam pridem nobis caeli te regia, Caesar,
inuidet atque hominum queritur curare triumphos,
quippe ubi fas uersum atque nefas: tot bella per orbem, 505
tam multae scelerum facies, non ullus aratro
dignus honos, squalent abductis arua colonis,
et curuae rigidum falces conflantur in ensem.
hinc mouet Euphrates, illinc Germania bellum;
uicinae ruptis inter se legibus urbes   510
arma ferunt; saeuit toto Mars impius orbe,
ut cum carceribus sese effudere quadrigae,
addunt in spatia, et frustra retinacula tendens
fertur equis auriga neque audit currus habenas.

The sun is the last of the *prognostica*, the weather-signs, that Virgil cites; and just previously the section appeared to be closing:

> denique, quid Vesper serus uehat, unde serenas
> uentus agat nubes, quid cogitet umidus Auster,
> sol tibi signa dabit. (461–3)

But it recommences with lines that move through ambiguity and metaphor into a different dimension altogether (463–8). Via transcending examples of the sun's prognostic function the peroration on civil war and the chaos of the present world is introduced. Jupiter's signs show their full potential; the extent of his concern for man is, it seems, revealed.

The pivotal ambiguity is *tumultus* (464) – supported by *instare*. At 311–34 there was a striking set-piece description of a Storm; the sun has in the lines immediately preceding 464 been considered as a prognosticator of bad weather (cf. e.g. 441ff. or 453–6); and *tumescere* (465) has previously been used in a literal context of weather (357). Thus the literal sense 'storm' for *tumultus* seems momentarily a reasonable assumption.[16] But *caecos* suggests something more sinister. *tumultus* emerges as a metaphor, developing through *tumescere* of 465 into *bella*. The epithets ease the transition; and adumbrate the nature of the *bella*. The 'covered', 'hidden' (*operta*) are naturally 'dark'; and *caecus*, often found meaning unequivocally 'dark', is obviously helped to contribute *its* association of 'hidden'. Both, in the context, obviously suggest sedition.[17] We rightly sensed a warning behind the military metaphor[18] – which in fact was prominent in that Storm of 311–34.

The conception of the sun changes to suit this change in dimension. He now explicitly commands a national attention and shows a transcending and national concern, becoming the anthropomorphic divine Sun, with prognostications to match. First in general he warns of those conflicts regrettably frequent and sinister, manifestly *civil* wars (464–5). And as a climax he gives his response to the assassination of Caesar, covering his head in pity for Rome – but also therein warning of the consequences to follow (466–8). Having moved from metaphor to reality in *tumultus*, we move from general to immediate and crucial particular in *ille etiam...ille etiam*.

This Sun and Caesar are so to speak of the same stature – a feeling which emerges from the balance and phrasing of 466.[19] There, while the Sun displays human emotion (*miseratus*), Caesar's dying (*exstincto*), given the context, manifestly magnifies in significance to suggest the extinction of a cosmic body.[20] The Sun covering his head – the action is one of mourning[21] – pities Rome on the death of an equal or equivalent. But the action *is* also prognostication. If the Sun *covers* his shining head in *darkness* (467 *caput obscura nitidum ferrugine texit*), the portentous significance after the *caecos tumultus* and *operta bella* portended in the past is obvious. All 464–8 turn on the ideas of light and dark, hidden and open. The world, it seems, had in Caesar a 'Sun' capable of preventing the covert darkness of civil war. At his eclipse, the heavenly Sun correspondingly reacts, removing his light: pitying Rome it may be, but warning her *people*, the *impia saecula*, who have abandoned the piety enjoined by the *Georgics*; showing them the 'darkness' they have produced – and the 'darkness' to come. The night feared for all time was real enough. But at the end of these five lines it is also a definitive symbol and portent of civil war.

I have left *fraudem* (465) for special comment. This is a stronger, more wide-ranging word than its English derivative might suggest. It summons from lexicographers glosses like 'harm', 'danger', 'crime' as well as 'dishonest conduct', 'deceit', and 'trickery'. It is something in this latter area that the context (*operta* following immediately) evokes. 'Treachery' to anticipate the 'treachery' of Caesar's killers, for example; or more generally the 'deceit' of insurrection. But the context does not confine the word. There seems to be indicated some basic fault, 'treachery', in the people which keeps surfacing in one form or another – symbolized (in a very different mood) at 502 by the perjury of Laomedon.[22] *fraudem*, and *impia...saecula* (468), are the beginnings of this idea, anticipating *luimus* and *periuria* of 502. While we witness the *Georgics*' military metaphor becoming reality, we appreciate also what dimensions are possible for man's guile (cf. p. 48). The Sun has had repeated occasion to warn of such *fraus*. The crime of Caesar's murder is the ultimate manifestation. There seems no doubt of the people's guilt or the Sun's consciousness of it. It should be stressed that the Sun's pity is for *Roma* as opposed to its people: the *saecula* are *impia* and frightened.

fraudem intensifies in retrospect the Sun's epithet *falsum* in 463 which expands (matching the movement of *sol* from weather sign to 'deity') from 'incorrect' to involve a suggestion of 'deceitful', 'treacherous'. The Sun is the obverse of this benighted generation. So, it would follow, was his equal – Caesar, whom they murdered. Additionally I would suggest that in this context of guilt and crime some moral tone emerges in *ferrugine*, a suggestion of moral corruption which Ovid at any rate seems to have felt the word could imply (see *Metamorphoses* 2. 798). The reaction of the Sun more pointedly mirrors the darkness of the world, and its prognostic significance ramifies. Some scrutiny of *ferrugine* is compelled, for it is not a common word – called 'puzzling' by one scholar.[23] Its basic function is obviously to convey *dark* colour. But the potential overtone suggested above, plus perhaps the simple associations which its root *ferrum* can relevantly contribute in the context, explain its selection.

From the Sun as prognosticator we move to other portents of disaster. The reaction is universal (469–88): the focus of the narrative shifts from the heavens to the broad divisions of the world and vague evocations of its beasts; from Aetna to the sky in Germany and to the Alps; there follow other portents which involve, more or less immediately, the World of the *Georgics* itself; and these mingled with signs more indefinable and unplaceable broaden back to the opening dimension, to portents in the heavens. Such is the build-up to the actual narrative of calamity.

Several lists of the portents supposedly following Caesar's death survive. Virgil's in fact is the earliest. There is considerable divergence of detail between it and later 'historical' sources, although in essence it may well be based on what was reputed actually to have occurred.[24] But whatever the 'truth', the choice of *which* portents to include, how to treat or embellish them, in what order to arrange and combine them, was Virgil's responsibility. This is Virgil's poetical account of the portentous foreshadowing of civil catastrophe that followed Caesar's assassination; it is Virgil I shall interpret.[25]

Both *obscenae* and *importunae* (470) signify 'boding-ill': cf. e.g. Virgil, *Aeneid* 12. 876 *obscenae uolucres*, 12. 864 *quae* (sc. *ales*)...*canit importuna per umbras*.[26] But both have other obvious senses; the dogs and birds anticipate in their epithets the horror of the deeds they portend. *obscenus* has general associations of 'hateful', 'disgusting', 'obscene': cf. e.g. *Aeneid* 7. 417 (Allecto) *frontem obscenam rugis arat*; and Virgil is playing on both areas of sense at *Aeneid* 4. 455 *uidit... fusaque in obscenum se uertere uina cruorem* (cf. Pease (1935) ad loc.). *importunus* comes close to 'cruel', 'savage': e.g. applied to a tyrant by Livy (29. 17. 20), to Catiline by Cicero (*Catiline* 2. 12). Such significations inevitably emerge in, and affect, this context. Just as, in this context, the signal for battle must be heard behind *signa dabant*[27] – ironically given by creatures of nature. Things have changed since 463, or 439.

Aetna erupts (471–3). The more ominous if one remembers that according to legend beneath Aetna lay trapped one or other of the type figures of violence (there were varying versions): e.g. the Giant

Enceladus (Virgil, *Aeneid* 3. 578–82) – or Typhoeus himself, son of Terra, whose buried anger, it was foretold, would violently boil over despite Jupiter's constraint in scenes of destruction very (and interestingly) similar to those here described: cf. Aeschylus, *Prometheus* 356–74. I mentioned the picture of Terra and her offspring above; it is perhaps hard not to sense mythical symbolism beneath the present portent.

But first we note the depth to the language. *efferuere* (471) denotes the 'boiling over' in heat and fire of Aetna. However, in the company of words evocative of military violence like *flammae* and *saxa*,[28] it also contains an impression, or suggests the colour, of things to come, the things it portends: cf. Virgil, *Aeneid* 9. 692f. *hostem | feruere caede noua*, or 9. 72 (*feruidus*) etc. The significance of *in agros* is intense. Built up by the narrative of Book 1, *agri* are by now in effect symbolic: they are after all the ground of the World of the *Georgics*; and 'living' – living enough to be 'pregnant' (cf. 2. 5 *grauidus...ager*). Hence emotive recipients of violence; and the portent as a whole deepens. *agri* here illustrates – in a simple way – an important technique; we shall see several more examples. A word, by repeated and significant mention in the poem, accumulates implicit but increasing resonance or meaning; and at salient moments (such as in this finale) all such meaning can be realized with explicit and climactic effect.

Cyclopum, now that we have moved into the Roman present, arrests. In such density of writing we should expect it to be more than a method of geographical location.[29] And, if we allow it, it is. Let us accept the full implication. The fields are in the portent the property of these monsters, and not of farmers. According to Hesiod[30] the Cyclopes are, like the Titans and Typhoeus, dreadful offspring of Earth. By other tradition[31] it was actually the Cyclopes who were domiciled in Aetna, forging thunderbolts for Zeus. Conflation has taken place, the Cyclopes (naturally enough) adopting the role of the Titans and Giants as symbols of savagery and by implication being *imprisoned* as such in Aetna. Beneath the surface signification of this portent there is thus an adumbration of another idea as we suspected above. In the boiling over of Aetna is the escape of symbolic monsters of violence – the Cyclopes – taking possession of the fields with the violence foretold for the anger of Typhoeus. *ruptis fornacibus* helps this picture, suggesting the *escape* of the Cyclopes. *fornax*, basically a furnace, is particularly where one smelts metal – precisely these monsters' job – as well as being poetically and more generally applied to volcanoes.[32] The picture is only adumbrated; it will not submit to tight logical analysis and the impression on the reader may be largely subliminal.

The sound of battle stirring in 471 is strident in 474. The basic import of the omen is obvious enough. But Germany particularly heard it and for Germany no doubt it was a tuneful sound. The portent has more specific implications than commentators mention: pointing to barbarians exploiting the coming civil strife, the threat of incursions – added repercussions to the murder of Caesar. This is indeed to be the case: *illinc Germania bellum* (509). The Alps tremble, shaken by earth-quakes: ominous in itself.[33] But this trembling also indicates *fear*. Both *motus* and *tremo* have emotional potential that interacts.[34] The Alps, long felt as the bulwark and frontier of unified Italy, tremble in fear at the prospect of the barbarian invasion threatened in the previous line.[35] Passages of Livy are instructive to compare for the feeling about the Alps (e.g. 5. 34. 6–7, 21. 30. 6–8, 41. 15); and with the recent com-pletion of Italian unity (cf. note 3), such a feeling must have been enhanced.

The portents become less distinct, ominously juxtaposing opposites (476–8): the *ingens uox* in silent, presumably sacred but also (simply) *rural*-sounding groves;[36] singularly-hued phantoms in darkness (*obscurum noctis*) pregnant because reminiscent of the Sun's eclipse (cf. 467f. *obscura...noctem*). We are not told what the voice said, nor who or what these *simulacra* were. Perhaps we can guess; if not we shall soon be in a better position. But then the *pecudes locutae* (478) strike immediately, provoking *infandum* (479). Here is the first of the portents that intimately involve the Country. In each case the essential component is sufficiently typical of the World of the *Georgics* to remind us of it and its normality. But what happens suggests rather a nightmare *Georgics*. We see in these portents pictures not so much of violence inflicted upon the Country which was the basic impression with Aetna, but its internal collapse, distortion, even perversion[37] – something more terrible; and a closer depiction in image of civil war.

However, before considering these in detail, I shall look ahead to the other portents unplaceable and more general like the *ingens uox* and the *simulacra* which are mingled with the specifically 'Country' signs. I take first 483–4 *nec tempore eodem | tristibus aut extis fibrae apparere minaces*. Key here are the framing adjectives *tristibus* and *minaces*. The former is comparable to *obscenus* and *importunus* above, combining a signification virtually equivalent to 'boding-ill' (cf. *Aeneid* 2. 184 *pro numine laeso | effigiem statuere, nefas quae triste piaret*, etc. and see Pease (1923), 389) with its more obvious emotional range. *minax* is correspondingly industrious: threatening for the future what will be 'threatening' in the present. Both thus, as usual, anticipate as well as forebode.

More dramatic is 480 *et maestum inlacrimat templis ebur aeraque sudant*. The line with its climactic *aeraque sudant* has an extraordinary impact. Yet the portent of 'sweating statues' in isolation might seem no more than a vague if awesome marvel – as e.g. in Cicero, *De Divinatione* 1. 98. The point is that in our line the emotional potential of *sudant* has been realized. The 'sweating statues' have been coupled with statues that are explicitly 'grieving' and do the overtly emotional thing of 'weeping'.[38] Hence the relevant emotional content or causation of *sudant* surfaces. These statues weep in grief, fittingly, for what the future holds; if they are sweating, it will be for the equally fitting reason of fear.[39]

These portents space the more or less immediately 'Country' ones, which start with the speaking cattle. *pecudes* are part of the *Georgics*. They have been mentioned already in Book 1 (see especially 4; cf. also 263, 444) and will recur as the poem proceeds – particularly (naturally) in Book 3; and each mention increases their emotive 'typicality'. But they do not normally *speak*. (Forced, so it seems, to speak, what had they to say? Again one wonders, again one might guess.) Then *sistunt amnes* (479): pointed in the context since we know the importance of water in the form of natural or artificial streams for the life of the land: cf. especially 106ff., and 269. In the Golden Age rivers ran with wine (132); the life they contribute to the World of the *Georgics* is more prosaic but still life. Worse follows. The Italian river Po, so to speak in an alien guise (*fluuiorum rex Eridanus* 482), runs riot *destroying* rather than vivifying – linked to the destruction of Aetna by Aetna's image of *undantem* (472). Admittedly rivers do not always run easy but ease was not after all Jupiter's will for man; and this destruction magnifies beyond all reason or expectation the floods of nature (cf. 115ff., 326f.).

And *what* is destroyed is emotive. 482f.: *camposque per omnis | cum stabulis armenta tulit*. The resonance of *campos* is basic: cf. *agros* in the Aetna portent. And the *armenta* with their *stabula* whom we have already met (355 *quid saepe uidentes | agricolae propius stabulis armenta tenerent*) are to become, increasingly, indicative members of this World: thus cf. e.g. 2. 515 (in the praise of the Farmer's life) *hinc patriam paruosque nepotes | sustinet, hinc armenta boum meritosque iuuencos*; and particularly of course in Book 3.

Perversion of the *Georgics*' norm is the point of or gives strength to *terrae dehiscunt* (479): *terra* is deeply emotionally charged, the very substance of the Country, in our minds from the first line of the poem

on. Against that norm, too, the frightfulness of *nec tempore eodem...
aut puteis manare cruor cessauit* (483ff.: again possibly Virgilian invention in its details, like the 'weeping statues') sharpens. *puteus* though
not 'built up' in the *Georgics*, manifestly belongs to ordinary, peaceful
life. When *cruor* ('gore') appears in the place of the expected[40]
normality, constant *water*, the horror fits into the pattern of perversion
and is thereby exacerbated. In fact *puteus* is more or less a symbol – like
armenta and *amnes* etc.

One does naturally first connect the *puteus* portent with others of the
Country. But 'wells' are not of course exclusively rural. As the open
evocation of civil war approaches, the signs that at once portend and
image it broaden again. In 486 the scene is *urbes*, with which *putei*
must, in view of the syntactical inextricability of 485 and 486, also
associate; the 'wells', then, start the shift. But the main portent of the
cities is that of the wolves – howling in them *per noctem* (again a recall
of the Sun's eclipse). In essentials here is a traditional portent. But *lupi*
are banes of the *Georgics*: cf. 130 *ille* (sc. *Iuppiter*)...*praedarique lupos
iussit*, 3. 407, 537, 4. 435. So the portent takes on a particular significance. A threat to the *Georgics*, wolves are a threat to peace, order and
the like. Hence what their presence in the cities portends for those cities
is clear. The 'wolves', also, facilitate the return to the scale of the beginning, combining in their portent the Country with the world of cities.

But 487–8 take us right back to the heavens, with signs unparalleled
in their profusion. Comets, plainly here the *belli mala signa* (Tibullus
2. 5. 71), the overtones of whose language (*diri* and *arsere*)[41] are a fore-
taste of the *bellum*. Thunderbolts falling[42] in a cloudless sky, which
admitted various interpretations,[43] but here as often evidence the anger
of Jupiter, his response to the *impia saecula* (cf. the remark above,
p. 48, on 328ff.); and more generally portend war: for again the sign
images what it portends. Violence (in the shape of *fulgura*) is intruding
into peace: the word *serenus* has in Book 1 been associated with peace
for the Farmer (cf. 100 *umida solstitia atque hiemes orate serenas*,
260, 340 *sacra refer Cereri laetis operatus in herbis | ...iam uere sereno. |
tum pingues agni et tum mollissima uina...*, 393, and 461 *unde serenas |
uentus agat nubes...sol tibi signa dabit*). And though there can be
insidiae in a *serena nox* (426), I suppose *that* is scarcely surprising; and
anyway the sun is prepared to help (424): on reflection (after 466ff.)
424–6 is a pregnant little passage.

So a circle has been completed in the portents and on various levels
we have been prepared, as the Romans were prepared, for the actuality
of civil war (489ff.). *ergo*: the portents were a consequence of the assas-

sination of Julius Caesar, and so of course is the disaster presaged and imaged in, and now fulfilling, those portents. Now we witness Virgil's most explicit portrayal of the destruction, collapse and perversion of the World of the *Georgics*. There is calculated surprise in 489 but obviously no lack of poetical or logical continuity. The actuality, like salient portents, is phrased in terms of the opposition of the Country and violence.

Lines 489–92 have been much discussed. Which two battles is Virgil referring to? I must propound my own (unfashionable) view summarily, leaving the reader to compare the accounts of other commentators. *iterum* is most naturally taken with *uidere*, though perhaps also by association with *concurrere*. At all events Virgil is indeed talking of two battles at 'Philippi'; and he means the two battles actually at Philippi itself in 42 B.C. approximately one month apart, the first ending in the suicide of Cassius, the second in that of Brutus.[44] Philippi was in Macedonia on the borders of Thrace: Emathia strictly a district of Macedonia could be extended poetically to signify all of it; Haemus is a mountain range in Thrace. The geography of the passage on this reading, though loosish, is plausible. Virgil is *not* confusing or conflating the sites of Philippi and Pharsalus (which was in Thessaly, approximately 170 kilometres S.W.): I should not hasten to impute to him such laxity or licence whatever subsequent poets – some possibly through misunderstanding these lines – allowed themselves.[45]

This interpretation most satisfactorily answers the claims of geography and syntax. But does it make poetical sense? Why should Virgil put two parts of what in the light of history is one battle at the heart of his finale when an apparently more powerful conceit might have been engineered with – for example – Pharsalus? Due consideration of the structure of this finale will lead to the solution. Its frame is the two Caesars, the murdered Julius erstwhile Sun of Rome and the new hoped-for redeemer, the young Caesar (466 and 503). The omens, stressed as happening at the time of (i.e. as a result of) Julius Caesar's murder (*tempore...illo* 469, *tempore eodem* 483), portend the *consequences* of it: civil war as here described, adequately epitomized in Philippi – whilst Pharsalus was past history, way outside the frame. But not just 'adequately': there is much more to it. The mood is changing (this I shall amplify below). The emphasis is shifting from the idea of due if horrible punishment coming upon the *impia saecula* for their wickedness, to bewilderment at a seemingly unending tragic process of crime begetting crime; to bafflement at the Gods' allowing such a thing; to an expression of desperate hope that the new Caesar (the balance in the finale to the old) will be able and be allowed by the Gods to call a halt. Therefore evocation of the two onslaughts on this self-same Caesar by his own suffering people becomes acutely pertinent – onslaughts led we remember by the protagonists of the destruction of the first Caesar. The tragedy of the Romans' fate is that the civil war which is their punishment (but we are less and less happy with this word) for the murder of Julius Caesar involves the murderers leading Romans against the new Caesar, who offers the only chance of escaping from precisely this sort of endless cycle of crime and punishment. That Romans should doggedly pursue this insane (cf. 481) attempt at self-destruction twice on the same field – and not learn from the blood already there – completes the tragedy. Philippi (other 'attacks' on the young Caesar before Actium could have been found) selects itself. We must not forget that these were indeed considered, or promulgated, as two substantial and separable battles at the time: such was Augustus' view – cf. *Res Gestae Divi Augusti* 1. 2 *qui parentem meum interfecerunt, eos in exilium expuli...et postea bellum inferentis rei publicae uici bis* (N.B.!) *acie*; historical perspective has allowed, for some commentators, the impact of contemporary events (spontaneous or contrived) to become dulled. Nor must we forget that this whole tragedy of self-destruction took place on a site recalling in its name healthily defeated Macedonians.

The shift in emphasis and mood becomes more apparent in *nec fuit indignum...*(491). Why was such horror not *indignum* in the Gods' judgement? True, there seemed a deep sin in the people (cf. *saepe monet fraudem* 465, *impia saecula* 468, and see above, p. 52); witness the ultimate manifestation, the assassination of Caesar, for which Jupiter appeared justly angry (cf. *fulgura* 488, above p. 57). So perhaps the Gods are right to inflict, or allow, such tragic suffering. Yet the emotional strength of the language (which I shall turn next to consider) expressing the suffering defies such unquestioning acceptance. *nec fuit indignum...* easily gathers to it a tone of bitter incomprehension. In short the statement is ambivalent. The state is intrinsically corrupt, it now murders Caesar, the Gods are angry, and according to tragic justice the guilty destroy themselves. But – *satis iam pridem sanguine nostro | Laomedonteae luimus periuria Troiae.* And is it justifiable to talk so generally of guilt? (With the ambivalence of *nec fuit indignum...* we may compare the famous *dis aliter uisum* at *Aeneid* 2. 428 with the note of Austin (1964) on it.)

Philippi watches the Roman conflict: *Romanae* and *Philippi* (490) are pointedly placed at either end of the line – *Schadenfreude* for ghosts or descendants. The language of the clash (*inter sese paribus*) stresses that this is civil war. The portents, and the premonition sensed in the military metaphor of the book, are vindicated. A detail clinches the latter: the language of the battle also recalls that Storm again (cf. above, p. 51):

> omnia uentorum *concurrere* proelia uidi
> quae grauidam...etc.   (318)

318 and 489 are the only occurrences of *concurro* in *Georgics* 1. The worst of wars has triumphed to mock the 'war' of the peaceful *Georgics*.

Understanding the intimate relation of finale and the body of the book is essential to a full appreciation of 491f. *bis sanguine nostro* | *Emathiam et latos Haemi pinguescere campos* – a superlative example of the technique expounded above, p. 54. The core of strength is in *pinguescere*. The basic idea of bodies fattening land is old;[46] but this is a transformation. A repeated theme of the book has been *pinguis* land or growth; what in the peaceful and sane world of the Italian *Georgics* constitutes it, or will produce it (interestingly the epithet in some of its collocations was probably novel enough particularly to catch the attention):[47] see 8 *pingui...arista*, 14, 64 *ergo age terrae* | *pingue solum* ...*inuertant tauri*, 80, 87, 105, 341; and the ironic use at 192 – which draws its effect from the previous examples. In all these *pinguis* accumulates an association with the fullness of the *Georgics*; and this accumulation is the basis of the horror conveyed by *pinguescere*. Here is an epitome of the obscene perversion of the *Georgics* that civil war conclusively is. Not only are the *campi* (cf. above, p. 56) of Italy neglected (cf. 507). Here is what richness of land now means: our *blood* – and the poet identifies in *nostro* (cf. now my remark above on guilt) – fattening broad fields; far away, in Emathia, in Haemus.

493–7 bring the *agricola* and war into direct confrontation, and at last there seems to be some optimism: a belief in the final victory of *diuini gloria ruris*. The warriors who fought each other will be gone: we are reminded of a Hesiodic Age, past and buried. The replacement it seems will be the Farmer and his Age: the World of the *Georgics*.[48] The Farmer may marvel at their *grandia ossa*, i.e. the remnants of a race of 'epic heroes', but they will be dead and he will be alive – *grandia* can take on a nice touch of irony. Nor are the warriors' *sepulcra*, we might think, exactly heroic; or indeed *sepulcra* at all.

The Farmer, performing his timeless task, will find the weapons of war eaten away with rust. Manifestly and immediately symbolic; but the symbolism is grounded in the poem. In the course of the narrative 'ploughing', and more particularly *aratrum* itself, has gained special significance. Unexpectedly the poem proper *begins* with the action of ploughing (43ff.),[49] throwing it into prominence. And the plough is the first of the Farmer's *arma* to be enumerated: 160ff. *dicendum et quae sint duris agrestibus arma...uomis et inflexi primum graue robur aratri – arma* which are summarized in lines of obvious wider potential significance *omnia quae multo ante memor prouisa repones,* | *si te digna manet diuini gloria ruris* (167–8). Of these *arma* it alone claims a passage (169–75) describing, impressionistically, its construction. The *aratrum* is fixed in the memory, prepared by the poem to evoke by itself the World of the *Georgics*;[50] and see too 19, 45, 98, 213, 261. It becomes a symbol of peace and productiveness. And already, I think, we sense that the seemingly formulaic (in essence) epithet *incuruo* makes its own contribution to this symbolism. The *aratrum* was *inflexum* at 162, *curuum* at 170; and the beginning of the description of the plough's construction (169–70) indicates the possible reasoning behind such a symbolic association: *continuo in siluis magna ui flexa domatur* | *in burim et curui formam accipit ulmus aratri.* The plough – like, more broadly, the general military metaphor – illustrates the channelling of man's *uis* without which the *Georgics* cannot exist. (The curved plough is again used in a synoptic vision at 2. 513.) Appropriate then for it to turn up the mouldering weapons. Appropriate too for the *rastra,* also listed among the Farmer's *arma* (164) – cf. too 94, 155 (in a passage of obvious 'military metaphor') – to knock the war helmets; here the ironic opposition of *grauibus* and *inanis* is obvious: *rastra* unusually but splendidly enjoy the full ramifications of *grauitas* while *galeae,* symbols of war, are not only literally 'empty' but empty in the sense of useless, worthless, vain. Indeed the right *arma* prevail.

These remarks on 493–7 are true enough so far as they go but they need qualification. The time envisaged sounds very remote: so remote it is phrased in terms that suggest a whole New Age. The present remains nightmarish. And in such a present to introduce a vision of optimism with *scilicet* – a word of most unfortunate ambiguity as a glance at 'Lewis and Short' shows – is not calculated to inspire confidence. Nor anyway is the vision itself totally unequivocal, a simple picture of *diuini gloria ruris* triumphing finally over *gloria militaris.* If War and the Farmer are opposites, there is no such easy opposition between Farmer and soldiers. The soldiers whose bones are turned up *were* once farmers – *squalent abductis arua colonis* – an alien race of heroes though they may seem in that distant future.

The disastrous present remains; the poem leads naturally into an emotional prayer to the Gods to save the state (498ff.). This balances the opening invocation but in very different mood. The Gods addressed are intimately connected with the Roman Commonwealth:[51] the *di patrii* obviously, then the *Indigetes*, i.e. probably heroes who have been granted divine honours for services to the people; then Romulus the deified founder, and Vesta whose cult was at the heart of Rome and whose eternal and symbolic flame had been brought from Troy (*Aeneid* 2. 296f.) – Vesta's relative clause involving an allusion to the Tuscan origin of the Tiber and a consequent balancing of *Romana* by *Tuscum* sufficiently and suitably adumbrates the Italianness of the Roman *patria*. But the prayer is not put quite in the way we expect. The Gods are asked not to *prevent* the *iuuenis*, the new Caesar, from reviving the *euersum saeclum*. He, it is implied, can possibly restore piety, justice, law, peaceful life – all that the *Georgics* propounds. Why on earth should they obstruct him? But it must be counted a real possibility. *saltem* (500) implies that in the past the Gods disallowed just such a saviour – the old Caesar. And already the *iuuenis* has been twice in tragic danger. What has become of the Gods – whose statues seemed in sympathy with, and fear for, Rome's plight? Of Jupiter who respected *pietas* and cared for man? If Heaven grudges (*inuidet*, 504) the new Caesar's attention to worldly matters at *this* juncture (*quippe ubi fas...*), where is the value of such a pantheon? It cannot simply be a circuitous form of flattery for Octavian. (*hominum*, 504; *mere* men perhaps, but Virgil emphatically cares about them.)

Problems are crystallizing. Where does lie responsibility, how do we apportion blame? For a time this seemed simple; we could say the Romans simply deserved what they were getting. But we have been increasingly appalled by the suffering and perplexed by the place of men and Gods in it. The apostrophe, first to the Gods and then to Caesar himself (deservedly in their company as the invocation at 25ff. shows) focuses, though barely answers, the perplexity. While *people* could be blamed for a crime, a guilt in the race supposed, and this accepted as a reason for divine anger and punishment (as seemed the case at 464ff.) the position was clear. But the poem is moving towards a less facile culprit: war rather than warriors, abstract and generalized forces of violence which must somehow be controlled if the World of the *Georgics* is ever to be attained. The attitude to people in the increasingly inexplicable chaos becomes correspondingly more sympathetic; and the Gods' role mysterious: to compare the beginning and the end of the book is illuminating.[52] Virgil does not really know *what* they are doing – except that if they are still punishing the Romans for some

primeval sin, enough is enough: *satis iam pridem sanguine nostro...*
Caesar, the new Caesar, is the only hope. He must *impose* the *Georgics*.

euerso...saeclo in 500 illustrates the shift in attitude. *euersum* itself
works like *pinguescere*, though less obviously; the verb, simply or in
compounds, is joined in Book 1 to the dominant and symbolic theme of
ploughing:[53] cf. 1f. *quo sidere terram* | *uertere*, 65 *pingue solum...fortes
inuertant tauri*, 119, 147 *prima Ceres ferro mortalis uertere terram* |
instituit; and in another sense at 98 *rursus in obliquum uerso perrumpit
aratro*. Thus *euersum* activates, at least subliminally, associations of the
World of the *Georgics*. But here it spells destruction. However, crucial
to note is the difference in emphasis to *impia saecula* of 468. They we
might say deserve what they get. But an *euersum saeclum*, though
evoking the perversion of the age, arouses sympathy; passively phrased,
it appears a victim. The same dimension of horror as in *euerso saeclo*
is involved in *quippe ubi fas uersum atque nefas* (505). But it is equally
impossible to apportion the guilt.

This is the general configuration as the book closes (505ff.). *tot
bella* face the young Caesar, not numerable concrete enemies. More
ominously, *tam multae scelerum facies*. The metaphorical picture with
facies is a nice touch: elusive faces of virtually personified *scelera*
instead of *scelerosi* with faces, identifiable and exposed to conventional
defeat. Then follow perhaps the most eloquent lines of the piece
(506–8): *non ullus aratro* | *dignus honos, squalent abductis arua colonis* | *et
curuae rigidum falces conflantur in ensem*. The disastrous state of Rome
is captured in three climactic sentences expressed in the basic imagery
of the poem. Caesar is shown the scorn, disruption and perversion of
the World of the *Georgics*. This is the reality; 494f. were a dream. The
centrally symbolic plough lacks honour. The hard-won fruits of *labor*
are lost, for the emotive *arua* ('fields') are now *squalida*, neglected,
their *coloni* led away even 'seduced' to become soldiers.[54] And the
sickle, which, naturally making a pair with the *aratrum*[55] and specifically belonging in the *Georgics* (it is mentioned in Book 1 at 157 and
348), has a comparable symbolism, is forged into a sword, conclusively
signalling the victory of the reality of war over the *Georgics'* metaphor.
rigidus must in the context involve the idea of *straight* rigidity.[56] It is
compelled to by its contrast with *curuae*; and this straightening symbolizes in itself, especially when we recall the symbolism implicit in
curuus, the epithet also of the plough (see above, p. 61), the perversion
that is civil war. But this is not the obvious significance of *rigidus* (see
note 56). Also contributed, in conjunction with *ensem*, must be its
common metaphorical associations: e.g. it is an epithet which Ovid

can apply to Mars (*Metamorphoses* 8. 20). Thus it further interacts with *curuae* reinforcing but conflicting with the aura of peace we sense to that word. In the epithets alone as well as in the conceit of the line we can find an epitome of the defeat of peace.

509 expands the reality of war – threats at either end of the empire. Perhaps it was not to be expected that the World of the *Georgics* would ever be understood there. But 510 moves home (*uicinae... urbes*). It pictures the breaking of *leges* in language (*ruptis*) which recalls the violence of Aetna; and again, still, civil war – and at home, anyway, understanding *was* hoped for. *arma ferunt*: but not the *arma* of the *Georgics* which precisely insists upon *leges* (see p. 49). All however is phrased in the generalized terms we have become accustomed to. And finally war moves into the cosmic picture of Mars rampant in 511ff. Such is the situation that faces the young Caesar: a vast, inexplicable chaos where simple apportionment of blame and responsibility is impossible. The finale opened with the Romans seeming cursed and guilty, to be punished; specifically they had murdered the old Caesar. But the consequences emerge, so to speak in the telling, to be too awful and tragically self-perpetuating for any easy explanation or comprehension. If Rome is expiating guilt when will it stop? If the Gods are just and care for Rome, surely her people have now suffered enough – and should not be grudged a saviour? Will the Gods watch the consequences of Julius Caesar's murder continue into further inexpiable crime? It is with fine-judged rhetoric that, as the apocalyptic vision of disaster gathers momentum, the notion of primeval sin finds its most explicit statement symbolized in the *periuria* of Laomedon (502); but phrased precisely so as to capture the Virgilian perplexity. Laomedon is prehistory but the blood of 501 is horrifically today's: *sanguine nostro* of 501 picks up the *bis sanguine nostro* of 491. Enough surely is enough: *satis iam pridem sanguine nostro* | *Laomedonteae luimus periuria Troiae*. Doubt indeed seems implicitly cast upon the whole idea of collective guilt, primeval or particular. The distinction of Rome and Romans implicit at 464ff. no longer stands up, and it is Mars who is now called *impius* not the people. And yet the people suffer, as has been brought strikingly home to us. In these circumstances only one thing emerges as certain. Hope for the future rests with the new Caesar who must somehow impose the controls that the *Georgics* needs for its existence. Somehow he must restrain *impius Mars*, whose *saeuitia* opens into the concluding picture of the chariot careering out of control. Initially seeming a general adumbration of the wildness of Mars's rampage, the picture particularizes. The chariot begins to seem

the state helpless in the grip of war – for there is no effective *auriga*. This there must be and of course it must be Caesar. He must – somehow – control the state, govern its warlike propensities: he must make sure that the *retinacula* are not unheeded.[57] Did not even the vine need them (265)?

Other implications are clearly involved in the simile; it operates on several levels. Generally adumbrating Mars's wildness, its *carceres* (the 'starting-barriers') intrude their other meaning 'prison': however *Mars impius* chooses to manifest himself, that manifestation must, it seems clear, be summarily dealt with. (Cf. the description of the clearly symbolic winds at *Aeneid* 1. 54: *luctantis uentos tempestatesque sonoras | imperio premit ac uinclis et carcere frenat.*)[58] When the simile particularizes, the chariot – the state – *is* still running out of control. The book sets in stark contrast the World of the *Georgics*, an ideal (poetically expressed) but to be considered as realizable, and the contemporary actuality. The only hope of replacing the one with the other we now know. The Romans must accept and obey the *auriga*. But we can hardly be confident about the future. The simile gives no signs that the people are yet willing to respond, or capable of it; civil war, as 510f. showed, persists. Nor can the hope residing in the *auriga* be very sure given a universe of inexplicable Gods and the precedent of Julius Caesar's assassination and the battles of Philippi.

So the conclusion of the book points towards a solution but with little optimism. And (a final thought) could Virgil have viewed the solution – the *imposition* of the *Georgics*, the effective *auriga* – without mixed feelings? It seems a solution if not of despair then at least of compromise, and containing its own dangers. War is clearly going to be necessary – even, likely, more civil war (cf. 510f.): a sad way to establish the *Georgics*. And the *auriga* image involves external or centralized control. That too needs pondering. Naturally, a *currus* is unworkable and unthinkable without an *auriga*. But the whole simile is as it were an alien addition, while the *Georgics* seemed to argue a way of life that worked through mutual respect and agreement, virtue and self-control. The *Georgics* was drawn with its own system of law and treaties – and the vintner applied his own *retinacula*. It is perhaps no more than a certain implicit equivocation; but one should not suppose that Virgil's Caesarianism was naive.[59] The tragedy of Philippi was that there Romans doggedly tried to destroy their one hope of salvation. But it was also the tragedy of, simply, a civil war. The degree of tragedy involved in a civil war is in proportion to the degree with which one is unable to exculpate either side. Book 1 ends therefore poised and rhetorical – and with a touch of ambivalence. The whole poem remains fundamentally rhetorical, a vision and a challenge; now arguing with greater enticement the way of the *Georgics*, now elaborating the threats to it from within and without. It sticks to the Caesarian solution; but the reservations or worries which we sense the poet may feel about it, these too persist, detectable in periodic signs of ambivalence and ultimately to be amplified in the last book, which reflects or should reflect the time when a realization of the World of the *Georgics* was at hand.[60]

5

David West

OF MICE AND MEN

Horace, *Satires* 2. 6. 77–117

'The Country Mouse invited the Town Mouse to dinner and gave him country produce to eat, figs, grapes and other tree fruits. The Town Mouse noticed the great poverty of the Country Mouse and invited him to repay the visit the next day. He took him into a rich man's pantry and let him feast on all kinds of meat and fish and even of cakes. In the middle of all this, the pantry woman came in and they fled in panic. The Country Mouse said to the Town Mouse "You can keep your high living and all these courses. I prefer to live frugally but in freedom and security."'

Aesop 314 Hausrath–Hunger

This trite little story with its tired moral coming pat at the end has little to offer the modern reader. Aesop is a 'decayed celebrity'.[1] The animal fable is all but obsolete. But still Fraenkel can write that the tale of the two mice at the end of Horace, *Satire* 2. 6 is 'one of the best-known and most-admired pieces of Roman poetry; there is therefore no need to praise it again'.[2] Goaded by this *non sequitur*, we ask whether this is just flummery. Is Horace so very different from Aesop? What is there to admire or to enjoy in this most-admired piece of Roman poetry?

> Ceruius haec inter uicinus garrit anilis
> ex re fabellas. siquis nam laudat Arelli
> sollicitas ignarus opes, sic incipit: 'olim
> rusticus urbanum murem mus paupere fertur   80

In the middle of all this [philosophical discussion at dinner], my neighbour Cervius keeps spinning his old wives' tales, but they are not so very far off the point. If some ignorant fellow speaks highly of Arellius with all his wealth and all his worries he starts up like this: 'Once upon a time, so they say, the Country Mouse entertained the Town Mouse in his pauper's hole. They were old

accepisse cauo, ueterem uetus hospes amicum,
asper et attentus quaesitis, ut tamen artum
solueret hospitiis animum. quid multa? neque ille
sepositi ciceris nec longae inuidit auenae,
aridum et ore ferens acinum semesaque lardi   85
frusta dedit, cupiens uaria fastidia cena
uincere tangentis male singula dente superbo,
cum pater ipse domus palea porrectus in horna
esset ador loliumque, dapis meliora relinquens.
tandem urbanus ad hunc "quid te iuuat" inquit, "amice, 90
praerupti nemoris patientem uiuere dorso?
uis tu homines urbemque feris praeponere siluis?
carpe uiam, mihi crede, comes, terrestria quando
mortalis animas uiuunt sortita neque ulla est
aut magno aut paruo leti fuga: quo, bone, circa,   95
dum licet, in rebus iucundis uiue beatus,
uiue memor, quam sis aeui breuis." haec ubi dicta
agrestem pepulere, domo leuis exsilit; inde
ambo propositum peragunt iter, urbis auentes

*family friends. The Country Mouse lived a hard life and kept a
tight grip on his property, but he could still ease off and relax when
he was the host. The long and short of it is that it wasn't his way
to be stingy with the chick-pea he had laid aside in a special place,
nor with the long grain of the oat, and he served in his own mouth
the shrivelled berry and half-eaten strips of bacon fat, all in an
attempt to overcome by this varied menu the fastidiousness of his
guest. But the Town Mouse did no more than sample with dis-
dainful tooth every separate thing put before it, while the master of
the house lay stretched out in this year's straw, eating spelt and
darnel and leaving the choicer dishes to his guest. At last the
Town Mouse turned to the Country Mouse and said " My dear
friend, what pleasure is there for you living hard on the ridge of
this precipitous forest? Come now, choose mankind and the city
rather than these wild woods. Trust me, make your way under my
escort, for creatures of the earth are allotted mortal souls, and
there is no escape from death for great or small. For this reason
my good sir, live richly, while you may, a life of pleasure, and as
you live remember how soon you are to die." Thus he spoke and
prevailed upon the Country Mouse, who leapt lightly from his
home; then together they accomplished the proposed journey, and*

moenia nocturni subrepere. iamque tenebat   100
nox medium caeli spatium, cum ponit uterque
in locuplete domo uestigia, rubro ubi cocco
tincta super lectos canderet uestis eburnos
multaque de magna superessent fercula cena,
quae procul exstructis inerant hesterna canistris.   105
ergo ubi purpurea porrectum in ueste locauit
agrestem, ueluti succinctus cursitat hospes
continuatque dapes nec non uerniliter ipsis
fungitur officiis, praelambens omne quod adfert.
ille cubans gaudet mutata sorte bonisque   110
rebus agit laetum conuiuam, cum subito ingens
ualuarum strepitus lectis excussit utrumque.
currere per totum pauidi conclaue magisque
exanimes trepidare, simul domus alta Molossis
personuit canibus. tum rusticus: "haud mihi uita   115
est opus hac" ait et "ualeas: me silua cauosque
tutus ab insidiis tenui solabitur eruo."'

Horace, *Satire* 2. 6. 77–117[3]

*eagerly under cover of night they crept into the city walls. Night
was already holding the mid-space of the sky, when together they
set their footsteps in the wealthy home, where the drapery dyed in
the scarlet juice of the oak berry gleamed on the ivory couches,
and where many courses remained from the great banquet of the
previous night, standing by in towering baskets. So then the host
made the Country Mouse stretch out on the purple draperies.
Then he rushed about, like a man with his tunic hitched up for
running, and kept the banquet going uninterrupted, performing
even the duties of the trusted house slaves, licking everything
before he served it. The Country Mouse lay back and basked in
the change in his fortunes, playing the part of a banqueter taking
his pleasure in the lap of luxury, when suddenly a great noise of
doors opening drove them both off the couches, and they ran in
terror all round the dining room, and nearly died of panic when
the lofty halls resounded with the barking of Molossian hounds.
Then the Country Mouse said "I can do without a life like this.
Goodbye to you. In my hole in the forest I shall live secure from
ambush and comfort myself with a frugal diet of vetch."'*

David West

A SIMPLE TALE? (79–81)

This is a country tale, told by a rustic at a country table, and it starts with an air of simplicity. 'Once upon a time' says Cervius, and the folk-tale atmosphere is heightened by the instant naming of the protagonists. Three of the first six fables of Aesop begin in the same way with the names of the *dramatis personae*. The rhythm of the verse adds to the impression of simplicity. *Incipiam* says Aeneas at Dido's banquet, and he begins the tale of the fall of Troy at the beginning of the second foot (Virgil, *Aeneid* 2. 13). Austin (1964) finds the pause magnificent. *Incipit* says Horace, and when Cervius begins his old wives' tale at the beginning of the sixth foot, this break also is unusual, but this time the effect is informal, rather than magnificent. Strong punctuation in the last two feet is incomparably more frequent in Horace's *Satires* than in other hexameter verse,[4] and usually where it occurs the tone is conversational: a few lines later for example, after *quid multa?*; in 10, in another fable; in 23, at the beginning of a remark and before the exclamation *eia*; in 51, introducing a parenthesis in a conversation; in 70 where a conversation is getting going, before *ergo sermo oritur*. This is not slack writing but a deliberate blurring of the hexameter rhythm where it is most assertive – at the end of the line, in order to achieve a vivid imitation of the direct speech of everyday life. Not simplicity, but a calculated illusion of simplicity. And those who call this a simple tale have been taken in.

Consider the word order in 80–1: the chiasmus (ABBA) in *rusticus urbanum murem mus* is followed by BAAB *ueterem uetus hospes amicum* where A is the country mouse in the nominative and B the town mouse in the accusative. Most people would think that double chiasmus with inversion might be enough ornament for two mice, but not Horace: in the first chiasmus, two cases of the same word (*murem mus*) are juxtaposed in the third and fourth place; in the second chiasmus, a similar polyptoton occurs with *ueterem uetus* in the first and second place. Polyptoton admittedly occurs in proverbs: *manus manum lauat*, *amicus amico*, 'you scratch my back and I'll scratch yours'. Horatian commentators have added this to their collections of colloquial language in this fable. But polyptoton (the repetition of the same word in a different form) is frequent also in the high style in tragedy and epic,[5] and the complexity of this rhetorical structure leads us to believe rather that the tone here is mock-heroic. The initial simplicity conveys the flavour of fable for a moment but swiftly modulates into bravura. The wit's the thing, and Horace is already putting us on our mettle to look for it.

This wit is based upon the anthropomorphic fallacy, and may be divided into three categories: dietetic, philosphical and literary.

MICE AND DIET (82–9, 102–111)

In Aesop the Country Mouse provided what was in the fields, figs, bunches of grapes and tree fruits; in Babrius, a few sodden roots of grain with black earth all over them; in Phaedrus, an acorn.[6] In Aesop then, it is a fruit diet; in Babrius a sordid country diet; in Phaedrus' version a sparse one. In Horace and only in Horace, the menu *chez* Country Mouse is divided into four distinct courses: the first, the chick-pea (vegetable); the second, the oat (farinaceous); the third, a dry berry (fruit); the fourth, bacon fat (the meat course). Mice do not have this kind of *table d'hôte*. This is an anthropomorphic joke, demonstrating the Country Mouse's eagerness to please his guest.

And his pathetic incapacity to do so. The chick-pea is no gourmet's delight, but the 'food of the poor',[7] used by Horace in *Satire* 1. 6. 115 to characterize his own simple standard of living. That gives the game away. The fabulists are content to devise a realistic diet for a country mouse; Horace is engaged in a much more complex and more humane creation. Plausible mouse fare, yes. But his menu also characterizes or caricatures the simple diet of a poor Italian countryman, and at the same time (and here is the great poetic virtuosity of this *uaria cena*) it enriches the characterization of the Country Mouse. He is strained and tight, but he can on occasion loosen up (typically[8] Horace points the metaphor by a contrast). This is Horace's general assessment: the dietetic details bring it to life: the chick-pea has been hoarded, kept in a special place, but he does not begrudge it to his guest. 'In England food for animals', wrote Dr Johnson of the oat, and the Italians would have agreed. The dry berry is also diagnostic. It is only a single berry. It is dry. Its species is not specified, perhaps not identifiable – a grape, for instance, would have been much more extravagant. The Country Mouse has obviously spared no effort in gathering this meal together. Nor in serving it. *Ore ferens* says Horace, and come to think of it, how else would a mouse carry food if not in his mouth? But by stating this vivid detail Horace gives a living picture of his comical conscientiousness as a waiter. And what about the bacon fat? *Lardum* is also simple country fare, but why is the meat course kept till last, contrary to Roman practice? Again the answer lies in characterization. A country mouse can get bacon fat only by robbing a farm or cottage. This delicacy is kept till last as the *pièce de résistance*. *Semesa* is a telling detail.

The lard has not been nibbled by the Country Mouse. That would destroy the characterization. This is rather the bacon fat remaining on the rind which the humans have rejected.

Commonsense has long been crying 'Stop'. We are seeing more in this piece than the poet ever dreamed of. We are joining the lemon-squeezing, the bagpipe-milking school of literary criticism. No. As so often in the interpretation of great poetry, commonsense is wrong. In this case it is wrong on general and on particular grounds: generally, because in classical literature there is a long line of character writers, notably Homer, Theophrastus, Menander and the under-rated Terence, and Horace knew about them, and had perceptiveness and humanity enough to continue the line; particularly, because we have a control in this instance. The weakest points in the above analysis are the interpretations of *acinum* as a 'pauperized' singular, and of *ore ferens* as an embodiment of the assiduity of the Country Mouse. After all the poetic singular is a cliché in Latin verse of all ages, a metrical convenience with no semantic force, and when a mouse carries a berry in its mouth, anybody who builds an edifice on it might well be advised to look to his marbles. Both of these interpretations, however, are guaranteed by comparable details in the Town Mouse's banquet at the end of the satire, and it is Horace who invites us to compare the two meals. The one begins in *paupere cauo* (80–1); the other *in locuplete domo* (102): in the one the Country Mouse is *palea porrectus in horna* (88); in the other he is *purpurea porrectum in ueste* (106). We are therefore encouraged to see the singular chick-pea, the singular oat, the singular berry and the plural but fragmentary bits of bacon-fat in the light of the multifarious delicacies of the contrasted banquet. With shrewd economy Horace does not expatiate on the urban menu, but three adjectives in two lines make all the point he needs, *multa*, *magna* and *exstructis* (104–5). Such a contrast with the country fare confirms that the singulars are not inert poetic tricks, but part of the character-ization of this piece. It is the mark of genius to touch the cliché into life. And what about *ore ferens*? How can the zoologically inescapable be dramatically significant? *Praelambens* (109) is our guarantee. It is typical of Horace's cheerful ingenuity that he turns the same physio-logical necessity to two different psychological purposes. What was a token of servile assiduity now becomes a manifestation of high fashion. The latest thing in society (Antony was the pace-setter according to Pliny, *N.H.* 21. 12) was the food-taster, *praegustator*. The Town Mouse is so *à la mode* that he performs even this exquisite service for his guest.[9] The slave characterization is carried through: the host bustles to and fro like a man with his tunic held up for running, like the slave waiters in *Satire* 1. 8. 23, and 2. 8. 70; and not only that, he even performs his duties like a house-born slave, tasting the dishes before he serves them. For surely a house-born slave would be more likely to be entrusted with this office than a recent recruit to the *familia*?

The four lines that remain of the country meal are typically Horatian in their density, every detail contributing to the dramatic delineation of the two characters. The Country Mouse has tried to tempt the jaded appetite of his guest by these varied courses. But how is Horace to demonstrate the fastidiousness of the Town Mouse in terms which accord with mouse anatomy while suggesting the choosiness of an over-sophisticated human being? *Tangentis male*, he can just bring himself to touch – but only *singula*, a single sample of every dish – and that *dente*, putting it to only one of his teeth in yet another effective use of the 'poetic' singular. In human terms he cannot bring himself to put these revolting scraps past his teeth. In mouse terms surely he would curl his upper lip? The wit lies in the economy of the detail by which Horace encourages the reader to fuse human face and fingers into this scene of sniff and whisker. Any fear that we may be over-interpreting the anthropomorphism is dispelled by the next words. We have just seen that in the town banquet that follows the Country Mouse is served by a *praegustator*, the very latest thing in *haute cuisine*; by contrast the Country Mouse is *pater ipse domus*, not because of any polyphilo-progenitiveness (he lives alone), but to dangle before our eyes the Roman *paterfamilias*. Only of course, the *pauper cauus* is not much of a *domus*, and he *has* no *familia*, else he would not have to do his own waiting at table (*ore ferens*). In 88, *palea porrectus in horna*, we see that the Country Mouse has gone to the limit, clearing out the musty old straw smelling of mouse dirt, and producing his sweetest and freshest to lie on. It is also there, as we have seen, as an amenity to be beggared by the sumptuous purples of the city banquet in 102–3 and 106 *purpurea porrectum in ueste*. And why *porrectus* in 88 and 106, which is used nowhere else of reclining at table? The *mot propre* for this elegant reclination on the left elbow leaving the right arm free for trencher work is *accumbere*. *Porrectus* refers rather to an unsupported, inert and fully extended position, not that there is anything abandoned about the demeanour of the Country Mouse at either supper, but surely because Horace is thinking of mouse anatomy. When a human being is said *accumbere* or *accubare* his characteristic outline is high-shouldered and low-rumped. Whether or not a mouse has elbows, his characteristic outline is low-shouldered and high-rumped. Hence not *accubans* but *porrectus* twice, and *cubans* only at 110 after the picture is drawn. And what about the diet of the Country Mouse? Two dishes he has to his guest's four and both of them grain, *ador loliumque*. But whereas the oat served to the Town Mouse was at least edible, *ador* appears not normally to have been eaten (it was an ancient type of wheat used for sacral purposes), and *lolium* was positively damaging (it was darnel, a weed resembling rye whose best use according to Pliny, *N.H.* 22. 160, was as a decoction with vinegar to heal impetigo. If eaten it caused blindness, if we can believe Plautus, *MG* 321, and Ovid, *Fasti* 1. 69). *Dapis meliora relinquens* is the last telling phrase in this series of anthropomorphic plays. '*Daps* is a solemn religious word originally used of a sacrificial meal' (Fordyce (1961) on Catullus 64. 79). This archaic splendour at the end of this scene is a wry comment on the hospitality of the Country Mouse. Such was his intention. We all know what a flop it was.

MICE AND PHILOSOPHY (90–7)

Now we leave the Country Mouse and the dietetic joke and turn to philosophy. The Town Mouse comes to the end of his patience. The well-meaning hospitality of the Country Mouse is rewarded not by anything so socially inept as a direct criticism of the bill of fare, but by a condemnation of his home on the wooded ridge. *Vis tu praeponere?* is blatant chivvying.[10] '*Do* prefer mankind and the city to the wild woods.' For those who have ears to hear (and it is for those he writes his *Satires*, as he explicitly says at the end of the first book), the echo is unmistakable. In Plato's *Phaedrus* 230D Socrates has been taken for a walk in the country by his young friend. As they go paddling down the Ilissus in their bare feet Socrates apologizes for his lack of interest in the country. 'Forgive me, my good friend. For I love to learn. *Trees* and landscapes are not going to teach me anything. Only *men* in the *city* can do that.' The implication is plain. The Town Mouse is a philosopher, not however a Myo-Platonist, but a fashionable Pseudo-Epicurean. *Dum licet* and *mortalis* are the jargon, amply illustrated in the commentaries. 'Eat, drink and be merry' is the standard text of this philosophy so foreign to the moral purity of Epicurus. Here we see a pretentious version of it. 'Since mortal lives are allotted to creatures of the earth, and there is no escape from death for great or small, therefore, my good friend, richly enjoy the good things of life while you may.' This is the only passage in Latin literature where *quocirca* is separated into two words with an insertion between them.

Such tmesis is a notorious feature of the elevated style of Ennius and is common in the didactic epic of Lucretius. The heavy punctuation before the fifth foot, 'the bucolic diaeresis', is another feature of the high style and an audible warning of approaching pomposity.[11] *Bone* is the philospher's button-holer in *Satire* 2. 3. 31, and an obvious reminder of the Platonic ὠγαθέ.

But there is more to the utterance of the Horatian rodent than verbal parody. The main wit of the passage is again anthropomorphic. Philosophy is rendered even more than usually incongruous by being expounded by a mouse. The great Socratic question of 92 has to be re-read with this in mind. How pretentious for a mouse, a *fera*, to speak disparagingly of the wild woods, *feris siluis*. How preposterous for one mouse to chivvy another into sharing the habitat of men. And it takes only a moment of reflection to realize that the term *terrestria*, 'creatures of the earth', is deliciously ambivalent, philosophically applicable to man, and literally true of mice. *Sortita* is another piece of cheek, blandly suggesting that mice have an equal stake with men in the spiritual lottery propounded by Socrates in the Myth of Er at the end of the *Republic*, or in the scurrilous travesty of it in Lucretius 3. 776–83. *Aut magno aut paruo* is also in the game, and *Epistle* 1. 3. 21–9 proves it. In that passage some of man's more solemn activities are expressed in terms which suggest businesses of bees. The culminating endeavour is philosophy. Now bees, as was well known to Horace's readers (see Virgil, *Georgic* 4. 149–50, 220–1), partake of the divine nature. So Horace, a notorious tease of philosophers, has his tongue far in his cheek when he refers to philosophy as 'heavenly wisdom' *caelestis sapientia*,[12] and the joke continues in line 28:

> hoc opus hoc studium parui properemus et ampli.
>
> *This is the work, this is the interest we should hurry along whether we be small or great.*

Opus, *studium* and *properare* are all bee words, and in such a context *parui et ampli* carries an allusion to the interplay of microcosm and macrocosm which is the poetic heart of this passage.

By a comfortable circular argument this interpretation of *Epistle* 1. 3. 28 may be held to confirm and be confirmed by a similar interpretation of *aut magno aut paruo* in the fable of the two mice. *Leti* clinches it. It is a high poeticism used by Horace on seven[13] other occasions, all in the *Odes*, and all serious. *Breuis* and *beatus* are part of the fun. We are to enjoy *breuis* because it brings into the same focus the brevity of the life of man and the brevity of the life of mouse; and *beatus*, because it can refer to wealth or bliss or both (cf. 74–6), and such ambiguities are meat and drink to philosophers.

MICE AND EPIC (97–105)

The Country Mouse (now called *agrestem* for the first time) has no armour to resist this battery of philosophical rhetoric (*uiue beatus, uiue memor*). He is up and away to a new life, and Horace is up and away to a new butt for his wit. From the complacent philosophizing of an urbane rodent, he moves to epic parody in 97–104. This time the key signature is *haec ubi dicta*, after the portentous bucolic diaeresis. The Country Mouse leaps lightly from his home, *exsilit*. The light leap of a mouse has only to be visualized to make us doubt the solemnity of the narrative. Whether or not mice leap lightly from holes there is no doubt that epic heroes frequently leap (cf. ὕψι δ' ἀναθρώσκων πέτεται, *Iliad* 13. 140, and a dozen entries under ἅλλομαι in Ebeling's lexicon to Homer).[14] There is another hint of burlesque in *ambo propositum peragunt iter*.[15] This might well have been predicated of Diomede and Odysseus setting out through the dark night when the stars have moved far on their courses, and more than two-thirds of the night has passed, as in the *Iliad* 10. 252–3 and 297; or of Nisus and Euryalus calling on the Trojan leaders when all the animals were relaxing their cares in sleep (*Aeneid* 9. 224). But in Horace of two mice? So too, a pair of warriors might well enter fortifications under cover of darkness, but surely we are required to notice that these two mice *crept* into the walls. So too, the inverted temporal clause is a standard epic motif:

> iamque rubescebat stellis Aurora fugatis
> cum...   Virgil, *Aeneid* 3. 521–2

> *And the stars had been put to flight and Aurora was beginning to blush when...*

In our passage *iamque*[16] (in bucolic diaeresis again) is mock-heroic. *Vestigia ponere* is mock-heroic, and mock-mouse. It would be a sadness to read this without thinking of the scuttering of mouse paws. Yet another ornament of the high style is the colour contrast[17] in *rubro ubi cocco | tincta super lectos canderet uestis eburnos*, a standard trick. Cf.

> Indo quod dente politum
> tincta tegit roseo conchyli purpura fuco.
>   Catullus 64. 48–9

Line 104 contains another epicism; κεῖτο μέγας μεγαλωστί says Homer (*Iliad* 16. 776), of Cebriones. *Ingentem atque ingenti uulnere uictum* says Virgil of Lausus (*Aeneid* 10. 842). Meanwhile Horace has written *magno magnum spectare catino* (*Satires* 2. 2. 39) of a fish on a dish and here of the scraps of last night's dinner. Nor should we fail to hear the portentous rhythms of 103–5. The Golden Line, by strict definition, consists of a pair of adjectives together, a pair of nouns together, and a verb between the pairs, but variants are very common. Virgil, *Georgic* 1. 494–7 will demonstrate a Golden Line preceded by three Golden Type lines:

> agricola incuruo terram molitus aratro
> exesa inueniet scabra robigine pila,
> aut grauibus rastris galeas pulsabit inanis
> grandiaque effossis mirabitur ossa sepulcris.

The first dozen lines of Catullus 64 contain half-a-dozen such lines juggling two pairs and a verb – fair game for the peroration of Horace's pseudo-epyllion in *Satire* 2. 6. 97–105.

Horace's *dénouement* is best savoured by comparison with other fabulists. 'When two mice were feasting in the larder', says Aesop, 'the pantry-woman came in and they fled in panic.' That's all. Bare and brief. No psychological interest. Babrius is more elaborate. 'As the Country Mouse was picking cheese out of a basket, the door opened. The Town Mouse jumped up and escaped into the depths of a tiny hole, squeaking incomprehensible instructions and jostling his guest. After a short wait he crept out again and was about to reach for a Kameraean fig when somebody else came in to get something. The mice went into hiding.' This is more interesting. We know what they are eating. We can enjoy the *sauve-qui-peut* reaction of the Town Mouse. But this is ramshackle writing. Why, for instance, does only the Town Mouse come out of hiding, although both go back into hiding a moment later? The main refinement is the double interruption, and the pointlessness of this is demonstrated by the greater discipline, drama and psychological insight of the Horatian ending. First a sudden noise – and this is a mouse-ear interpretation of the event: then the mice off the couches and scuttling all round the dining-room: the muricentric view of the catastrophe is continued with the height of the house and the barking of the dogs. Aesop tells us that the intruder was the pantry-woman, and scholars have asked who it was in Horace. But no answer has been agreed. There is no answer. This is a dramatic omission, showing Horace's grasp of mousy realities. The mice are not interested; nor is Horace. Nor is there time or taste for any second intrusion and second concealment, nor for any new psychological development like the jostling of the Country Mouse. Horace moves swiftly with the two historic infinitives *currere* and *trepidare* to the vigorous colloquialism of the Country Mouse's farewell, which is the conclusion and the climax of the fable and of the satire. *Haud mihi uita est opus hac.* He's had enough.

THE FABLE AND THE SATIRE

Hoc erat in uotis writes Rudd at the beginning of his chapter on 2. 6, 'This is a poem about wishes.' It is not. Nor even about prayers. Horace, in the country, starts by expressing his satisfaction with the country and expostulating against the hectic round of city life. A passer-by in the city asks him to use his influence with Maecenas, and Horace modulates to an amusing description of their relationship, admitting the pride he takes in it while claiming that it is conducted at a purely trivial level. At line 60 he breaks into the trivialities with a cry of longing for country life, *O rus quando ego te aspiciam*, and this leads to a description of a country supper-party which is the setting for our fable. 'The over-all unity of this poem consists in a humorous balance of satisfaction and dissatisfaction, country and town.' This 'moral dialectic', carefully analysed by Brink,[18] forms the sounding-board for the fable at the end, and greatly increases its resonance. The Town Mouse is Horace or, to be exact, one aspect of the *persona* Horace is presenting, and the Country Mouse is another. Take just the last line, the moral of the fable. *Tutus* and *tenuis* clearly relate to Horace himself as presented in the rest of the poem (e.g. 1–3, 15, 18, 63–4, 71, 79). *Tenuis* is a common adjective for the simple life in Horace and Horace elsewhere connects the simple life with simplicity of diet.[19] *Viuitur paruo bene* (*Odes* 2. 16. 13). This is the life Horace claimed to live and to love. It is the inspiration of much of his poetry, including this satire. So the fable is humane and intelligent; full of good-humoured mockery depending largely on the anthropomorphic joke, at the expense of pretension in philosophy and literature; and an amusing extension and reflection of the main concern of this poem. This 'simple tale' is not a lonely pipe, but a large orchestra cunningly deployed.

HORACE AND HENRYSON

Aesop and Babrius and Phaedrus have been quoted in this essay and always to demonstrate the greater wealth and wit of the Horatian version. But detail apart, Horace's poetry is, as we have just argued, more powerful because the fable is not a free-standing anecdote but an integral part of the great personal satire whose theme it supports and extends. This same argument applies against modern versions of this fable. The best of these is by Robert Henryson (1425?–1500?), in his 'Morall Fabillis of Esope the Phrygian'. Although the 'Taill of the Upon-landis Mous and the Burges Mous' is self-contained and has nothing of the intimate personal significance which the Horatian fable derives from its setting in *Satire* 2. 6, it is a brilliant poem in its own right.

Its political and social allusions have recently been elucidated by MacQueen (1967), and if he is right the poem contains also symbolic references to religion. The mice are the enemies of Christ; the cat is Fortune as well as Death; and the spenser or butler may be the Providence which governs Fortune.[20] These theories may shock the soberer imagination of those of us who study Latin literature and are unfamiliar with such arcane equations. But there is another striking difference between Horace and Henryson: Henryson's mice are female! The great joy of the poem lies in its devastating observation of the social behaviour of women.

Typical is the meeting of these two Scotch wifies, laughing, and weeping, and embracing and then walking side by side into the house.

> For quhylis they leuch, and quhylis for joy they gret
> Quhylis kissit sweet, and quhylis in armis plet:
> And thus they fure quhill soberit was their mude,
> Syne fute for fute unto the chalmer yude.

But they soon have their difficulties. There are even traces of cattiness:

> 'Sister, is this your daylie fude?'
> 'Quhy not,' quod scho, 'is not this meit richt gude?'
>
> 'Na, be my saule, I think it bot ane scorne.'
> 'Madame,' quod scho, 'ye be the mair to blame;
> My mother said, sister, quhen we war borne,
> That I and ye lay baith within ane wame:
> I keip the rait and custome of my dame,
> And of my leving in to pouertie,
> For landis haif we nane in propertie.'
>
> 'My fair sister,' quod scho, 'haif me excusit.
> This rude dyet and I can nocht accord.
> Till tender meit my stomok is ay usit
> For quhylis I fair als weill as ony lord.'

We are reading a comedy of manners, of feminine manners. Gone are the urbanity, the philosophy, the literary play, the wit of male conversation.

Horace's protagonists are sophisticated males: in Henryson we have a feminine genre scene. This profound change appears to have its origin in a grammatical accident. Henryson's model was French.[21] In French the word for mouse is *la souris*. Throughout any French narrative the appropriate demonstrative pronoun would be *elle*. Even if a Frenchman wishes to denote a specifically male mouse, he uses the feminine noun, *la souris mâle*, and if he subsequently wishes to refer to him he uses the pronoun *elle*. In early French fabulists this tale is told of *les deux souris*, and they are feminine in gender. So Haudent (died 1557?) 'D'une souris de ville et d'une autre de village'. So Marie de France (late twelfth–early thirteenth century)

> La suriz de vile demande
> S'ele ot iluec point de viande.
> Cele respunt: 'J'en ai asez;
> Venez avant e sil veez.'

Henryson, using French sources, has female mice and a female genre scene. It therefore looks as though Henryson's female characterization was sparked off by an accident of French gender. Some confirmation of this theory may be found in the fables of Corrozet (1510–68), Boursault (1638–after 1701), and Le Noble (1643–1711), who have preserved the male sex of the classical sources, but at the cost of changing the species. They wrote about rats. So La Fontaine 621–95:

> Autrefois le rat de ville
> Invita le rat des champs...

Kiessling–Heinze (1960) note in their commentary that Horace's Town Mouse criticizes only obliquely and by implication. Henryson's mice are women, and Scotswomen speak in cataracts of acid. The ladies behind MacDiarmid's Jean, Tam O'Shanter's Kate and Dunbar's Twa Mariit Wemen and the Wedo have driven their menfolk to a prodigious output of anti-feminist and quasi-anti-feminist poetry in which Henryson's Twa Mice take an honoured place.

6

John Bramble

CVI NON DICTVS HYLAS PVER?

Propertius 1. 20

Hoc pro continuo te, Galle, monemus amore,
   (id tibi ne uacuo defluat ex animo)
saepe imprudenti fortuna occurrit amanti:
   crudelis Minyis dixerit Ascanius.
est tibi non infra speciem, non nomine dispar,   5
   Theiodamanteo proximus ardor Hylae:
huic tu, siue leges Vmbrae sacra flumina siluae,
   siue Aniena tuos tinxerit unda pedes,
siue Gigantea spatiabere litoris ora,
   siue ubicumque uago fluminis hospitio,   10
Nympharum semper cupidas defende rapinas
   (non minor Ausoniis est amor Adryasin);
ne tibi sit duros montes et frigida saxa,
   Galle, neque expertos semper adire lacus:
quae miser ignotis error perpessus in oris   15
   Herculis indomito fleuerat Ascanio.
namque ferunt olim Pagasae naualibus Argon
   egressam longe Phasidos isse uiam,
et iam praeteritis labentem Athamantidos undis
   Mysorum scopulis applicuisse ratem.   20
hic manus heroum, placidis ut constitit oris,
   mollia composita litora fronde tegit.
at comes inuicti iuuenis processerat ultra
   raram sepositi quaerere fontis aquam.
hunc duo sectati fratres, Aquilonia proles,   25
   hunc super et Zetes, hunc super et Calais,
oscula suspensis instabant carpere palmis,
   oscula et alterna ferre supina fuga.
ille sub extrema pendens secluditur ala
   et uolucres ramo summouet insidias.   30
iam Pandioniae cessit genus Orithyiae:

a dolor! ibat Hylas, ibat Hamadryasin.
hic erat Arganthi Pege sub uertice montis
   grata domus Nymphis umida Thyniasin,
quam supra nullae pendebant debita curae   35
   roscida desertis poma sub arboribus,
et circum irriguo surgebant lilia prato
   candida purpureis mixta papaueribus.
quae modo decerpens tenero pueriliter ungui
   proposito florem praetulit officio,   40
et modo formosis incumbens nescius undis
   errorem blandis tardat imaginibus.
tandem haurire parat demissis flumina palmis
   innixus dextro plena trahens umero.
cuius ut accensae Dryades candore puellae   45
   miratae solitos destituere choros,
prolapsum leuiter facili traxere liquore:
   tum sonitum rapto corpore fecit Hylas.
cui procul Alcides iterat responsa, sed illi
   nomen ab extremis fontibus aura refert.   50
his, o Galle, tuos monitus seruabis amores,
   formosum Nymphis credere uisus Hylan.

Four versions of the story of Hylas, ward of Hercules, abducted by the
water-Nymphs, have been preserved from antiquity, those of Apollonius Rhodius, Theocritus, Propertius, and Valerius Flaccus.[1] Study
of the first two makes an important preliminary to analysis of the
twentieth poem of the *Monobiblos*, Propertius' first book of elegies.
Valerius is of little help, offering nothing in the way of information
about the state of the myth before late Republican times, since he
merely reworks Apollonius, with Virgilian phraseology, into a
monotonously grandiose pastiche.[2] Besides Theocritus and Apollonius,
the Hellenistic poets Nicander and Euphorion appear to have treated
the theme, but sadly little can be discovered of their manner.[3] Still, for
once we know a good deal about the Greek background to a production
of Roman Alexandrianism – enough to place in relief the aims and
methods of the Latin poet. Latter-day adherents of the New Criticism
of the thirties, with their fond belief that a blank mind facing an anonymous text will register impressions of value, will no doubt disapprove
of the invocation of extrinsic criteria. All I can say is that I am happy
to have my response prejudiced by historical considerations, believing

as I do that mortal texts cannot be analysed according to immortal principles.

Working within the Alexandrian tradition, the young Propertius was bound to produce a personal angle in a mythological narrative: since the time of Callimachus, this type of composition had been marked by eccentricity and editorial intervention. Judging from the frequency of polysyllabic pentameter endings, 1. 20 is an early work,[4] written at a time when innovation and experiment claimed the attention of Latin poets, the period of the *Eclogues*, the *Epodes*, and the *Amores* of Gallus. In Propertius' love elegies, exemplary myth is retailed from the unexpected viewpoint. How much more important in a narrative proper to avoid the banal and the conventional, in order to maintain the title of modernist. Virgil mentions the story of Hylas in the sixth *Eclogue*, paying special attention to the echo motif and the description of the fountain of the Nymphs: given the status of this composition as a catalogue of themes suitable for treatment by, or already treated by, Roman Alexandrianism, there is a chance that the story had already received one Latin version. By the time of the third *Georgic*, Virgil could include the myth amongst the tales that everyone knew.[5] Seeing that the theme had already undergone a certain amount of literary anatomization in Rome, if it had not been actually treated *in extenso*, the demands on Propertius' originality would have been great. A poet writing at the end of the miniature epic's period of domination, when the revolutionary creed expounded by Callimachus had hardened into an orthodoxy, had to cater for exacting and sophisticated tastes. Above all, variety in narrative technique had to be combined with a novel version of the myth.

To judge from the literary–theoretical creed implied in his divergences from Apollonius,[6] Theocritus would have found himself at home in the company of Propertius. Though not as yet an avowed follower of the Callimachean poetic, Propertius, like Theocritus, writes in a manner which is quite at the other end of the scale from the sustained monochrome elevation of epic. Sequence is abandoned for tonal juxtaposition, panorama for irregular focus. Diction is eclectic, an imbalanced mixture of epicism and less ambitious, sometimes lyrical forms, while characterization is ironic and psychologically probable. Gone is the attempt to impress with a consistently urgent sense of moment: flexibility replaces inflation.

Concentrating briefly on Theocritus, we see that he has broken off a portion of the *Argonautica* and welded it into an organic episode, giving it a unity which it did not possess in the original. Two protagonists are singled out, Hercules, comic and credible thanks to detraction from his unwieldy heroic status, and Hylas, sentimentally transformed from Homeric squire into fetching *naif*: the most significant omission is the intrusive Polyphemus of Apollonius, whose presence was only explicable in terms of aetiological factors outside the scope of the main theme. The Argonautic background is only sketchily delineated, being required to act as no more than a foil to a low-key account of love and separation, a contrast, like the normally heroic stature of Hercules, to events carefully divested of Apollonius' inappropriately even epic colouring. Emphasis is on the love of Hercules for the boy, the concrete details of landscape – neither of these accentuated by Apollonius – and the moment of abduction. The only remaining epic feature – and this, significantly, was dropped by Propertius – is a lion simile.[7] All that Apollonius can offer to rival Theocritus is his description of Hylas when seen, or rather as seen by the Nymph – 'And the boy she perceived close at hand with the rosy flush of his beauty and sweet grace. For the full moon beaming from the sky smote him' (lines 1229ff.) – a coyly erotic touch which is quite out of harmony with its context.

Theocritus prefaces his narrative with a fifteen line introduction, in which his address to Nicias implies that there is no great gap between ordinary erotic involvement and the loves of legendary heroes. To illustrate his contention, he brings on Hercules (lines 5–6), 'the brazen-hearted son of Amphitryon, who withstood the fierce lion', and then undermines the pompous phraseology with the simple statement that he loved a boy. He exchanges the cumbersome genealogical inset of Apollonius for a single line describing Hylas' attractive appearance, and continues the tension between high and low in an uneven account of the various times of day (lines 10ff.): 'He never left him, neither at midday, nor when Dawn's white horses ran back to the abode of Zeus, nor when the chirping chickens scurried to their bed on the smoke stained rafters at the flapping of their mother's wings.' In the description of evening, with its homely picture of the hen and her chickens, he seems to catch something of the protective relationship of Hercules to the youth, expressing its comic incongruity through juxtaposition to the conventionally poetic image of the chariot of Dawn.

Having equated the heroic with the human, Theocritus now forgets Nicias and seems to return to the level of epic. But pastoral touches inserted amidst the succession of exotic proper names and geographical details remind us that our poet is not simply another chronicler of the Argonauts: mention of the time of year occasions a reference to lambs finding pasture, while the heroes make a couch out of rushes and sedge, realistic replacements for Apollonius' colourless leaves. After line 35 the main narrative begins, soon halted by a static *descriptio fontis*, later regarded as a primary component of the story, as shown by *quo fonte* in the sixth *Eclogue* (line 43), but nonetheless absent from Apollonius' account. Propertius was later to better the bucolic poet, ignoring naturalism in an attempt to make the spring suggestive of the relationship between lover and beloved. Three lines follow, 43–5, which create another static vignette, this time of the dances of the water Nymphs, who are now three in number, and catalogued by name in a line of their own – a more rounded, more decorative arrangement than that of Apollonius, whose single anonymous Naiad is left behind by her companions apparently in the interests of nothing more than the illusion of faithfulness: in his theoretically sanctioned pursuit of 'truth' the epicist omits nothing, and places nothing in relief. Immediately love causes the Nymphs to grasp the arm of Hylas as he lowers the pitcher, and the next minute he joins them in the water. To lighten what might have been a tragedy, his fall is compared to that of a star – the nautical setting of the simile prepares for the departure of the Argonauts – and our last glimpse of him is sitting on the knees of the Nymphs, receiving comfort, lines 49ff.: 'And he fell headlong into the dark water, as when a fiery star falls headlong from the sky into the sea, and one of the sailors says to his companions "Make ready the tackle. The breeze is set for sailing." The Nymphs held the weeping boy on their knees, comforting him with gentle words.' Linear narrative sequence is minimal, emphasis being concentrated on a few specially selected items. Romance and distance are the keynotes of this section, both aimed at producing an image of a painless, dreamlike world where incidents have none of the banal or relentless logic of everyday life.

Realism returns in the description of Hercules' reaction at 55ff., a passage which relies for its point on the juxtaposition of elevated diction and allusion, heralded by the enormous patronymic *Amphitryoniades*, with normal erotic psychology. The distance of the previous section now has the function of increasing the sense of separation: the massive Hercules can do nothing to recover his beloved, lost irretrievably to another existence, as idyllic, alien and irrational as that of childhood. 'Though near, he seemed very far away.' All that he has to console him is the boy's answer to his cries, 'a thin voice from the water' (lines 59–60). We are not even told the content of the reply: Hylas might just as well not care. Hercules, alone and bereaved, is thrown back on the only resources which myth allowed him, to become a figure of fun, almost a child's vengeful caricature, with his Scythian bow and uncouth bellowing. Epic gifts and accomplishments are not merely useless when faced with loss: they are ridiculous. Were it not for the lion simile which, though consonant with the other grandiose elements in the passage, upsets the balance with the realistic vein – it looks like a survival from the animal similes of Apollonius – the section would be a subtle study in the emotions, laid bare and exaggerated by their attribution to a figure traditionally impervious to the finer nuances of human feeling. With a contrast between Argo, 'the ship of the thirty benches' (line 74), and the image of Hercules ignominiously reaching Colchis on foot, Theocritus ends his account on the same incongruous note as he began.

There could be no question of Propertius' returning to the ramshackle construction of Apollonius: to award equal weight to all incidents was to produce a fatal dispersion of interest, raising background to the same level of importance as action. Once more epic had been surpassed by the shorter, more selective composition, which dispensed with consistency of tone and even balance. The pitfalls of Apollonius' method of composition are seen, for instance, in the overloaded sentence at 1234ff., where Hylas dips his pitcher in the stream, leans to one side, the water fills the pitcher, the Nymph takes hold of the boy wishing to kiss him, draws down his arm, and pulls him into the water. There is no centre of gravity, no foreground: we have hardly progressed from the step-by-step, one-dimensional style of continuous narration described by Auerbach in Homer.[8] The task which faced the Roman was one of adapting the myth to the circumstances of his addressee – something which mattered less for the pastoral poet, whose narrative only purported to exemplify a general proposition – and producing an account which would rival his predecessor in finesse, yet remain sufficiently distinctive as to have the appearance of an independent creation. To meet these requirements, Propertius invents a Hylas who is in constant danger from would-be seducers, not simply because of his beauty, but also because of an innocence which to the onlooker, if not to himself, is more assumed than real. Where in Theocritus the emphasis was as much on the reactions of the lover as on the actual abduction, the centre now shifts to the boy, his wanderings, and his liability to seduction. From line 25 to 48 there is not a single mention of Hercules. Nor is there any hint in the narrative itself of the agonies he suffered. The address to Gallus is now the place for explicit allusion to the pain attendant on loss. A more personal note enters the history of the myth: Propertius' Hylas is a disguised version of Gallus' favourite, described in such a way as to show that the addressee should not harbour illusions about youth and simplicity. Whim is the dictating factor in the boy's behaviour, the thing which causes him to be heedless of the feelings of his lover.

Sixteen lines of introduction, the last two transitional, prepare for the relation of the cautionary tale, to be picked up by the final couplet. At the very beginning of the poem we find the dominant theme: Gallus' affair runs the risk of breakdown. Propertius, concerned with its furtherance – *pro continuo...amore*, 'so may your love continue' – has written the poem as a piece of advice to a careless lover: *uacuo* and *imprudenti* in lines 2 and 3 show how negligent Gallus can be. If the addressee is one and the same as the inventor of Roman love-elegy,[9] and there is no good reason to believe that he is not, there is an obvious irony in this adoption of the stance of *praeceptor amoris*: the younger poet has the effrontery to tell the experienced elegist how he should conduct his affair. Also the contrived learning of the composition gains point: one poet converses with another in the shared idiom of their craft.

Specificity and generalization, respectively the hallmarks of the first and second couplets, meet in lines 5–6, where myth is conflated with actuality:

> est tibi non infra speciem, non nomine dispar
> Theiodamanteo proximus ardor Hylae.

After direct address and axiom supported by recondite allusion, a fusion of past and present which authoritatively forebodes the same end for the Gallan Hylas as befell his legendary counterpart. But his prophetic ambitions lead Propertius astray. Unless we posit irony, or a concealed clue to the name of Gallus' boy,[10] the patronymic *Theioda-manteo* must be regretted as senselessly ponderous, an unfortunate incursion into the language of epic. More successful, since obviously parodistic, are the high-flown geographical references of lines 7–10, where the intention seems to be one of accommodating the rivers of Italy to the status of the distant *Ascanius*, and so continuing the tone of generality, the impression that the events of myth can repeat them-selves today, even in our own country:

> huic tu, siue leges Vmbrae sacra flumina siluae,
> siue Aniena tuos tinxerit unda pedes,
> siue Gigantea spatiabere litoris ora,
> siue ubicumque uago fluminis hospitio...

A further irony is that these rivers, in their Hellenized, almost epic guise, belong to fashionable parts of Italy: urban wit modernizes legend, converting what might have been only a sophisticated pastoral background into a Riviera of ersatz sublimity. Having implicitly equipped the Italian countryside with mythological hazards, Propertius draws a direct parallel at lines 11–12, as earlier in the couplet on the Gallan Hylas:

> Nympharum semper cupidas defende rapinas;
> non minor Ausoniis est amor Adryasin.

Contemporary Italy is equated with mythological Greece, partly with flippant nationalism – irony at expense of the fact that Rome wished to boast the annexation of as many things Greek as possible – partly to presage the fate of the new Hylas, here as yet only portrayed as the passive object of advances from Gallus' rivals. Legend now thoroughly intermingled with reality, Propertius concludes his introduction by repeating his warning, couching it in terms of the experience of Hercules, and using the desolate landscape which so frequently formed the back-cloth to the laments of the abandoned elegiac lover, 13ff.:

> ne tibi sit duros montes et frigida saxa,
> Galle, neque expertos semper adire lacus:
> quae miser ignotis error perpessus in oris
> Herculis indomito fleuerat Ascanio.

Like the *deserta loca* and *frigida rupes* of 1. 18, or *sola sub rupe* and *gelidi...saxa Lycaei* at *Eclogue* 10. 14–15, or again *rupe sub aeria* and *gelidis...sub antris* at *Georgic* 4. 508–9, the harsh mountains, cold rocks and unsympathetic river here serve as correlatives to mood: the conventionality of the device is apparent from the fact that once deployed it ceases to be functional.[11] Into this picture of an inhospitable nature, Propertius has introduced an allusion to the labours of Hercules: *indomito...Ascanio* represents the river as an erotic trial which has not been surmounted, so paralleling Theocritus' intimation that the hero might withstand the lion of Nemea, but has no defences against love. With the formula *namque ferunt olim*, abruptly demarcating present from past, we are projected into the company of the Argonauts. Lines 17–20 are a compressed counterpart to the somewhat lengthy geographical catalogue of Theocritus, written more in the allusive manner of Catullus 64, where an ornate but brief itinerary prefaces the narrative. We are led to expect more in this grandiose vein, but Propertius cannot allow too much distance to intervene between the myth and the situation it illustrates. More of this convoluted exotic manner would have made his story tangential to his purpose, as well as importing an alien element of continuity. Typical of the learned style is the etymological play in the juxtaposition *Pagasae naualibus* (line 17). Pagasa, the name of the port in Thessaly near which the Argo was built, was, according to Strabo, derived from ναυπηγία τῆς 'Αργοῦς, 'the place where the Argo was built': hence *naualibus*, 'shipyard'.[12] Lines 21–2 are a partial concession to epic, the equivalent of Apollonius 1. 1182–4 and Theocritus 13. 33, but differentiated from the elevated tone of the preceding passage by the interlaced word order of 22: 'mollia composita litora fronde tegit'. As if to insist that this medium is the couplet, not the hexameter, Propertius abbreviates his unit of composition, imparting a note of finality and completion.

This static feeling recurs at 25–30, the first *tableau* in the story of Hylas, after the slight elevation, again modified by intricate *iunctura*, of the transitional lines 23–4. Zetes and Calais are additions to the myth, no doubt imported in order to suggest that Gallus' Hylas is also open to homosexual seduction. Their persistence is mirrored by the repetitions, *hunc...hunc...hunc*, followed by *oscula...oscula*, as well as by subdivision of the massive *Aquilonia proles* into the persons of the sons of the North wind:

> hunc duo sectati fratres, Aquilonia proles,
> > hunc super et Zetes, hunc super et Calais,
> oscula suspensis instabant carpere palmis,
> > oscula et alterna ferre supina fuga.

Given these two couplets of concerted gymnastic assault it is surprising that Hylas manages to make an escape. Propertius' interest seems to be formal rather than pictorial, his aim one of producing an impression of mobility without recourse to obviously visual methods.

Hylas' immunity, however, is short-lived: line 32, perhaps an imitation of Alexander Aetolus,[13] enlivened by the reduplicated *ibat* and the prophetic exclamation *a dolor*, seals his fate. That the responsibility for seduction is his own comes out in the long description of the fountain at 33–42, a passage whose central placing is an indication of importance. The actions of the Nymphs are relegated to a mere three lines, emphasis now being squarely focused on Hylas and the fountain in a development of the formal *descriptio loci*. Here it emerges that he is too inquisitive, too easily diverted, and too much in love with beauty, albeit that beauty is his own (39–42, cf. also *nullae...debita curae* in 35):

89

> quae modo decerpens tenero pueriliter ungui
> *proposito florem* praetulit *officio,*
> et modo *formosis* incumbens nescius undis
> *errorem blandis* tardat *imaginibus.*

Exchanging the realistic pastoral detail of Theocritus for a more generalized vignette, in which only apples, lilies and poppies are listed, Propertius sacrifices accuracy – poppies do not grow near water – in order to include the poets' favourite contrast between red and white: *candida purpureis,* an ornamental juxtaposition of form, enhancing the brocade-like qualities of the text. It might also be the case that poppies have been chosen for their associations with forgetfulness. With its unreal, artificial atmosphere, the garden here is reminiscent of the allegorical landscapes of later Latin poetry – the bowers of Venus of Reposianus and Claudian.

Propertius has carefully represented Hylas as more interested in the flowers than in his 'duty', and delineated his narcissistic fascination with his own appearance, introducing erotic colour to remind the reader of the dangers besetting Gallus' affair. First, Hylas neglects his obligation to his lover. With *officium* in the sense of 'favour', we can compare Ovid, *Amores* 1. 10. 45–6:

> omnia conductor soluit mercede soluto;
> non manet officio debitor ille tuo

where the customer is absolved from further involvement after paying for sexual favours; also *Amores* 3. 7. 23–4:

> at nuper bis flaua Chlide, ter candida Pitho,
> ter Libas officio continuata meo est

where the poet, talking of the favours he has bestowed on women, remembers his previous potency. Here in Propertius, the erotic colour of *officium* is only latent, but nonetheless evocative of a situation where Gallus could be straightforwardly spurned by his *puer delicatus.* His Hylas neglects a promised favour – and transfers his interest to the flowers. But Propertius writes *florem,* not *flores.* Of course, on the primary level the reference is to the flowers recently described. But given the frequency of *flos iuuentutis* and similar expressions in Latin, it is tempting to infer that Hylas is portrayed as so involved with his own pretty face that he disappoints the hopes of his master. On this interpretation, the transition to line 41 is neater: the meaning of *formosis,* inexplicable without recourse to the image of his reflected appearance, is more immediately apparent if the previous line has prepared us for Hylas' fascination with himself. To those who object that *nescius*, backed up by the collocation *tenero pueriliter*, stands against any aspersions on Hylas' innocence, it could be answered that the boy is unsure of the identity of the person he sees in the spring – an uncertainty which makes his faithlessness the greater.

Most editors take line 42, one of the best in the whole *œuvre*, 'errorem blandis tardat imaginibus', as a reference to the aimless delay which interrupts the mission.[14] But given the picture of a narcissistic young boy, more interested in his own good looks than in the claims of his master, it would not be inapposite to detect another level of meaning in *errorem*, namely, an insinuation that the youth is perverse in his self-admiration. For *error* can be used of the mental derangement induced by love: witness, for example, Virgil, *Eclogue* 8. 41 *ut uidi, ut perii, ut me malus abstulit error*, Ovid, *Amores* 1. 2. 35 *Blanditiae comites tibi erunt Errorque Furorque*, 1. 10. 9 *nunc timor omnis abest animique resanuit error*, and *Metamorphoses* 10. 342 *retinet malus error amantem*. If we interpret along similar lines here, Hylas' interest in his own beauty – *florem* – rather than in obedience to his master – *officio* – becomes an *error*, a sexual deviation in which he too readily indulges. At *Metamorphoses* 3. 407ff. Ovid wrote up an analogous story, that of Narcissus, in more forthright terms, using the word in question twice, at 431 and 447, both times with something of the sense found here. It is perhaps worth asking if the two poets knew the same version, especially since Propertius' line 42 is not paralleled by anything in Theocritus or Apollonius: from the collection of myths prepared for the use of Gallus by Parthenius, a Greek poet from Nicaea of Callimachean affiliations, we see that it was acceptable to conflate one legend with another – a procedure obviously helpful to a poet in search of novelty.

The boy is finally seduced by his own appearance. But other temptations, embodied in the landscape, have already tried his constancy. Critics have failed to notice the ominous nature of *nullae . . . debita curae* at 34–5:

> quam supra nullae pendebant debita curae
> roscida desertis poma sub arboribus.

On this phrase Postgate (1926) writes in his commentary 'The labour of its cultivation has claims on the plant which must be satisfied', adding on *desertis* 'The trees had been planted and abandoned and cultivation had renounced its claim.' Correct, at a literal level. We appear to be in the midst of some kind of Golden-Age landscape: the fruit and the trees are free from all ownership. But why has Propertius chosen this particular mode of expression? Again, I think we can discern an erotic undercurrent. For *cura* can denote the lover's object of concern – the beloved. At *Amores* 1. 3. 15–16, for example, Ovid maintains his fidelity with *non mihi mille placent, non sum desultor amoris: | tu mihi, si qua fides, cura perennis eris*, and at Horace, *Odes* 2. 8. 8 Barine is the *publica cura* of the youth. Propertius' fruit 'owes nothing to any object of concern'. On an amatory interpretation of *curae* the implication is that the fruit is free from all 'attachments': since they have no obligation to any object of affection, the apples are capable of conferring their uncommitted allegiance on Hylas. Through the pathetic fallacy, the description of nature in terms of human moods and emotions, the landscape is transformed into a garden of temptation. The warning to Gallus is ironically incorporated into the description: 'Beware, Hylas is wandering into the abode of the Nymphs, a place where even the fruit on the trees is seductive.' Although he has warded off the more obvious physical threats of Zetes and Calais, and although he is not directly attracted to the Nymphs themselves, Hylas is placed by lines 33–42 in a situation which prepares for his seduction. He is not fickle as regards open overtures from people other than Gallus. But he is not the complete innocent. If Gallus lets him out of his sight, he will succumb to a curiosity which leads to compromise.

The *dénouement* is perfunctory. It is typical of epyllion style and elegiac narrative technique that a coincidental episode, almost entirely devoid of action, should claim the centre of attention, while essentials are left to form a bare supporting framework, themselves often presented from an unexpected angle. A couplet is devoted to the complicated physical details of Hylas' stance by the spring – as earlier at 27ff., Propertius seems to require acclaim for dealing with intractable material – then three lines describe the actions of the Nymphs, now only secondary figures, the sense being carried over at 46–7 from pentameter into hexameter, so producing a rare moment of continuity. These lines are far more condensed than their counterparts in Apollonius and Theocritus: only a participle is used to depict the love of the Nymphs; the institution of their dancing is taken for granted; it is not explicitly stated that they pulled Hylas *into* the water – only *through* it. Such allusiveness is very much in the manner of the Alexandrians, taking background information for granted, and focusing on a few oblique details: the beauty of Hylas, the ease with which he enters the water. Like Theocritus, Propertius is at pains to allay any feeling of tragedy, carefully following *leuiter* with *facili* to give an unearthly quality to the boy's disappearance. Without the use of similes, he achieves his predecessor's effect of remoteness simply by means of adjectival constructions. This same effect is continued by the three lines 48–50, where Hylas gives a cry, and Hercules answers, only to hear an echo from the fountain. The boy disappears into thin air. Propertius dispenses with the traditional antics of the bereaved Hercules, packing all the sense of separation into line 50: 'nomen ab extremis fontibus aura refert.' Then, after this pathetic elegiac diminuendo, a final couplet linking end to beginning. But now there is none of the brashness inherent in the earlier treatment of the contemporary Hercules and his love: our ultimate response is to the myth, to a story of loss, made the more final and absolute because of Hylas' carelessness.

7

Guy Lee

OTIVM CVM INDIGNITATE

Tibullus 1. 1

Diuitias alius fuluo sibi congerat auro
    et teneat culti iugera magna soli,
quem labor assiduus uicino terreat hoste,
    Martia cui somnos classica pulsa fugent:
me mea paupertas uitae traducat inerti   5
    dum meus assiduo luceat igne focus.

Ipse seram teneras maturo tempore uites
    rusticus et facili grandia poma manu,
nec Spes destituat sed frugum semper aceruos
    praebeat et pleno pinguia musta lacu.   10
nam ueneror seu stipes habet desertus in agris
    seu uetus in triuio florida serta lapis,
et quodcumque mihi pomum nouus educat annus
    libatum agricolae ponitur ante deo.

Others can pile up wealth for themselves in yellow gold
and own great acres of cultivated land –
those whom continual work scares when the enemy is near,
whose sleep is routed by the blare of army trumpet-calls.
My poverty should transfer me to a life of inaction   5
so long as my hearth gleams with continual fire.

I would plant the tender vines myself when time was ripe
and the tall fruit-saplings with easy hand – a peasant.
Nor would Hope fail me, but ever provide heaps
of produce and fill the vat with rich must.   10
For I offer worship wherever a solitary stake in the fields
or old stone at the crossways bears a garland of flowers,
and the first of every fruit the new year raises for me
is laid at the feet of the farmer god.

Flaua Ceres, tibi sit nostro de rure corona   15
    spicea quae templi pendeat ante fores,
pomosisque ruber custos ponatur in hortis
    terreat ut saeua falce Priapus aues.
uos quoque, felicis quondam, nunc pauperis agri
    custodes, fertis munera uestra, Lares.   20
tunc uitula innumeros lustrabat caesa iuuencos;
    nunc agna exigui est hostia parua soli.
agna cadet uobis, quam circum rustica pubes
    clamet 'io messes et bona uina date!'

Iam modo, iam possim contentus uiuere paruo   25
    nec semper longae deditus esse uiae,
sed Canis aestiuos ortus uitare sub umbra
    arboris ad riuos praetereuntis aquae!
nec tamen interdum pudeat tenuisse bidentem
    aut stimulo tardos increpuisse boues;   30
non agnamue sinu pigeat fetumue capellae
    desertum oblita matre referre domum.

At uos exiguo pecori, furesque lupique,

Golden Ceres, there would be a crown from our land for you – 15
of corn-ears, to hang on your temple door.
And a red Priapus would stand guard in the orchard
to scare the birds with his savage sickle.
You too, Lares, receive your gifts, as the guardians
of a property once prosperous, now poor.   20
Then a slaughtered heifer purified countless steers;
now a ewe-lamb is the small offering of a meagre estate.
To you a lamb shall fall and around her the young peasants
can shout 'Io, send good harvest and good wine!'

If only, now at last, I can live content with a little   25
and not surrender forever to the long road,
but avoid the summer risings of the Dog under the shade
of a tree by streams of water going past!
Not that I'd be ashamed to handle a mattock sometimes
or reprimand the slow oxen with a goad.   30
Nor would I mind carrying home in my arms a lamb
or a kid abandoned by its forgetful mother.

But spare my meagre stock, you thieves and wolves!

parcite; de magno est praeda petenda grege.
hic ego pastoremque meum lustrare quotannis   35
    et placidam soleo spargere lacte Palem.
adsitis, diui, neu uos e paupere mensa
    dona nec e puris spernite fictilibus:
fictilia antiquus primum sibi fecit agrestis,
    pocula de facili composuitque luto.   40

Non ego diuitias patrum fructusque requiro
    quos tulit antiquo condita messis auo:
parua seges satis est, satis est requiescere lecto
    si licet et solito membra leuare toro.
quam iuuat immites uentos audire cubantem   45
    et dominam tenero continuisse sinu!
aut, gelidas hibernus aquas cum fuderit Auster,
    securum somnos igne iuuante sequi!
hoc mihi contingat: sit diues iure furorem
    qui maris et tristes ferre potest pluuias.   50

O quantum est auri pereat potiusque smaragdi
    quam fleat ob nostras ulla puella uias!

You should seek plunder from a large flock.
Here I am accustomed to purify my shepherd every year   35
and sprinkle kindly Pales with milk.
Gods, be with me, and despise not gifts
from a poor man's table and from clean earthenware:
a peasant, long ago, invented earthenware,
shaping cups out of pliant clay.   40

I do not ask for the wealth of my fathers and the yield
which garnered harvest in time past brought my grandfather.
A small crop is enough — enough if one can rest on a bed
and lighten the limbs on the accustomed mattress.
How pleasant lying there to listen to the wild winds   45
and confine a mistress in tender embrace!
Or in wintertime, when Auster scattered freezing waters,
to pursue sleep in safety, aided by a fire!
Let this come true for me. He who can bear the sea's fury
and the sad rain deserves to be rich.   50

O perish all there is of gold and emerald
sooner than any girl weep for our travels.

te bellare decet terra, Messalla, marique
  ut domus hostiles praeferat exuuias:
me retinent uinctum formosae uincla puellae   55
  et sedeo duras ianitor ante fores.

Non ego laudari curo, mea Delia; tecum
  dummodo sim, quaeso segnis inersque uocer.
te spectem suprema mihi cum uenerit hora,
  te teneam moriens deficiente manu.   60
flebis et arsuro positum me, Delia, lecto,
  tristibus et lacrimis oscula mixta dabis.
flebis: non tua sunt duro praecordia ferro
  uincta nec in tenero stat tibi corde silex.
illo non iuuenis poterit de funere quisquam   65
  lumina, non uirgo sicca referre domum.
tu Manes ne laede meos, sed parce solutis
  crinibus et teneris, Delia, parce genis.

Interea, dum fata sinunt, iungamus amores:
  iam ueniet tenebris Mors adoperta caput;   70
iam subrepet iners aetas, nec amare decebit,

It is right for you, Messalla, to make war by land and sea
so that your town-house can display enemy spoils.
But I am held prisoner – in the chains of a beautiful girl,   55
and sit in front of a hard door – the janitor.

I do not care for glory, my Delia. If only
I am with you, they can call me indolent and useless.
Let me gaze at you, when my last hour comes;
let me hold you, as I die – in a failing grasp.   60
You will weep when I too, Delia, am laid on the bed of burning,
and you will give kisses mixed with bitter tears.
You will weep. Your heart is not bound in hard iron
and no flint stands in your tender breast.
No young man, no unmarried girl will be able   65
to return home from that funeral with dry eyes.
Do not grieve my ghost, but spare your unbound hair
and, Delia, spare those tender cheeks.

Meantime, while fate allows, let us join loves.
Tomorrow death will come, with head covered – in darkness,   70
or useless age creep up, and it will not be right

dicere nec cano blanditias capite.
nunc leuis est tractanda Venus, dum frangere postes
    non pudet et rixas inseruisse iuuat.
hic ego dux milesque bonus. uos, signa tubaeque,   75
    ite procul: cupidis uulnera ferte uiris,
ferte et opes. ego composito securus aceruo
    dites despiciam despiciamque famem.

to make love or pretty speeches when the head is white.
Fickle Venus must be handled now, while breaking doors
is no disgrace and picking quarrels a pleasure.
Here I can lead and soldier well. Standards and trumpets,   75
away with you! Bring wounds to greedy men.
Bring wealth too. Carefree myself, with pile put by,
I shall despise the rich, and I shall despise hunger.

THE CONTEXT

Works of art (it is a truism) reflect the age of their creation – or rather they presuppose that age; for reflection suggests a clear image visible to anyone looking in the mirror, but in the case of a poem written in the past the image will often be obscure or distorted unless one can shine the light of knowledge upon it. That knowledge is what the poet takes for granted in his readers – knowledge of history, society, culture, literature.

It helps to get Tibullus into perspective if one remembers that his first collection was published in late 27 or in 26 B.C., i.e. very early in the principate of Augustus, after Virgil's *Eclogues* and *Georgics*, after Horace's *Satires* and *Epodes*, after Propertius 1, but before the *Aeneid*, before the *Odes* and *Epistles*, before Propertius 2–4 and Ovid's *Amores*. The book is thus the second surviving collection of Latin love elegies, the *Amores* of Gallus, inventor of the genre, being lost. Its date of publication is arrived at as follows: on the one hand, Messalla's Gallic triumph, one of the themes of Tibullus 1. 7, is firmly dated by the *fasti triumphales* or official records of triumphs to 25 September 27 B.C.; on the other hand, Propertius 2. 5. 21–6 is a direct allusion to Tibullus 1. 10. 51–64 (see Solmsen (1961), 273–5) and Propertius 2 was published in 25 B.C. (see Camps (1967), p. v).

This was a time when fortunes could still be made by serving under a successful general. What Caesar had done earlier for his chief engineer Mamurra (see Catullus 29) was only an exceptional example of the regular practice, as we may learn from Cicero's letter recommending to Caesar the thirty-five-year-old lawyer Trebatius Testa (*Ad Familiares* 7. 5) and from his letters to Trebatius advising him to make the best of a golden opportunity: for example, 'Balbus assures me you are going to be rich', 'I can congratulate you at last. I was very worried by your letters in the early months because you seemed to me sometimes (forgive my saying so) irresponsible in your longing for the city and its civilization, sometimes indolent, sometimes faint-hearted in the performance of your military duties (*timidus in labore militari*)' (*Ad Familiares* 7. 16. 3 and 17. 1). Similarly, Horace's friend Iccius hopes to get rich in the forthcoming campaign against Arabia in 26 B.C. (*Odes* 1. 29). These non-professional military tribunes and prefects were sometimes a liability; there is a well-known passage in Caesar, *De Bello Gallico* 1. 39, which describes how exaggerated rumours of the size and courage of the Germans started a panic in his army: 'It began with the military tribunes, the prefects of the auxiliary troops, and the rest who had followed Caesar from Rome *amicitiae causa* with little experience of soldiering.' Tibullus, an *amicus* of Messalla, appears to have been no more fond of *labor militaris* than Trebatius, suffered from homesickness and had dreams of getting out and of making do on his reduced estate.

He wishes he could live content with a little, choosing as his own an ideal preached by most of the philosophical schools of the day. Listen to the Epicurean Lucretius, whose great didactic poem had been published some twenty-five years before:

> quod siquis uera uitam ratione gubernet
> diuitiae grandes homini sunt uiuere parce
> aequo animo, neque enim est umquam penuria parui.
>
> 5. 1117–19
>
> *But if anyone steer his life by true reason*
> *it is great wealth for a man to live frugally*
> *with an even mind, for there is never shortage of a little.*

And here is Cicero putting forward a basically Stoic view some fifteen years before in his *De Officiis* 1. 69–70 and 72:

> 'But there are today and have been in the past many people who sought the serenity of which I speak by withdrawing from public affairs and taking refuge in a life of leisure – among them philosophers of fame and distinction, and some serious-minded and responsible men who could not tolerate the

behaviour of the people and their leaders and who lived, not a few of them, on the land in the enjoyment of their family estates. Such men have the same aim as kings – to want for nothing, be their own masters, and enjoy freedom, a word whose essential meaning is living as one likes. So those who seek power and the men of leisure I spoke of share a common object, but the former think they can gain it by possessing great wealth (*opes magnas*), the latter by being content with what is their own, albeit little (*si contenti sint et suo et paruo*). Certainly neither of these views deserves our disrespect, but the life of leisure is easier and more protected, making fewer demands on others and causing less trouble, whereas the life of those who devote themselves to great actions and the service of the state contributes more to humanity and earns greater fame and prestige.'

'Statesmen no less than philosophers – perhaps indeed even more so – need high ideals and a disregard for the world (*despicientia rerum humanarum*), serenity of spirit and a sense of security (*securitas*) if they are not to be overcome by worry.'

This second passage throws light on the colour of the words *securus* and *despiciam* in the last two lines of Tibullus's poem.

Later in the same book Cicero discusses various occupations and professions and reaches the significant conclusion that 'of all the ways of earning money none is better or pleasanter than farming, none more productive or better suited to a free man' (*De Officiis* 1. 151). But by farming he means running one or preferably more large farms, managing an estate on which the work would be done by tenant farmers or hired labourers or slaves. How then does Tibullus, a Roman knight, come to picture himself as planting vines and fruit-trees, wielding a mattock, driving a bullock-cart or a plough, looking after lost kids and lambs? There was at this time a romanticization both of the country as a refuge from the complexities of modern life and of countryfolk as living more genuine and satisfying lives than other people – a romanticization which goes back to Virgil's introduction of pastoral poetry into Latin and which is in part, perhaps, a reaction to the 'urbanity' of Calvus, Catullus, Cinna, the so-called Neoterics, and to their contempt for the 'witless land' (*rus infacetum*). Evidently Tibullus knows and admires Virgil's *Eclogues*, published in about 38 B.C.; for example, lines 19–20 of his poem look like an unconscious combination of two Virgilian phrases, *felix quondam pecus* from *Eclogue* 1. 74 and *custos es pauperis horti* addressed to Priapus at *Eclogue* 7. 34, and sure enough Priapus has appeared in Tibullus's line 18, immediately before the couplet in question. He has also read the *Georgics*, probably published in 29 B.C.: *flaua Ceres* comes from 1. 96 where the phrase occurs for the first time in extant Latin literature as a translation of the Homeric *xanthe Demeter* (*Iliad* 5. 500); similarly the adjective *spicea* is first found at *Georgics* 1. 314 in the phrase *spicea messis*. But Tibullus is no thoughtless imitator swept away by the powerful influence of a major poet, for we notice that each Virgilian phrase has been altered in one or more respects; even *flaua Ceres* is no exception, for although the two words are unchanged their case is different – vocative in Tibullus for Virgil's nominative.

Tibullus's respect for the ancestral ways of the country and in particular his observance of the ancient religious rituals are also in harmony with Virgilian attitudes. The couplet 11–12 describing his worship of the god of boundaries Terminus in the form of a stock or stone (cf. Ovid, *Fasti* 2. 641–2) reminds us of Virgil's admonition at *Georgics* 1. 338 *in primis uenerare deos* and can be regarded at the same time as a contradiction of Lucretius's lines

> nec pietas ullast uelatum saepe uideri
> uertier ad lapidem   (5. 1198–9)
>
> *And there is no piety in being often seen*
> *with head covered turning towards a stone.*

There had been a religious revival in the second half of this century and in 28 B.C., as he records in *Res Gestae* 20. 4, Augustus with the Senate's authority saw to the restoration of no less than eighty-two temples in the city.

Tibullus has also read Horace's *Epodes*, published about 30 B.C.; *Epode* 2 in particular has made a strong impression on him:

> Beatus ille qui procul negotiis
>   ut prisca gens mortalium
> paterna rura bubus exercet suis
>   solutus omni faenore
> neque excitatur classico miles truci
>   neque horret iratum mare...   (1–6)
>
> *Happy he who far from business*
> *like the early race of men*

> *works paternal lands with his own oxen*
> *released from all usury*
> *nor is roused a soldier by the fierce trumpet-call*
> *nor shudders at the angry sea...*

The reader will have noticed that some of these motifs reappear in Tibullus's elegy and a look at the remainder of Horace's *Epode* will discover other parallel detail which it would be tedious to specify here.

Evidently too Tibullus has read Propertius's first collection, published some three years before his own and known from its opening word by the title of *Cynthia*. The theme of the lover's death has occurred there in poems 17 and 19 – notably in the first of these at lines 19–24 where the girl pays him the last rites:

> illic siqua meum sepelissent fata dolorem
> ultimus et posito staret amore lapis,
> illa meo caros donasset funere crinis
> molliter et tenera poneret ossa rosa,
> illa meum extremo clamasset puluere nomen
> ut mihi non ullo pondere terra foret.

> *There if some fate had entombed my passion*
> *and the last stone stood on my buried love,*
> *she would have given precious hair to my dead body*
> *and laid the bones softly on rose-petals,*
> *she would have cried my name over the final dust*
> *that earth might be weightless upon me.*

Similarly the lover's refusal to accompany a noble friend on service overseas is the theme of Propertius 1. 6, where there is the same dismissal of military glory and choice of the warfare of love:

> non ego sum laudi, non natus idoneus armis;
> hanc me militiam fata subire uolunt.   (29–30)

> *By nature I am unsuited for glory and for arms;*
> *this is the soldiering that fate wills me to undergo.*

So when Tibullus appears before the world in the character of an impoverished landowner who having taken up a military career in order to make his fortune now dreams of leaving the army, settling down on the remains of his family estate and living a simple, ritual, country life, he is working within a circle of ideas and attitudes that were of particular interest and importance among his contemporaries; and when he pictures himself as dying in the presence of the girl he loves and imagines her mourning at his funeral, or when he chooses love in preference to military glory and yet nevertheless implies that love itself is a form of warfare, he is similarly taking over romantic ideas which were dominant in contemporary elegiac poetry and yet still new enough to have retained a freshness of appeal which they have largely lost in the twentieth century. Tibullus, like most poets, shows his originality in the individual way in which he presents or (better) re-presents, and combines, a range of ideas that were, as we say, 'in the air' when he wrote.

THE STRUCTURE

One of these ways has to do with the structure of his poems. A contemporary reader in 26 B.C. would have noticed immediately that this new poet works on a bigger scale than Propertius in Book 1; his shortest elegy, the seventh, contains sixty-four lines and is twelve lines longer than the longest in the *Cynthia*; in fact he writes elegies of the length of Virgil's *Eclogues*. How does he make them so long? Well, sometimes he does it by joining together disparate main themes, and the opening poem is an excellent example of this.

The contrast between life in the army and life on the land is implicit throughout the first part of the poem, which for the purpose of this argument we can define as lines 1–40. But there is a different theme in the second part of the poem, which, again for the purpose of this argument, can be defined as lines 51–78. Tibullus the peasant farmer now appears as Tibullus the lover. True, the contrast with the army is continued but the choice now is not between the army and the land or between future fortune and present poverty, it is between money or rather, from line 53 onwards, military glory, and a girl. When you come to think of it the first and second parts of the poem have nothing in common except the themes of war, money and inaction (*inertia*) – *uitae inerti* in line 5 being picked up at line 58 by *quaeso segnis inersque uocer*. There is even a concealed contradiction between the two parts, for the first is explicitly set in the country whereas the second is implicitly set in the town. Implicitly, because it goes without saying that if Tibullus is Delia's prisoner and doorkeeper, then he must (if only in imagination) be in Rome and not on his country estate, for women of Delia's kind, women like Gallus's Lycoris and Propertius's Cynthia, do not live buried lives in country towns or country houses. Most readers however are unaware of the lack of real connexion between the poem's two parts, not to mention their latent contradiction. This must mean that Tibullus has succeeded in making a plausible unity out of them. The question is how does he manage it? Clearly the crucial passage is the join between them, viz. lines 41–50 – and at this point let me ask the reader to re-read lines 25–40 and 51–60 so as to have a clear idea of the width of the gulf to be bridged.

So far then we have two disparate wants put side by side: the first – I want a simple country life; the second – I want Delia. How does Tibullus modulate from one to the other? Let us look at his answer in detail. Lines 41–2 tie up firmly with the first part by referring back to line 19 and the opening. There is in *fructus* a slight pun – 'fruits' and 'profits'; in the first meaning it echoes *frugum* of line 9. In lines 43 *seges* picks up this first meaning and the whole phrase *parua seges satis est* varies the earlier phrase *contentus uiuere paruo* (25). *Lecto* introduces a new idea, but it has been prepared for by line 4 and it is very natural for the soldier sleeping on the ground or on some form of portable bed (*grabatus*) to miss the comfort of his *lectus* at home. One remembers Catullus's *Sirmio*, describing his pleasure at being back home at last after serving on the staff of Memmius in the province of Bithynia-Pontus:

> o quid solutis est beatius curis
> cum mens onus reponit ac peregrino
> labore fessi uenimus Larem ad nostrum
> desideratoque acquiescimus lecto?   (31. 7–10)

> *O what greater bliss than troubles cancelled*
> *when mind lays down the load and wearied*
> *by foreign service we have come to our own Lar*
> *and relax in the longed-for bed?*

Cubantem at the end of line 45 makes an easy connexion with *lecto* and *toro* in the preceding couplet; and if the wild winds are the equinoctial gales, this indoor autumn scene contrasts with the outdoor summer idyll in the first part. The pentameter (46) adds a new dimension to the picture. So far in the elegy Tibullus has been alone, farming his land in isolation, his shepherd the only other human being mentioned (35). Now, however, we have a *ménage à deux*, and the transition is managed very simply – by means of two parallel clauses, both dependent syntactically on *quam iuuat*, in which two infinitives, 'to hear' and 'to hold', and two adjectives, 'ungentle' and 'tender', contrast with each other.

The autumn gales are followed by the winter rains of the next couplet, Auster the south wind leading on from *uentos*, *aquas* introducing another 'element', *fuderit* contrasting with *continuisse, gelidas* opposed like *aquas* to *igne* in line 48. *Hoc mihi contingat* makes it clear that what precedes is wishful thinking and that the poet is not yet in fact living in the country with his *domina*, perhaps not in the country at all, despite the reader's first impression that *hic* in line 35 is to be taken literally. The rest of the couplet (49–50) returns to the theme of money; at the same time *tristes pluuias* looks back to line 47 and *furorem maris* springs from the idea of travel that has come in the first part at line 26. This leads easily and naturally into the next couplet, which begins what we have called the second part of the poem, for in that couplet the theme of wealth is varied into gold and emeralds (gold reminiscent of the opening line), the theme of travel is repeated in *nostras uias* (echoing 26 *longae uiae*) and the new theme of love reappears after its seemingly casual introduction in line 46 – only now as *quam fleat ulla puella*, arising perhaps by unexpressed metaphor out of *tristes pluuias*, a girl's tears being another sort of rain (cf. Ovid, *Amores* 3. 6. 68).

The introduction of Messalla, Tibullus's patron, in the next couplet is important because it serves several purposes: it is an implied dedication to him of the whole book of poems; it enables an entertaining contrast to be made between the duty of a patrician and that of his equestrian dependant (in what way 'entertaining' I hope to show later); patrician *noblesse oblige* allows a change-over from the theme of money to the theme of military glory, which is rejected by the poet in favour of love; Messalla's *domus* in line 54 is his town house as opposed to his *uilla* or country house (for the opposition cf. Columella, *De Re Rustica* 1. 1. 18 *qui agrum parauit domum uendat*) and thus we are neatly transported from the country to Rome. The connexion backwards is firmly made, however, by *marique* (cf. *maris* in 50), by the theme of war, and perhaps too by the mere sound of the last word of the couplet, *exuuias*, for it rhymes with *uias* and *pluuias* at the end of the two preceding couplets.

However that may be, *exuuias* and *domus* make an easy connexion with what follows, for 'spoils' suggests 'prisoners of war' and 'prisoners of war' the contrasting image 'prisoner of love', in which the girl takes the place of the victorious commander. Town house and fetters suggest the door-keeper, a slave who was sometimes kept on a chain (cf. Ovid, *Amores* 1. 6. 1). The vivid present indicatives here contrast with the prevailing subjunctives of the first part and suggest that Tibullus actually is in the town, but of course he need not be, even as the *persona* of this poem – any more than Propertius or his poetic *persona* was actually at Lanuvium in 4. 8. 48 when he says *Lanuuii ad portas ei mihi solus eram* 'I was alone alas at the gates of Lanuvium', for it is clear from the context that he was only there in his thoughts, in a daydream.

In short, the transition from solitary country bliss to Delia is brought about in five steps: first, *lecto* (43); then, *dominam* (46); then *ulla puella* (52); then a particular girl unnamed (55) and finally her name, *mea Delia* (57). The change-over from land to love is managed so gradually and naturally that the reader is probably unaware of it until he has read the whole poem and stops to analyse it, and even then he can point to no roughness or awkwardness at the join nor can he remove any couplet without leaving an obvious gap.

This unity is strengthened by the ending (73–8), which succeeds in drawing together most of the themes that have appeared in the poem. At 73 the theme of love and youth introduces the idea of violence in love. The idea of violence leads into the figure of love as a form of war and then back to real war with its standards and trumpets – *tubae* echoing *classica* of the opening. *Cupidis* prepares the way for *opes* in 77 and we are back to the theme of wealth with which the elegy began and which has re-entered during its course almost in the manner of a refrain. The image of the heap at the end of 77 suggests not only produce, recalling *frugum aceruos* in 9, but also money, recalling *diuitias congerat* in 1; the first meaning brings back the theme of life on the land, which has not appeared in the second part of the poem. *Securus* contrasts with the dangers of active service (*uulnera* in the line before, cf. line 3) and also contrasts with *famem*. The last line recapitulates the themes of wealth and the simple life, for *famem* too, like *aceruo*, reminds one of lines 9–10. In this way the last two couplets cleverly unite four of the themes the poem has dealt with – war, money love, and life on the land, though it must be admitted that the last is only hinted at in *composito securus aceruo* and implied in *despiciam famem*, and also that the theme of honour is not alluded to – unless one argues for its implied presence in *despiciam*.

THE POETRY

We tend to regard Tibullus as the poet of sentiment and wishful thinking, whose art is tinged with a gentle and nostalgic melancholy, its essence perhaps distilled in such couplets as 11–12, 31–2, 45–6, 59–60, 69–70 of this elegy; and we are right to think so. But he also has another side, as I hope to indicate in what follows, though the reader should here be warned that we are stepping on to controversial ground.

Line 3 is hardly complimentary and it is strange that the soldier on the make is said to be scared of hard work *uicino hoste*. Does this hint that he is not only a coward but work-shy too? If it does and if, as we are told in line 4, he can't even sleep in peace, Tibullus must be making fun of him.

What is the point of line 5? If we consult the concordances to Caesar and Cicero's speeches – works all published before Tibullus's elegy – and the concordance to Livy, whose *History* began to appear in the 20s B.C., we shall find that *traducere* is common in military contexts for troop movements and that it can also be used of 'transferring' troops or individuals from one side or front or unit to another, as at Cicero, *Philippics* 10. 6 *legiones ad rem publicam traduxit*, 11. 26 *hinc si Brutus erit traductus ad aliud bellum* and Caesar, *De Bello Gallico* 6. 40 *nonnulli ex inferioribus ordinibus reliquarum legionum uirtutis causa in superiores erant ordines huius legionis traducti* (where S. A. Handford translates 'had been promoted'). Further, if we consult the *Thesaurus Linguae Latinae* we shall find that the adjective *iners* is not uncommon in military contexts, where it means *sine uirtute bellica* (see *iners* column 1309 lines 1–30). Now the construction of *traducat* in Tibullus is analogous to that found in the passages quoted, the dative *uitae* being a poetic variant for the prose idiom of preposition with accusative; moreover lines 3–4 provide a military context. It can therefore be argued that this verb and adjective would keep their military associations and that we have here an example of Tibullan wit; for the idea of poverty transferring, or promoting, the poet to a life of inaction is fresh, pointed and pleasantly paradoxical; as a rule poverty recruited people for a life of action in the army.

Does Tibullus mean it when he calls himself in line 8 *rusticus?* The word carries associations of boorishness, like 'peasant' in English, e.g. Cicero, *De Senectute* 75 *non solum indocti sed etiam rustici* and Virgil, *Eclogue* 2. 56 *rusticus es, Corydon*. And if he is not quite serious in so describing himself, is he really quite serious about leaving the army or is he perhaps indicating to his audience that what follows, though serious in tone, is intended as the expression of a nostalgic mood merely?

Certainly from 9 to 45 the tone is serious but at 46 we wonder about *continuisse*. Is this simply a metrically convenient alternative for *tenuisse*, the regular word in such a context, e.g. Catullus 45. 1–2 *Acmen...* | *tenens in gremio*, Tibullus 1. 5. 39 *saepe aliam tenui*, Propertius 2. 22. 37 *altera me cupidis teneat foueatque lacertis*, Ovid, *Heroides* 3. 114 *te tenet in tepido mollis amica sinu?* If that is so, then the usage is unparalleled. But we can find a parallel for the syntax, i.e. the construction of the active verb *continere* with a personal object (other than the reflexive pronoun) and a locative or ablative of place: for example Cicero, *De Haruspicum Responso* 6 *ferro alios fugaret, alios domi contineret*, Caesar, *De Bello Gallico* 1. 48 *exercitum castris continuit*, and *TLL* s.v. col. 703. 23ff. gives other examples of the word *in re militari*. It seems rather a strong and restrictive word to use of an embrace and one can argue that Tibullus is using a military form of speech in an unexpected and therefore entertaining way.

I have translated the next couplet as though the same thing were happening there. *Somnos sequi* is striking (perhaps an extension of such a prose phrase as *otium sequi* at Cicero, *Pro Murena* 55); in many military contexts in Caesar and Livy we should find it natural to translate *sequi* as 'pursue'; besides, the phrase here is reminiscent of *somnos fugent* at line 4, where there is certainly a military metaphor. *Iuuare* too occurs in military contexts in Caesar and Livy, and *securus* in Livy and Tacitus later. The point of this pentameter may be the use of paramilitary vocabulary in a witty way. And if this were so, there would be a military overtone in *fuderit* in the hexameter. *Fundere* is common *in re militari* (*TLL* s.v. col. 1568. 6off.), and it happens that Latin uses the same verb for what English calls 'routing' the enemy and 'pouring' water. The military overtone of *fuderit* might be evoked by the military use of *continuisse* and the paramilitary metaphor *somnos sequi*. Here is an English example of what is meant:

> Stiffen the sinews, *summon up* the blood,
> Disguise fair nature with hard-favour'd rage

and

> When to the sessions of sweet silent thought
> I *summon up* remembrance of things past.

The different effect of the same verb in each context is noticeable; in the second the legal word 'sessions' evokes a latent legal overtone in 'summon' which is not perceptible in the non-legal context of the first quotation.

At line 55, after the explicit reference in the previous couplet to Messalla as a victorious commander, the word *retinent* could hardly fail to recall the slightly sinister military sense it has on occasions, especially as it is here combined with *uinctum*: e.g. Cicero, *In Verrem* 2. 2. 65 *nuntium miserunt se a praetore retineri*, Caesar, *De Bello Gallico* 3. 9 *legatos retentos et in uincla coniectos*, Livy 28. 35 *duos pro obsidibus retineri ab Scipione iubet.* Here again Tibullus appears to be exploiting a military idiom.

And he achieves a similar effect with *sedeo* in 56. The word is used of forces and commanders encamped somewhere, e.g. Cicero, *Pro Sestio* 52 *ad portas sedenti imperatori,* Livy 10. 20. 6 *ad Volturnum flumen sedere hostem.* It is also used of anyone who sits idly by, doing nothing, e.g. Cicero, *Ad Atticum* 9. 12. 3 *ego ipse sedeo.* Both senses are present in Livy 44. 13 *consul ne segnis sederet tantum in agro hostico* and both senses are glanced at in the Tibullan passage, where the second sense leads on naturally to *segnis inersque,* words of military disapproval; *laudari* in 57 refers of course to military glory.

Between this couplet and the next (59–60) there appears at first sight to be a lack of connexion unparalleled elsewhere in this elegy, a poem remarkable for its internal coherence. Why is death suddenly brought in? The reason must surely have something to do with the contrast between lover and soldier explicit in lines 53–8; that contrast must somehow be continued implicitly in what follows. Fisher (1970) says the point of 59–68 is that the soldier killed on active service has to be buried in foreign soil, unaccompanied by the grief of those near and dear to him. This is surely right for lines 61–8 but it still leaves unanswered the question why death is suddenly introduced after the couplet 57–8 which is about glory and disgrace. Is not the point likely to be that whereas the soldier may be required to die a 'glorious death' (*dulce et decorum est pro patria mori* as Horace was to write later) Tibullus *segnis inersque* would sooner die an inglorious one, gazing at Delia in his last moments rather than at some enemy or comrade? If that is so, it is interesting that the point is not made explicitly but implied and that the implication is lost on any reader unaware of the associations of certain words in 57–8.

In line 70 there is an ambiguity about *tenebris* which I have tried to represent in the translation. This ablative could go with the verb and mean 'in the dark', cf. Tibullus 1. 2. 25 *en ego cum tenebris tota uagor anxius urbe* and 1. 6. 59 *haec mihi te adducit tenebris,* but it can also be taken with the participle *adoperta.* The image is mysterious and memorable, suggesting various things, among them how we cover the face of the dead and how the Romans covered their heads in mourning. Suicides by drowning did the same before jumping into the river (Horace, *Satires* 2. 3. 37, Livy 4. 12. 11, Ovid, *Amores* 3. 6. 79) and so did Caesar when his murderers drew their daggers (Suetonius, *Julius* 82). (Compare also above, p. 52 n. 21.)

At line 75 we find an explicit example of the application of military terminology to love – *hic ego dux milesque bonus*. But this conceit of the lover as a kind of soldier is not introduced here quite out of the blue; it has been prepared for by the use of military metaphors at lines 5, 46 and 55, if the arguments I have put forward are found convincing.

Finally, lines 51–2 are helpful pointers to the tone of the poem as a whole. The couplet expresses an extreme hyperbole: any girl's tears as the legion marched away would be a greater disaster for the poet than the loss of all the gold and emeralds in the world. To borrow a term from music, this is the galant style of poetry, elegant and sentimental, but intended to be taken with a pinch of realistic salt.

Tibullus is a better poet than he seems at first reading and probably belongs to the class of those whom foreigners have difficulty in appreciating because of their limited knowledge of the language. It cannot be for nothing that Quintilian rates him the best of the love elegists. He is particularly interesting because, like Cornelius Gallus, the inventor of Latin love elegy and later the first Prefect of Egypt, he was not only a poet but a soldier too and had experienced a way of life unknown to the civilians Propertius and Ovid. The product of his time, he shares certain attitudes and beliefs with the poets who were his contemporaries and reacts against others, but the resultant mixture in him is individual and the poetic sensibility we feel through the medium of his Latin is unique. We glimpse a character of some complexity, not to say contradiction: an *urbanus* with a hankering after *rusticitas*; a religious man devoted to the gods of the country and a sensual man devoted to a girl of the town; a respecter of tradition and the ancestors who nevertheless rejects the code of his class by putting love before honour; a precise and disciplined craftsman and a dreamer governed by his feelings; a romantic who sees himself rescuing young animals, who hates to see a girl cry but derives luxurious pleasure from the thought of her tears over his corpse, who can't bear to think of her scratching her cheeks or tearing her hair in traditional mourning but thoroughly enjoys the prospect of breaking down her door and starting a rough-house – perhaps even with her, because love is a kind of war. Such are the outlines of the poetic character discernible in this elegy.

But does the poem give us the man? Very significant, to my mind, is the epitaph he writes for himself in the third poem of Book 1, a poem apparently dominated by his fear of death and his love for Delia:

> Hic iacet immiti consumptus morte Tibullus
> Messallam terra dum sequiturque mari.   (55–6)

> *Here lies Tibullus wasted by ungentle death*
> *as he followed Messalla by land and sea.*

Contrast Propertius 2. 13. 35–6:

> qui nunc iacet horrida puluis
> unius hic quondam seruus amoris erat

> *He who is now vacant dust*
> *was once the slave of one passion.*

> (Pound's translation)

Propertius wishes to be remembered as Cynthia's lover, Tibullus as Messalla's lieutenant. The inscription is revealing and we notice how the two names it contains are placed together – *Tibullus/Messallam.* If we could have asked Tibullus which meant more to him, his friendship with Messalla or his love for Delia, it looks as though he would have replied, in the words of 1. 5. 31, *Messalla meus.*

APPENDIX

DIFFERENCES FROM POSTGATE'S OXFORD TEXT

2 *magna* MSS: *multa* Diomedes: Freising Excerpts (10th century): Paris Excerpts (12th century).

The *iugerum*, we are told, is a fixed measure of area and cannot correctly be termed 'great' or 'small'. Moreover we find *multa iugera* at Tibullus 2. 3. 42 and Ovid has two clear allusions to our Tibullan line at *Fasti* 3. 192 *iugeraque inculti pauca tenere soli* and *Ex Ponto* 4. 9. 86 *et teneat glacies iugera multa freti*. Besides, with regard to the sound of the line it is argued that *multa* goes better than *magna* with *culti* and *iugera*.

But we are not talking about the singular *iugerum*; the plural makes a difference. *Magna* is much less obvious and more likely to have suffered change than *multa*. As for the Ovidian allusions, allusions by definition are not exact quotations and *multa* in Ovid may equally well have come in from Tibullus 2. 3. 42, supposing he could not have thought of it himself. Admittedly there is no exact parallel for this use of *magna*, but are poets never to be allowed a *hapax legomenon* or a new combination of words? We find in Cicero *magnae decumae*

(*In Verrem* 3. 88) and tithes are a fixed proportion; in Sallust and Horace *magnae legiones* (*Catiline* 53 and *Satires* 1. 6. 4) and a legion has an official establishment; in Virgil *magni menses* (*Eclogues* 4. 12) and a month has a limited number of days; in Valerius Flaccus *magna regum milia* (*Argonautica* 5. 273) and a thousand is an ordinal number; in Statius *spatiosa iugera* (*Thebaid* 5. 550) and Postgate (1922) says this 'does not help much'. Are there exact parallels for the last three of these? And as for the sound of it, does not *iugera magna* with the long open *a* suggest a vaster estate than *iugera multa*? The evidence of Diomedes, grammarian though he is, carries no weight in a case like this, for he is simply quoting the couplet as an example of the elegiac metre and he may well be quoting from memory; in any case his MSS offer the corruption *conserat* for *congerat* in the hexameter.

All in all, it seems better to be conservative here and stick to the direct MS tradition (even though it starts, for us, in the fourteenth century), especially as this means choosing a less obvious and more interesting reading.

> 5 *uitae* MSS: *uita* Freising Excerpts: Paris Excerpts: G(uelferbytanus, 15th century).

Traducere, as we have seen, is a common word in military contexts. With the ablative here it would mean 'lead me along an inactive life', probably, as Postgate (1922) maintains, with the suggestion of being paraded in a procession. But the dative *uitae* has been shown to give excellent point and has the support of the direct MS tradition. Then why hesitate to accept it, especially as the Freising Excerpts offer *meum* for *meus* in the pentameter?

> 25 *iam modo iam possim* Freising Excerpts: *iam mihi, iam possim*
> OCT: *iam modo non possum* MSS.

The easiest correction of the direct tradition is *iam modo nunc possim* and it was made by the humanists, but one is dubious about the divorce of *iam nunc*. Schneidewin's *mihi* does not fit well with the rest of the poem: first, because the soldiers of the opening also live partly for themselves, amass money for themselves at any rate; secondly, because later in the poem Tibullus will be living for Delia quite as much as for himself. On the other hand the Freising Excerpts here give excellent sense; the repetition of *iam* is emotional and thoroughly suitable in the context, cf. Seneca, *Dialogue* 4. 29. 3 *iam enim iam audisti?*, Valerius, *Argonautica* 8. 108 *iamque omne nefas iam spero peregi*. For *modo* introducing the main sentence cf. Tibullus 1. 6. 67 *sit modo casta doce* 'only teach her to be chaste'.

35 *hic* MSS: *hinc* OCT.

Postgate (1922) describes *hic* as 'without sense'; his conjecture *hinc* means in full *de meo exiguo pecore* i.e. with a victim taken from my small flock. But what exactly is wrong with *hic*? As Fisher (1969) argues, following Dissen (1835), the excellent nineteenth-century editor, *de magno grege* suggests other estates and the purpose of *hic* is to bring us back to the poet's. One can add that the word does not have to imply that he is actually there (though he *may* be), any more than *hic* at 1. 3. 59 proves him to be in Elysium. But the purification of the shepherd *does* imply that of the flock too, because we know from Ovid, *Fasti* 4. 786 *cum duce purgat oues*, that both were purified at the festival of Pales i.e. the Parilia. There is therefore nothing to be said for changing *hic* to *hunc* (sc. *gregem*) or *hoc* (sc. *pecus*).

48 *igne* MSS: *imbre* Paris Excerpts.

A famous crux. For the confusion cf. Catullus 62. 7 *ostendit Noctifer imbres* (T: *imber* V), where the correct reading *ignes* was first printed by the humanist Palladio in 1496 (but strange to say not accepted by Scaliger in 1577). *Imbre* is very tempting and at first sight more poetical. On the other hand it is winter and the lovers could do with a fire; moreover the contrast between *gelidas aquas* and *igne* in this couplet is parallel to that between *immites* and *tenero* in the previous one. Some supporters of *igne* have used the argument that *fuderit*, being a perfect tense, indicates that the downpour has stopped. This contention is not watertight! The tense can be taken as the sort of perfect that leaves open the question of completion of the action: a good example of such a perfect is to be found at Cicero, *Tusculan Disputations* 2. 52 *si dens condoluit, ferre non possumus?* 'if a tooth aches, can we not bear it?'

59–60 The MS tradition begins each line with *et*. Postgate (1924) accepts the humanist correction *te* in 59 but retains *et* in 60. But the repeated *te*, picking up *tecum* in 57, is superior: first, because the effective emotional repetition continues in 61ff.; secondly, because Ovid's adaptation of the line at *Amores* 3. 9. 58 *me tenuit moriens deficiente manu* (Nemesis speaking) has most point if the original was *te teneam* here.

ACKNOWLEDGEMENTS AND BIBLIOGRAPHICAL NOTE

In the discussion of context and structure I owe much to Reitzenstein (1912). I am grateful to Mr J. A. Crook for the reference to Trebatius, to Professor K. F. Quinn for pointing out the connexion between lines 4 and 48, and to Mr W. A. Camps for some forceful objections to an earlier version of this study.

Hanslik (1956) argues that in real life Tibullus was not poor, because Horace in *Epistles* 1. 4. 7 says the gods have given him wealth, and because in the first elegy of Book 2 he appears as a substantial land-owner: we are therefore to take as poetic fiction the statements in lines 19 and 22 about Tibullus's reduced estate. But apart from the fact that wealth is a relative term, the argument assumes no change in Tibullus's circumstances during his lifetime. But Maecenas gave Horace a Sabine farm; was he the only patron to enrich his *amici*? Why should not Messalla have enriched Tibullus – especially after the triumph *ex Gallia*? Hanslik also argues that the elegy was written while on active service with Messalla in Aquitania. He does this by taking line 26 and 75 *signa tubaeque* more literally, 35 *hic* and 55–6 *me retinent... sedeo* less literally than previous readers. The idea has its attraction, provided one distinguishes between appearance and reality: we cannot know the actual place of composition but we can accept the dramatic scene of the monologue as a tent somewhere in Gaul if we so wish.

Fisher (1970) gives a very thorough and instructive analysis. But is it quite fair to say of the opening 'These lines provide nothing less than a summary of the entire piece: all that follows is an elaboration of elements found in verses 1–6' (p. 767)? Where, we may ask, is the love theme? Implicit in *inerti*? But the reader cannot know that yet; he refers *uita iners* to the following description of country life. And where is Messalla and the change of theme from money to military glory? Nor is it convincing to argue that the rough-house at 73–4 takes place in the country because at 1. 10. 53–4 some peasant, after a country celebration, lays in to his wife: Delia is married (1. 2. 41), yes, but not to a peasant – she lives in Rome (1. 3. 9) and is probably a freedwoman (1. 6. 67–8).

at the end of a book of poetry and including some personal details of the poet's life or background, together with a mention of the poet's name. In this way a kind of 'copyright' was established. The last eight lines of Virgil's *Georgics* are an excellent illustration. Here in *Odes* 3. 30 we are admittedly given no reference to Horace's own name; but since we are given three lines dealing with his local territory and a hint of his successful career (*qua...ex humili potens*, 10–12), we may conclude that in this last ode of all Horace intended there to be some similarity to the *sphragis*-motif.[3]

These same three lines, however, have recently been subjected to a rather different interpretation. Epitaphs as found on tombstones conventionally mentioned the place of a person's origin and details of his career,[4] exactly as we see in lines 10–12; and it has been argued that this ode belongs to the category of epitaph poems, composed (as it were) for Horace's own grave.[5] A good case can be made for this thesis. It was also conventional for epitaphs to refer to the *merita* a man had performed during his life,[6] and these too we are given in line 15 (see below, p. 126). Yet such features on their own would not be conclusive in deciding whether this poem is indebted to the epitaph form; the opening of the poem is decisive. Horace calls his poetry a *monumentum*, more everlasting than bronze and higher than the pyramids. The two objects with which the *monumentum* is compared are both memorials to the dead: bronze plaques adorned the tombs of the dead in Italy, while the pyramids are of course the tombs of the Egyptian kings. It is thus likely that the *monumentum* is itself a memorial to the dead, especially since we know that one of the commonest meanings of the word is 'tombstone'. By means of a strong and vivid metaphor Horace sees his lyric poetry as the tombstone which will cause him to be remembered by future generations. Moreover, the first two words of the poem, *Exegi monumentum*, bear a striking resemblance to inscriptions commonly found on Roman tombstones, such as *hoc monumentum feci* or *hoc monumentum apsolui*.[7] Horace's *Odes* are his tombstone, and this final ode, the epilogue, is the epitaph inscribed upon them.

That Horace decided to write his epilogue in the form of an epitaph is not unexpected. On the one hand writers had long expressed a desire for literary immortality,[8] and this might occur naturally in an epilogue (thus in the epilogue to Book 2 of the *Odes*); on the other hand tombstone inscriptions conventionally proclaimed either that the tombstone was itself immortal[9] or that the words inscribed thereon would live for ever.[10] It was therefore inevitable that sooner or later poets would combine literary immortality and the writing of epitaphs, and this is

exactly what we see in one or two poems in the Greek Anthology[11]
and in Ennius' epitaph:[12]

> Nemo me lacrimis decoret nec funera fletu
> faxit. cur? uolito uiuus per ora uirum.

But Horace is always full of invention and surprises, and this ode is no
exception. In visualizing his poetry as his *monumentum* and the present
poem as its inscription he has invented not only a new image but a completely new context for his claim to immortality.[13] We may also care to
observe how, in his fusion of the epilogue and epitaph forms, Horace
has produced a characteristic shock for his readers. Although we would
be wrong to brand Horace a strict Epicurean, nevertheless one of the
distinctive qualities of his poetry, and one which has appealed so much
to generations of readers, is his popular Epicureanism. We might well
have expected a hint of his philosophy to reappear in this epilogue,
a natural place in which to sum up those aspects which have marked the
poet's work as a whole. Instead, however, we are given five glorious
opening lines describing Horace's pride in his *monumentum*, his
metaphorical tombstone; this was the exact opposite of Epicurean
docrine, which held that the wise man will be indifferent to statues and
will not concern himself with his tomb![14]

The ode concludes with a prayer to the Muse (lines 14–16), making
this the third poetic form (along with those of the epilogue and epitaph)
to be considered in an analysis of *Exegi monumentum*.[15] But our
awareness of the form or category of a poem should not blind us
(as it blinds some scholars) to even more important considerations, the
words and imagery of which a poem consists.

THE POEM ITSELF

In the long and impressive first sentence, which stretches into the
second stanza through the medium of an ascending tricolon,[16] Horace
says that his *monumentum* is

> aere perennius
> regalique situ pyramidum altius.

What does *situ* mean? The noun *situs* can mean either 'site' or 'decay'.
Here the word is usually taken to mean 'site'. The commentators admit
that the usage is unusual, but the expression can be defended on two
counts. There would be little point if Horace compared his *monumentum*
to a decayed ruin, and besides he may have wanted the unusual noun

situs = 'site' to stick in our minds and evoke thoughts of the common sepulchral inscription *hic situs est*.[17] Such a suggestion would be in harmony with the epitaph form discussed above. Some critics, however, have maintained that *situ* means 'decay'.[18] Horace would be using the word in a proleptic sense, 'higher than the pyramids which themselves must soon decay'; and the adjective *regali* provides a pleasing oxymoron 'royal decay'. If 'decay' is the right meaning, Horace's lines gain added lustre by recalling Simonides' famous poem on the dead at Thermopylae (lines 2–5):[19]

> εὐκλεὴς μὲν ἁ τύχα, καλὸς δ' ὁ πότμος,
> βωμὸς δ' ὁ τάφος, πρὸ γόων δὲ μνᾶστις, ὁ δ'
> οἶκτος ἔπαινος·
> ἐντάφιον δὲ τοιοῦτον οὔ τις εὐρὼς
> οὔθ' ὁ πανδαμάτωρ ἀμαυρώσει χρόνος.

> *Theirs is a glorious fortune and a noble lot:*
> *for grave they have an altar, for mourning remembrance,*
> *for pity praise. Such a burial decay shall not darken,*
> *nor time the all-conquerer.*

Simonides contrasts the heroes' metaphorical burial (ἐντάφιον) with physical decay (εὐρώς) in much the same way as Horace contrasts his metaphorical *monumentum* (his poetry) with physical decay. Scholars have long debated which meaning *situ* must have in Horace's poem;[20] but surely the truth is that the word's meaning changes as our reading of the poem progresses. We initially take it to mean 'site', for the reasons given above; but as we remember Simonides and see the references to destruction in lines 3–5, the meaning 'decay' is activated.[21] Horace's lyric poetry is full of such ambiguities, this ode more than most.

In lines 3ff. Horace proceeds to prophesy the future of his *monumentum*: it will survive rain and wind. An American critic, writing on the Pindaric style of Horace, has said that here he 'undoubtedly had in mind' Pindar, *Pythian Odes* 6. 7–14:[22]

> ὕμνων|θησαυρός...
> τὸν οὔτε χειμέριος ὄμβρος ἐπακτὸς ἐλθών,
> ἐριβρόμου νεφέλας
> στρατὸς ἀμείλιχος, οὔτ' ἄνεμος ἐς μυχοὺς
> ἁλὸς ἄξοισι παμφόρῳ χεράδει
> τυπτόμενον.

A treasure-house of songs . . .,
which neither the rain-storm from abroad,
that relentless army of shrieking cloud,
nor the wind with its swirls of dust will strike
and drive into the corners of the sea.

In Pindar both rain and wind are depicted in terms of violence: his adjectives (ἐριβρόμου, ἀμείλιχος, παμφόρῳ, 'shrieking', 'relentless', 'carrying-everything-along-with-it') provide the background to this idea, an idea which is pictured most vividly in his verbs (τυπτόμενον, ἄξοισι, 'struck', 'drive'). In Pindar these actions are common to both the wind and the rain – by their sheer force they will attempt to sweep away the treasure-house of songs into the sea. Horace, however, is different. His verb, *diruere*, like Pindar's ἄξοισι, refers to both wind and rain; but whereas Pindar's ἄξοισι is a precise action ('drive'), Horace's *diruere* ('destroy') is not. We are left to discover from elsewhere in Horace's sentence the *manner* in which his wind and rain attempt their destruction. The clue lies in his use of adjectives. Horace's wind is violent (*impotens*), like Pindar's; but his rain is *edax*, an adjective which implies the gradual gnawing-away of the rain, not its violence. When the ancient commentator on Horace's poem, the third-century Porphyrio, remarks 'conrumpens *ui* tempestatis', he has not looked closely at the words used by the poet. Gnawing rain is the potential destroyer of bronze memorials and the pyramids; to appreciate the full force of Horace's poetry, we must examine the interaction of these three elements more closely.

What happens when *imber edax* gets to work on pyramids? Over a long period of time (the *innumerabilis* | *annorum series* of 4–5) it gnaws gradually at the stone. Now the wearing away of stone by water is an extremely common motif with a long heritage in classical literature, but as far as we can judge, no writer before Horace had used this particular image to illustrate mortality or immortality.[23] The first readers of this poem must have been struck by what was a novel application of a familiar idea. Next, what happens when 'gnawing rain' gets to work on bronze? When water comes into contact with *iron*, the iron rusts away. Propertius uses the image of water on stone to illustrate the way he wears down his loved one, and to it he joins the image of iron which eventually rusts; forty years later Ovid also linked the two ideas to describe his exile at Tomi on the shores of the Black Sea.[24] Now bronze, of course, is not the same as iron and does not actually rust; but it does decay in much the same way, and such technical writers as

Tony Woodman

Columella and the elder Pliny use the word *robigo* ('rust') of bronze as
well as of iron.[25]

Horace thus has two precise ideas before his mind, quite different
from anything in Pindar: water wearing away a stone memorial and
'rusting' a bronze memorial. His own *monumentum*, however, will be
able to withstand both these fates. The idea appealed to Ovid, who
years later coupled two similar images to contrast with the immortality
of his poetry (*Amores* 1. 15. 31–2, 41–2):[26]

> ergo cum silices, cum dens patientis aratri
>   depereant aeuo, carmina morte carent...
> ergo etiam cum me supremus adederit ignis,
>   uiuam, parsque mei multa superstes erit.

Also *Ex Ponto* 4. 8. 47–51:

> carmine fit uiuax uirtus, expersque sepulcri
>   notitiam serae posteritatis habet.
> tabida consumit ferrum lapidemque uetustas,
>   nullaque res maius tempore robur habet.
> scripta ferunt annos...

But in Ovid water is not mentioned specifically: it is *aeuum* or *uetustas*
(admittedly *tabida*) doing the damage. Horace is superior for his
immediacy and vividness, a point to which we shall return below
(pp. 127–8).

The reason why Horace's *monumentum* will not be destroyed by the
violence of the wind or the rusting of the rain is that the *monumentum* is
only metaphorical: the *monumentum* is his poetry, which in literal terms
can clearly neither rust nor be blown away. But we must remember that
rust and the blowing wind have metaphorical applications too. Catullus
and Ovid use the metaphor of 'rust' to describe something which has
fallen into disuse,[27] while Tacitus uses it to describe an obsolete style.[28]
Horace is perhaps indicating that his verses will never 'rust' in as much
as they will be continually read and their style will appear forever fresh.
We see this idea repeated later in the poem with the words *usque ego
postera | crescam laude recens* (7–8), where the adverb *usque* (as some,
but not all, of the commentators remark) qualifies *recens* as well as
crescam. Similarly when Horace refers to the wind attempting to
destroy the *monumentum* which is his poetry, he perhaps had in mind
the motif of a person's words being scattered on the wind. The motif is
extremely common in ancient literature to express the idea of 'speaking
in vain'; but this will not be the fate of Horace's poetry.[29]

With lines 6–14 we move into the second section of the poem, which is again formed around an ascending tricolon (balancing that in lines 1–5): (a) *non...moriar...uitabit Libitinam* (1½ lines), (b) *usque...pontifex* (2½ lines), (c) *dicar...modos* (4½ lines). Within this second section, lines 6–9 are important in forging a link between the first five lines and the latter portion of the ode. For the sequence of thought in these fourteen lines is as follows: 1–5 I have completed a *monumentum* which will be indestructible; 6–9 however (a contrast, since the building of a *monumentum* implies death), I shall not all die (*non omnis moriar*, a negative statement) but rather I shall grow in acclaim (*crescam*, a very positive assertion); 10–14 my claim is one of originality.[30] It will be noticed how in lines 1–5 Horace is talking about his poetry, but in line 6 says *multaque pars mei* and in line 7 *ego* (placed in an emphatic position). Almost imperceptibly Horace has changed ground to become identified with his own poetry. The change is intentional. A tombstone, however durable, carries only the name of its dedicatee:[31]

> sepulcri similis nil nisi nomen retineo.

But in Horace's poetry it is the essence of the poet himself which lives on.[32]

The sequence of thought analysed in the previous paragraph calls to mind a similar progression of ideas in the fifth book of Lucretius, lines 306–37. In the first part of this section Lucretius is discussing the mortality of monuments and, if any reliance can be placed on the notoriously corrupt line 312, is comparing their mortality to the mortality of man (306–7, 311–12):[33]

> denique non lapides quoque uinci cernis ab aeuo,
> non altas turris ruere et putrescere saxa...?
> denique non monumenta uirum dilapsa uidemus,
> quaerere proporro sibi sene senescere credas?

Both monuments and man, he concludes, are equally susceptible to decay and death. He then attempts to prove that the world is in fact still young, and he introduces events which preceded the Trojan Wars but which had no poet to immortalize them (328–9):

> quo tot facta uirum totiens cecidere neque usquam
> aeternis famae monumentis insita florent?

The process of culture and civilization, says Lucretius, is still developing; the nature and system of the world have only recently been discovered, and he himself is the first to describe them in Latin (335–7):

denique natura haec rerum ratioque repertast
nuper, et hanc primus cum primis ipse repertus
nunc ego sum in patrias qui possim uertere uoces.

When Horace wrote *Odes* 3. 30 he may well have had in mind this passage of thirty lines from Lucretius.[34] The similarities are unmistakable, but Horace, as so often, tempers and alters the rigid doctrine of Lucretius to suit his own more realistic view of the world. Whereas Lucretius, if we may trust line 312, compares the mortality of monuments to the mortality of man,[35] Horace compares the mortality of monuments to his own *im*mortality. Horace's claim gains added weight if we allow for a 'corrective' allusion to Lucretius. Lucretius picks up the literal use of *monumenta* in 311 by a metaphorical use of the word in 329, *aeternis famae monumentis*. His subject now is poetry and its power to make men immortal, and we may wonder whether the coincidence of this particular metaphor and idea here provided the germ of Horace's first few lines – although Lucretius' metaphor lacks the immediate impact and brilliantly original context of Horace's confident claim *Exegi monumentum*.[36] It is true that when Lucretius moves on to talk of his own originality (336–7) he is simply repeating a claim often heard elsewhere in ancient poetry,[37] and we have no need to assume that Horace in lines 10–14 is alluding to Lucretius; yet the sequence of thought in both poets is so similar that we may like to think that when Horace wrote his claim to originality he had an eye on Lucretius also.

In lines 10–14, the third section of the poem, Horace defines his claim to immortality. He begins by stating the locale where he expects his claim will be remembered (10–12):

dicar, qua uiolens obstrepit Aufidus
et qua pauper aquae Daunus agrestium
regnauit populorum...

I shall be spoken of where the violent Aufidus roars
and where Daunus, poor in water,
reigned over his wild people...

He is referring to the territory of Apulia, where he was born, through which the River Aufidus runs, and which in ancient legend was ruled over by king Daunus. The king is called 'poor in water' because Apulia was famous for its poor water-supply: Horace calls the region *siticulosa* ('thirsty') at *Epodes* 3. 16. But why does Horace stress the aridity of Apulia in this way when he has already pointed out that the territory is blessed by a river which is both violent (*uiolens*) and noisy (*obstrepit*, in counterpoise to *tacita* in line 9)? These two features of Horace's native landscape seem at first sight paradoxical, but the paradox is there to stimulate our imagination. Horace intends to emphasize the river, to make it stand out: it is a force of nature to be compared with the forces of nature in line 3. There the gnawing water and violent wind were attemptive destroyers of his *monumentum*, whereas here the violent rush of water in the Aufidus symbolizes the locale where above all Horace and his poetry will be preserved. The contrast is helped by the echo of *impotens* (3) in *uiolens* (10): the violence of nature in the second half of line 3 is destructive, in 10 it is preservative. And we may also like to see in *regnauit* (12) an echo of *regali* (2):[38] the lofty royal pyramids will eventually crumble, but Horace will live on in a place which has its own proud royal heritage, preserved in legend and in Horace's own poetry.

In the previous paragraph we translated the repeated *qua*-clauses as if they qualified *dicar* ('my reputation in Apulia will be to have introduced Greek poetry into Italy'); but most of the commentators take these clauses with *deduxisse* in line 14 ('my reputation will be to have introduced Greek poetry into Italy from my homeland Apulia'). If we translate this latter way, Horace is describing not his proposed fame but his actual achievement, which must be seen in terms of his humble birthplace. There is a very similar idea to this in the first stanza of a later ode, 4. 9 (and compare too *Epistles* 1. 20. 20–1, quoted below, p. 126):

> Ne forte credas interitura quae
> longe sonantem natus ad Aufidum
>   non ante uolgatas per artis
>   uerba loquor socianda chordis.

But how, on this interpretation, do we explain the paradox of lines 10–11 which seemed to throw so much emphasis on the river? We must remember that in the ancient world water was frequently a symbol of literary inspiration: the Greeks had their fountains of Hippocrene and Castalia, while Horace himself could address his Muse as one 'quae *fontibus integris* | gaudes' (*Odes* 1. 26. 6–7).[39] Horace appears to be saying that he took his inspiration from the river which ran through his native territory. King Daunus, despite the region's natural resources, was helpless (11–12): he could not utilize the river and himself remained *pauper aquae* (a metaphorical way of saying that he lacked poetical inspiration), while his people remained uncultured (*agrestium*).

Horace, on the other hand, was able to draw inspiration from his local river. As a result he is now *potens* (12) – and here we may see another echo of *impotens* in line 3. In its immediate context the wind is 'violent' (like the wind in Pindar's ode and like the Aufidus itself); but now it comes to have its other meaning of 'impotent' (as in *Odes* 2. 1. 26). Horace has become *potens*, and the forces of nature are 'powerless' to resist him.

Thus we can no more settle upon a definite, static meaning of *impotens* in line 3 than we could of *situ* in line 2 (above, pp. 117f.); nor can we be conclusive as to the exact reference of the *qua*-clauses in lines 10–12. We must just assume that Horace knew what he was doing and intended these ambiguities to give his compact ode a wealth of extra meaning lying beneath the surface.[40]

In the last three lines of this third section (12–14) Horace eventually specifies his poetic claim, although the language which he has used to express himself simply confirms the pervasive equivocalness of the whole poem:

> ex humili potens
> princeps Aeolium carmen ad Italos
> deduxisse modos.

What does *deduxisse* mean? Is it a metaphor from founding colonies, from a victorious general celebrating a triumph, or from the spinning of fine thread? Each of these possibilities has been canvassed by scholars,[41] but one of them seems immediately attractive. In the last two lines of the poem Horace appears to see himself as a victorious general being crowned by the Muse (see below, pp. 126–7). The technical term for taking to Rome for a triumph is *deducere*, as in *Odes* 1. 37. 31–2 '*deduci superbo* | non humilis mulier *triumpho*'.[42] Horace would be saying: 'the first to have brought Aeolian song (that is, the lyric poetry of Sappho and Alcaeus, who both wrote in the Aeolic dialect) to Italian music in triumph'.[43] We are thereby neatly prepared for the more explicit triumph-image in lines 15–16. At the same time it is impossible for us to forget that Horace, like the so-called 'new poets' of the previous generation (of whom Catullus was one) and like his famous contemporaries Virgil and Propertius, was strongly influenced by the early third-century Greek poet Callimachus, who had insisted that poetic style should be λεπτός (the Latin equivalent is *tenuis*).[44] This style was achieved only through a continual process of perfecting and refinement, and a metaphor which came into fashion with Callimachus' Latin followers to describe this process is *deducere* = 'spin', found in Virgil's *Eclogues*, Propertius, and elsewhere in Horace's own work.[45] In the context of the poem itself we take *deduxisse* to be part of the triumph-image, but our knowledge of the literary background to which Horace belonged means that we cannot exclude the notion of 'spinning' (that is, producing finely wrought work) from our minds.

The Callimachean language of *deduxisse*, if we accept it, confirms other hints of Callimachean technique elsewhere in the poem. We agreed (above, p. 116) that the opening words *Exegi monumentum* strongly resemble tombstone inscriptions, but the verb *exigere* also became fashionable with the Augustan poets to describe the same process of poetic refinement as *deducere*: the usage is found in Propertius, Horace's *Epistles*, and in Ovid.[46] We can now also see the phrase *ex humili potens* (12), about which a little has already been said (above, p. 116), in sharper focus, with the help of another famous ode, 2. 16. In the fourth stanza of that poem Horace describes a characteristically simple outlook on life, saying that frugal living is essential for inner happiness:

> uiuitur paruo bene cui paternum
> splendet in mensa tenui salinum.

> *He lives well on little whose family salt-cellar*
> *gleams on a sparely laid table.*

The following stanzas elaborate this theme by contrast and example in a typically Horatian manner until we reach the final stanza of the ode, where Horace claims to be content with his own small lot because he has his poetic powers:

> mihi parua rura et
> spiritum Graiae tenuem Camenae
> Parca non mendax dedit et malignum
> spernere uolgus.

> *But to me Fate is consistent,*
> *in giving me a little farm, the spare spirit*
> *of the Greek Muse, and a taste*
> *for rejecting the common crowd.*

The adjectives *parua* and *tenuem* in the final stanza clearly echo *paruo* and *tenui* in the fourth: Horace is drawing an analogy between his mode of living (which is *tenuis*) and his poetic principles (which are also *tenues*). Horace regularly portrays himself as a devotee of the simple life, and the *tenuitas* of Callimachean style is practised throughout his work:[47] here in *Odes* 2. 16 the two themes have become fused into one, his way of life is mirrored in his poetic technique. This fusion of ideas is found elsewhere in the *Odes*,[48] and we may like to see it also in the phrase *ex humili potens*. Horace, though *potens*, is still *humilis* (or *tenuis*) in both his life and poetic technique.[49] This is a note we might well expect to be sounded in an epilogue poem, comparing the last poem in the first book of Horace's own *Epistles* (lines 20–1):

> me libertino natum patre et in tenui re
> maiores pennas nido extendisse loqueris.

The final section of the poem (lines 14–16) is a prayer to Horace's Muse the function of which can only be understood if we appreciate the climactic tone of the section just ended: *princeps Aeolium carmen ad Italos | deduxisse modos*. Knowing that many other poets had claimed their work to be original (see above, p. 122 and n. 37), we may tend to dismiss Horace's claim as merely conventional, especially since in some respects his *Odes* had been anticipated by earlier Latin poetry such as that of Catullus. But we must remember that there is one respect at least in which Horace's *Odes* are almost completely original, their metres.[50] Modern poetry tends to disregard the importance of formal versification, but to the ancients regular metre was an essential feature of poetic craftsmanship. The difficulty of adapting the heavier vocabulary of the Latin language to the lighter metres of Greek lyric poetry must have been a supreme test of sustained effort and poetic competence, and for this one achievement alone Horace could feel justifiably proud at the result.[51]

Now that Horace has come to the end of his three books of lyric poetry and they are about to be published, his pride shows itself (14–15): *superbiam | quaesitam meritis*, 'the pride which has been won by my own merits'. The commentators differ as to whose *merita* are being referred to, Horace's or the Muse's, but the whole tone of the poem indicates that these are Horace's *merita*, nor must we forget that epitaphs commonly referred to the *merita* of the dead person (see above, p. 116). Since this poem is Horace's epitaph, there would seem to be no question that these are his *merita*. If, on this interpretation, we sense that Horace's attitude is overbearing, he tempers it by offering his newly won pride to the Muse: *sume superbiam*. The verb contains the notions of 'putting on' (a crown or cloak, for example) and 'taking for one's own'.[52] The Muse must assume Horace's *superbia* and make it her own; in return, meanwhile, she must garland Horace's head with a Delphic laurel (*cinge*, 16, activates the latent sense of 'putting on' in *sume*). The crowning of the poet's head with laurel recalls the procedure of Roman triumphs;[53] Propertius too was soon to see himself as a victorious general (3. 1, especially lines 19–20 for crowning).[54] The image is grand and majestic, but here again Horace does not permit extravagance to creep in: he addresses the Muse as *uolens* (16), a word which, as the commentators point out, belongs to the respectful language of prayer-ritual. Indeed the prayer as a whole is 'a perfect antidote to the expression of personal pride' and 'seems formally to close a whole period of the poet's work'.[55]

THE FAME OF THE POEM

When Horace published his first three books of *Odes* in 23 B.C., *Exegi monumentum* had an immediate impact. Propertius concluded the second elegy of his third book with a passage which is clearly influenced by, and probably written in rivalry of, Horace's poem (lines 17–26).[56] Later there was Ovid too (see below), then Seneca, St Jerome, Shakespeare possibly, Ronsard, Herrick, the eighteenth-century writers Klopstock and Derzhavin, Pushkin, and a whole host of others.[57] We may briefly consider the case of Ovid to emphasize by comparison the quality of Horace's ode.

Ovid's most well known aspirations to poetic immortality occur in the epilogue to his *Metamorphoses*, where the language is clearly borrowed from this ode of Horace (15. 871–9):[58]

> iamque opus exegi, quod nec Iouis ira nec ignis
> nec poterit ferrum nec edax abolere uetustas.
> cum uolet, illa dies, quae nil nisi corporis huius
> ius habet, incerti spatium mihi finiat aeui;
> parte tamen meliore mei super alta perennis
> astra ferar, nomenque erit indelebile nostrum,
> quaque patet domitis Romana potentia terris,
> ore legar populi, perque omnia saecula fama,
> siquid habent ueri uatum praesagia, uiuam.

Ovid does not specify what he imagines his immortal construction to be, *opus* being a weak word commonly used of any literary composition. This lack of precision is not improved by the assortment of objects which might attempt to destroy the *opus*. *Iouis ira* (presumably 'lightning') and *ignis* are consistent enough, but what about *ferrum* and *edax uetustas*? It is hardly a compliment to himself if Ovid says that a mere sword (*ferrum*) will not destroy his *opus*.[59] And in describing age as *edax* Ovid is returning to a metaphor he had used several hundred lines earlier in this book of the *Metamorphoses* (234–6):

> tempus edax rerum, tuque, inuidiosa uetustas,
> omnia destruitis uitiataque dentibus aeui
> paulatim lenta consumitis omnia morte.

He looks at time and old age in human terms (he even addresses them), as if they were a man with sharp teeth who attacks monuments and the like.[60] Horace, on the other hand, has chosen from the start a single metaphor, *monumentum*, which he imagines as being attacked by the immediate, natural forces we should expect, rain and wind. It is only when we have reached this stage of the image that Horace predicates the metaphors *edax* and *impotens*. Cecil Day Lewis once wrote that in his opinion 'image-patterns must in fact *be* patterns and not random assemblages of word pictures'.[61] The consistency of detail in Horace's opening metaphor presents a much more imaginative and compelling picture than the imagistic fragmentation of Ovid.

Horace was proud of his lyric poetry, and rightly so. He saw fit to end *Odes* 1–3 with a poem about his poetry which in its depth, grandeur, delicacy and suggestiveness surpasses even the finest odes he had already written. When in the latest standard commentary on the *Odes* we read, 'Poetry is not the best subject for poetry and Horace's greatest odes are not written simply about themselves', *Exegi monumentum* will refute this judgement every time.[62]

9
EPILOGUE

The contributors to this book are practising Latinists. Most of them, as far as the editors are aware, have no specialist knowledge of the recent history of literary criticism. The twentieth century has seen an explosion of theories, methods and controversies in this field.[1] It may be useful in this epilogue to review these essays, written as they are in all innocence, to see how Latin scholarship has been affected by these developments. We have heard the rumblings of the great critical storms of the century, and the waves have beaten on our shores. But have they reshaped the coastline?[2]

The traditional activities survive. Chiasmus and polyptoton are never far from our thoughts, and we cannot often manage a page of Latin without invoking ascending tricolon with anaphora. West catches the tone of voice in a particular verse pause. Kenney and Cairns are both interested in the lengths of sentences and words, and the relationship of these to the verse measure, the one plotting the emotional level of Lucretius' writing, the other throwing light on Catullus' Alexandrianism. Williams fastens on the parallel clauses in *Eclogue* 4, traces the mannerism to Theocritus, and concludes that Virgil is asserting his pastoral identity in a poem which has risen so far above the conventional form. These are all traditional techniques, or extensions of them. The modernity lies in the purposiveness of their use. The inert categories have disappeared – there is no 'genitive of the rubric' or 'dative of work contemplated'. Every discussion of syntax and metrical structure is dedicated to the one purpose of heightening our awareness of the interaction between the thought and the verse, of allowing us to hear the tone, tension and pace of the poetry.

Textual criticism, the ancient citadel of classical scholarship, still stands. But even here the same principle has taken command. In Lee's textual appendix it is the poetic effect of *magna* which scores over the dull and obvious *multa*; the wit in the metaphor of *uitae* tells against *uita*; and even the tiny detail of *hic* against *hinc* strengthens a transition of thought in a composition where so much of the poetic interest depends upon transitions of thought. When Kenney reads *tendere* for *tollere*, and Cairns *gaudente* for *gaudete*, again the reasons are firmly grounded in the poetry.

Of all the controversies which have divided the literary critics of this century, none has attracted more passion than the question of the role of historical data in the interpretation of poetry. On the one hand we read: 'The work of art has been treated as autonomous and self-explanatory, and the pure critic has tried to concern himself with the poem as it can be explained purely in terms of itself and himself.' On the other hand Helen Gardner, to whom we owe this brief description,[3] herself prefers to acknowledge that poems are influenced by such considerations as the literary tradition or by events which took place during the lifetime of the poet:

> 'Every work of art is the product of a point in space and time, in so far as it would certainly have been different if it had appeared in any other place and time. It could not have been what it is but for the art which went before it. We ourselves see it through our knowledge and experience of what has come after it. It is historical also as the product of a mind which grew through particular experiences and not through others.'

Where now do Latinists stand between these two different points of view?

In literary history the comparison between a poem and the tradition behind it is especially common in the study of Latin poetry, where creative imitation is the poetic law. Bramble is happy to have his response to a poem conditioned by considerations of literary history, dismissing the 'fond belief that a blank mind facing an anonymous text will register impressions of value'. But there are dangers. Some scholars have clearly felt that the existence of a Greek model greatly reduces the stature of a Latin poem, an attitude which has led to a general disparagement of Latin poetry. 'It is a remarkable defect in Roman poetry that it is to so great an extent an imitation of Greek models and not the result of native inspiration', wrote T. E. Page in 1895. 'Mangelhaft also lateinisches' is the conclusion of Klingner in 1956, pithily expressing an attitude which distorts even some of the best of modern commentaries.[4] But mercifully most Latinists are moving away from this and recognize that the dependence of writers upon their predecessors in no way precludes originality. When Cairns discusses Callimachus, or Williams and Bramble call upon evidence from Theocritus, their purpose is to achieve a sharper definition of, and a juster feeling for, the poetry of Catullus, Virgil and Propertius. A similar purpose informs the attempt by West to illuminate Horace's treatment of the fable of the mice by comparing it with later versions by La Fontaine and Henryson, while Woodman cites Ovid to emphasize by comparison the quality of Horace. Generic studies are an expanding branch of literary history, represented most notably in this book by Cairns. It is only when we are aware of the conventions of a genre that we can fully appreciate the originality of Catullus or any other writer.

The importance of contemporary history is most conspicuous in the political poems, the *Eclogue* and *Georgic*. Williams and Lyne show again and again how the details of these poems and their emotional tone are to be connected with the emergence of Octavian. Our whole concept of the Messianic *Eclogue* is revised if we accept that the unnamed child saviour was meant to be taken *either* as the putative son of Octavian's dynastic marriage *or* as the putative son of Antony's dynastic marriage. This would be a panegyrical ambiguity worthy of the poet 'whose every word, let it only be possible', according to Henry,[5] 'is imbued in the quintessence of an *adulatio in potentes*'. The background of contemporary thought is equally important. Witness the Epicurean implications of *homo* elucidated by Kenney, or the philosophical flavour of *despicere* and *securus* detected by Lee, who stresses the importance of what the poet took for granted in his readers – knowledge of society, culture, the ideas which were 'in the air' at the time.

On this evidence Latinists agree with Helen Gardner in setting a poem in its literary, historical and cultural contexts. But we have retreated from the naively biographical approach of Victorian scholarship. In his biographical note Lee differs from Hanslik (1956) on questions relating to the life of Tibullus, but both scholars are aware that Roman poets have a way of making poetic capital out of their claims to poverty. Again Lee cautiously reformulates Hanslik's thesis that Tibullus' first elegy was written in Aquitania, in terms of the dramatic scene of the monologue. Most of the contributors talk of the character or characteristics of their poet, but all of them would presumably distinguish between the historical character now irretrievably lost and the *persona* projected by the poet in his writings, Lee's 'poetic character'. The only exception to this that we have observed is the interpretation of Tibullus' epitaph, where Lee has deliberately and profitably defied both the law of the biographical fallacy and Dr Johnson – 'In lapidary inscriptions a man is not upon oath.'

'Lemon-squeezing' is T. S. Eliot's emotive description of the close reading which is the other hallmark of modern literary criticism.[6]

Ambiguity, imagery, nuance, structure are among its key concepts.
Yet Northrop Frye has also observed that in the *Cratylus* of Plato 'we
are introduced to the ironic techniques of ambiguity, verbal association,
paronomasia, and the apparatus now being revived by criticism to deal
with the poetry of the ironic mode – the criticism which, by a further
refinement of irony, is called "new" criticism'.[7] Latin writers dealt
with such topics from a theoretical point of view,[8] while modern
scholars like A. J. Bell (1923) and W. B. Stanford (1939) were sub-
jecting both Latin and Greek poetry to rigorous analyses along these
lines at about the same time as W. Empson published *Seven Types of
Ambiguity* (1930). In our texts Bramble finds a piquant irony in
Propertius' geography; there is no lack of it in Horace's fable of the
two mice. Lee finds active ambiguity in the poetry of Tibullus and his
very title suggests the importance of paradox; for Woodman *Exegi
monumentum* is pervasively equivocal. 'Accumulated nuance' is an extension of this approach. Lyne's analysis of *Georgics* 1. 463ff. posits that
'a word, by repeated and significant mention in the poem, accumulates
implicit but increasing resonance or meaning; and at salient moments
in the poem all such meaning can be realized with explicit and climactic effect'. Kenney applies this technique backwards in Lucretius.
It is only when we reach 5. 1207–8 in a continuous reading of the poem
that we can appreciate to the full the originality and the irony of
Lucretius' magnificient image in 1. 64–5. There are two extremes of
error possible in this approach: to see too much, as do some of the
modern American Latinists – Empson himself said that 'we have to
exercise a good deal of skill in cutting out implications that aren't
wanted in reading poems'; and to see too little – according to
Nisbet and Hubbard, Horace 'does not evoke more than he says'.[9]
Readers may wish to place us at various points between Scylla and
Charybdis. We the editors had better abstain.

Imagery presents the same double danger. If we do not see the
metaphors (and metaphor was recognized by ancient theorists as an
essential ingredient of poetry), we see too little. If we accept the most
egocentric symbolist interpretations we see too much. Lee's elucidation
of the military metaphor in Tibullus is original work, but in line with
traditional exegesis. Lyne goes further, because his poem is different.
The *Georgics* is a political poem and an agricultural poem. It is the
clear duty of the critic to explore the relationship between these two
levels of meaning. Similarly, Roman prophecies and prodigies corres-
pond visually, verbally and substantively with the realities they
presage, and Williams and Lyne are bound to search for these corre-

spondences. The first *Georgic* 'argues piety, order, peace, productive-ness, *life* – in reaction to chaos, destruction and war. It does so though the metaphor of the Farmer.' This is what the poem is doing, and Virgil himself opens the door to symbolic understanding of his key concepts. Among the most original and daring of these interpretations in this book are Lyne's on the rivers and the reins, and on the curved plough, where he argues that it illustrates the channelling of man's *uis* without which the *Georgics* cannot exist. Similar is Bramble's analysis of the rape of Hylas. 'Sometimes in boyish fashion, picking a flower with his tender nails, he preferred a flower to the duty that lay before him; and sometimes forgetfully leaning over the lovely waters, he slowed his wandering steps to enjoy the reflections.' Thus, in a prosaic translation, Propertius 1. 20. 39–42. Bramble invites us to see running underneath this a symbolic suggestion that the reflection is Hylas' own, that the flower is his own beauty, that his duty is sexual obedience to his master, and that the wandering is the sexual deviation of narcissism.

Poetic structure is determined by responsions either of thought, sound, imagery or number. Kenney shows that Lucretius 1. 62–79 exemplifies a structure, common in ancient literature, called 'ring-composition'. The final lines 78–9 sum up the argument of the paragraph by returning us to the point of departure in line 62. Cairns demonstrates a more stylized and complicated instance of the same technique in Catullus 31. Here the whole poem can be seen as a series of concentric rings constructed around line 7, the pivot: lines 5–6 and 8–10, which complement each other thematically, form the first ring, lines 4 and 11 the second, lines 1–3 and 12–14 the third. Williams accepts a different formulation for *Eclogue* 4, which is seen as units of seven lines, with variations in the central prophecy (lines 18–45 = 28 divided into units of 8, 11 and 9).

The modern literary critic will note the amorality of Latin scholar-ship, and the undergraduate may find that it is irrelevant to contem-porary life. It is true that there are no Marxist or Christian interpretations, no Leavisite severity, no attempt to ameliorate present-day life or to draw conclusions about it from these poems. The nearest we come to this is when Lyne argues that the *Georgics* is an emotional response to a historical situation which is timeless, and Kenney finds in Lucretius some burlesque of bureaucratic hypocrisy. Such passing comments apart, these critics fix their minds on the poems and the world that produced them, rarely looking at the modern world or the minds of modern readers. Adverse evaluation (again a stock feature of the Leavis school) is not frequent. Williams thinks Virgil's self-coloured

NOTES

VENVSTA SIRMIO

The most important modern expositions of Catullus 31 are contained in the commentaries of Fordyce (1961), Kroll (1968) and Quinn (1970). Two recent articles on poem 31 – Baker (1970) and Witke (1972) – do not, in my view, further our understanding of it. The latter indeed obscures the poem by arguing that there is 'a sexual relationship between "uenusta Sirmio" and Catullus' (240), a notion for which I find no evidence in the text.

In the preparation of this analysis, I was aided by the valuable advice of my colleague, Mr J. R. G. Wright, and also by numerous editorial observations, both stylistic and factual.

1 The 'Alexandrian' movement is so called because it flourished mainly in the city of Alexandria during the third century B.C., although its effects naturally became more widespread in the course of time. Its most influential champion was Callimachus (c. 305–240 B.C.), but another famous name associated with it is Theocritus (c. 300–260 B.C.). Through dissatisfaction with the dominance of inflated epic poetry, these poets advocated 'lower' forms such as didactic, pastoral, epigram, hymn and 'miniature epic' (*epyllion*). The features we chiefly think of as 'Alexandrian' are those listed above: literary polish, erudition of all kinds (literary allusions, antiquarianism, science, geography, etc. – Callimachus' most famous poem was called Αἴτια, 'Origins'), originality of theme and treatment, a personal approach. The movement, which is sometimes referred to also as 'Hellenistic', had a notable contemporary opponent in Apollonius (see above, p. 83 and n. 6).

Although Alexandrian poetry was known at Rome early (e.g. to Ennius), 'Alexandrianism' as such had no major influence upon Latin poetry until the middle of the first century B.C. Thereafter its effect was extensive, a famous instance being the 'new poets' such as Catullus himself: see in general Wimmel (1960) and Clausen (1964). The essays in this book demonstrate in particular the influence of Callimachus upon Catullus (above) and upon Horace (above, pp. 124ff.), and of Theocritus (who, despite having written narrative poems, encomia and epigrams, was regarded by Romans as the founder of pastoral poetry) upon Virgil (pp. 32ff.) and Propertius (pp. 83ff.).

2 Cairns (1969).

3 Denniston (1952), 7.

4 Assonance is the close repetition of similar vowel sounds; homoeoteleuton occurs when words or clauses have a similar ending (from ὁμοιοτέλευτον).

5 Also known as 'tricolon crescendo', i.e. a series of three syntactically parallel clauses so arranged that they are in ascending order of mag-

nitude. The parallelism is often marked by anaphora, with the repeated word sometimes in a different case, gender or number in each colon. See further Fraenkel (1957), 351 n. 1.

6 Cairns (1972), 122.

7 Such encomiastic techniques are especially frequent in Pindar, e.g. the beginnings of *Pythians* 6, 8, 11; *Nemeans* 2, 7, 8.

8 It is possible that *ludius* (actor etc.), derived from *Lydius*, may have generated false popular etymologies linking *Lydius* and *ludere*. But Varro's etymology of *ludius* was correct (cf. Walde–Hofmann s.v. *ludius*). For a false etymological link between *Phrygius* and *fruges* see Lucretius 2. 611–13 and West (1969), 105–6.

9 Quinn (1970), 184–7.

10 Quinn (1970), 187.

11 Fordyce (1961), 170–1.

12 Fordyce (1961), 170.

13 On genres in general Cairns (1972); on the *epibaterion*, 59 ff., 211ff. References to Menander Rhetor are to the page and line numbers of Spengel (1856).

14 E.g. *Odyssey* 13. 352–60; 16. 11–67, 190–234; 17. 28–60; 23. 205–350; 24. 345–55.

15 430. 12ff.

16 Virtue in general is often treated in antiquity (especially in rhetorical contexts) as consisting of four particular virtues: justice, bravery, self-control, wisdom.

17 E.g. Aeschylus, *Agamemnon* 506–7; Seneca, *Agamemnon* 392–3.

18 Commonly found in the *prosphonetikon* (welcome-home speech): see Cairns (1972), 22.

19 Cairns (1972), 235ff.

2   *VIVIDA VIS*

1 Cf. Kenney (1971), 25–7.

2 The carrying over of the sense and construction from one verse to the next.

3 The order noun–epithet can of course be used deliberately for an effect of surprise, as is done by Juvenal at e.g. *Sat.* 1. 49–50 *exul ab octaua Marius bibit et fruitur dis | iratis*; but the device is effective precisely because the sequence is abnormal.

4 See Fowler (1970), 62–7; and for Latin poetry in particular cf. Moritz (1968), 116–31; G. Williams (1968), 233–9.

5 Cf. Kenney (1971), 13.

6 The imagery of 1. 62–79 is the subject of an extended analysis by D. West (1969), 57–63. The extent of my debt to West's excellent discussion will be evident.

7 This of course is Stoic, not Epicurean, doctrine.

8 Cf. Friedländer (1941), 19 = (1969), 339–40.

9 The term embraces, but is much wider than, what we call puns. The Latin word for it is *adnominatio* (Quintilian, *Institutio Oratoria* 9. 3. 66).

10 'The ancients did not consider a pun as degrading the dignity of

poetry. When Cassandra in her frenzy invokes Apollo as ᾿Απόλλων ἐμός, we know that she means Apollyon, "my destroyer"; and Aeschylus elsewhere in a splendid poem calls Helen of Troy ἑλέναυς "robber of navies"... Plato, our earliest grammarian, made no distinction between a pun and etymology' (Chapman (1920), 83). Cf. Fraenkel (1950) on Aesch. *Ag.* 687, Kenney (1971) on line 364.

11 Lucretius does not mention Apollo, slayer of the Python, presumably because to have done so would have duplicated and hence weakened the effect of the Hercules passage.

12 In a long and carefully organized poem such as the *De Rerum Natura* no part can be read in detachment from the whole: *Lucretium ex Lucretio interpretari* must be the first principle of the critic. But neither is the poem as a whole totally autonomous: Lucretius wrote for a sophisticated and highly literate audience, and clearly took for granted their acquaintance with a wide range of earlier poetry (see the useful discussion by Rudd (1964), 226–31). This is one of the things entailed in being a *doctus poeta*: cf. Kenney (1970), 366–92.

13 Familiar in Ennius' famous line *unus homo nobis cunctando restituit rem.* Elsewhere (6. 652) Lucretius uses the normal classical prosody *homŏ.*

14 In v. 66 *tendere* is rightly preferred by D. West (1969), following Lachmann (1882) and some other editors, to the *tollere* of the MSS. (*a*) The suggestion of the bending of a bow is appropriate to the generally martial character of the imagery, whereas *tollere* (though by no means inappropriate) is in comparison commonplace; (*b*) Nonius' citation is specific, being designed to illustrate the sense *tendere = derigere* (cf. Timpanaro (1970), 355–7). In favour of *tollere* is Ov. *Met.* 1. 86, quoted above.

15 The heroes in the *Iliad* habitually scowl at each other, and the Myrmidons, terrified by the divine arms of Achilles, dare not look at them, οὐδέ τις ἔτλη | ἄντην εἰσιδέειν, ἀλλ᾿ ἔτρεσαν (*Il.* 19. 14–15). Cf. Horace, *Odes* 1. 2. 39 *acer et Marsi peditis cruentum | uultus in hostem.*

16 Since it was *nefas* to look upon the face of a god: Livy 1. 16. 6, Ov. *Fast.* 6. 7–8, Seneca, *Epp. Mor.* 115. 4, Lucan 1. 598, etc.

17 The reading of v. 70 is far from certain. Priscian's *effringere* is good in itself, being *vox propria* for bursting through gates (see *TLL* s.v.), and preserves the metre. *perfringere* seems intrinsically nearly as good (cf. 72 *peruicit*...74 *peragrauit*; the repetition of the prefix would be characteristic of Lucretius), but requires, as does *confringere*, the transposition of the words *animi uirtutem* to save the metre. If *effringere* is right, it emphasizes the paradox that a sortie should *break* out of a besieged city: D. West (1969), 60.

18 Bentley's *fana* (which Lachmann (1882) accepts) spoils the point; it is worth mentioning as an example of what is apt to happen when even the best critics do not attend to the context and the argument as a whole.

19 'The resolution of a complex expression into its parts' (Moore (1891), 273); 'figura, cum una res in duas diuidatur' (Servius on Virg. *Aen.* 1. 61 *molemque et montes = molem montis*).

20 'Diaeresis occurs where the end of a word is also the end of a foot' (Platnauer (1951), 18).

21 A deliberate contradiction in terms for effect, as in Horace's *splendide mendax*. Behind the obvious sense of *immensum*, 'the immeasurable', lurks 'the untraversable' (*metior* commonly = 'traverse'); and Epicurus has surveyed *the whole of it*.

22 The 'foraging expedition' of D. West (1969), 60, diminishes *peragrauit* too much. Dr Woodman aptly compares Flor. 1. 33. 12 *D. Brutus...peragratoque uictor Oceani litore.*

23 On theme and variation in Lucretius cf. Kenney (1971), 25; and on the employment of the beginning of the verse to help in defining grammatical structure ibid. on lines 1–4.

24 Paragraphing is of course a modern editorial device, unknown in ancient books. Lucretius is at pains to distinguish the divisions of his argument by repeating key words and themes at the beginning and end of each section, as here: see next note.

25 The term stems from Homeric criticism (Willcock (1964), 142 n. 2), but the thing itself is not confined to the oral epic. Cf. Kenney (1971), 30n.; also above, pp. 7–8.

26 Is it fanciful to detect a hint of parody in the suggestion of an *aition*? As an Alexandrian poet such as Callimachus might explain a current rite or custom whose origins go back to the mythical past (cf. e.g. Callim. *Hymn* 2. 104), so Lucretius explains man's present enlightenment as founded on the heroic feats of Epicurus. On *aitia* see also above, p. 2 n. 1.

27 The Epicurean system had (somewhat oddly) a place for gods, but they did not intervene either in the workings of the universe or in the affairs of mankind. The real god of the Epicureans was Epicurus himself, so called by Lucretius at 5. 8 *deus ille fuit, deus* and prefigured as such here through the familiar conception of the conqueror as god–liberator (cf. Ogilvie (1965) on Livy 2. 16. 1).

28 Using standard argumentative formulae: *illud in his rebus* (80) = 'this point'; *quod contra* (82) = 'on the contrary'.

29 Aesch. *Ag.* 228–47; cf. Euripides, *I.A.* 1100ff. There was a famous painting of the scene by Timanthes (Pliny, *N.H.* 35. 73; cf. Cic. *Orator* 74). A fine wall-painting at Pompeii in the house of the Tragic Poet shows Iphigenia being lifted by two men while Calchas stands knife in hand, apparently indecisive, and Agamemnon hides his face; the latter detail is in Pliny's account of Timanthes' picture and in Euripides (*I.A.* 1548–50). The use of such *exempla* from myth and from poetry was familiar in the diatribe, to which Lucretius was considerably indebted: cf. Teles 33ff. Hense.

30 For exact statistics of the patterns preferred by Lucretius in the first four feet of his hexameter see Duckworth (1969), 39–42 and Table 1. The use of enjambment and dactylic rhythms in 'bridging' passages between episodes is characteristic of Ovid in the *Metamorphoses*.

31 An arrangement ABB'A', which when tabulated becomes

$$\begin{matrix} A & \times & B \\ B' & & A' \end{matrix}$$

hence the name chiasmus, from the Greek letter Chi (Χ).

32 = *ingredi*, for the sake of the metre; the usage has an archaic ring.

33 The phrase repeats and varies *ductores...delecti*, itself an epicizing variation on a common cliché (cf. *TLL* s.v. *deligo²*); Dr Woodman aptly compares Catull. 64. 4 *lecti iuuenes, Argiuae robora pubis*. For the construction cf. e.g. 1. 315 *strata uiarum*; and for the generally poetical character of this usage in Greek see the passages collected by Headlam–Knox (1922) on Herod. 1. 67.

34 In view of παρθενοσφάγοισιν and παρθενίου θ' αἵματος at *Ag.* 215, also *uirgineos* at v. 87, it is tempting to suggest that *uirginis* at v. 84 is doing double duty, looking forward to *Iphianassai* and implying the terrible inappropriateness of the sacrifice of *this* virgin to a virgin goddess.

35 According to the version of the story dramatized by Euripides in the *Iphigenia in Aulis*, which is clearly what Lucretius has in mind, she had been told that she was being brought to Aulis to marry Achilles. See Munro (1873), end-note on vv. 95–100. *uittae* and *infulae* are not consistently distinguished (cf. Daremberg–Saglio s.vv., Latte (1960), 385 n. 4), but the sacrificial associations of *infula* are clear: Varro, *L.L.* 7. 24, Liv. 2. 54. 4; contrast Plaut. *Mil.* 792. For similar ideas in later poets cf. Bramble (1970), 31 n. 2.

36 *ex utraque pari malarum parte* = (apparently) *pariter ex utraque malarum parte*, i.e. *parte* does double duty. It has been suggested that there is in these words a specific and ironical reference to the Roman custom of dressing the bride's hair in six plaits, three a side.

37 *genibus* is most easily understood as intrumental ablative, with *petebat*; *summissa* is present middle in sense = *se submittens*.

38 Cf. Sallmann (1972), 78–80. He makes some interesting points, but his interpretation of *petebat* seems to me obscure and strained.

39 The commentators on vv. 93–4, following Lambinus, compare for the sentiment of v. 94 Eur. *I.A.* 1220, but the two verses taken together constitute a specifically epic touch. Cf. Hom. *Il.* 5. 53–4 ἀλλ' οὔ οἱ τότε γε χραῖσμ' Ἄρτεμις ἰοχέαιρα, | οὐδὲ ἑκηβολίαι, ἧσιν τὸ πρίν γ' ἐκέκαστο 'but then Artemis availed him nothing, nor his former skill with the bow', 16. 837, Virg. *Aen.* 10. 319–20 *nihil illos Herculis arma | nec ualidae iuuere manus genitorque Melampus*, Ov. *Met.* 6. 95–6 *nec profuit Ilion illi | Laomedonue pater*.

40 Lucretius has adapted and exploited the Greek ritual of holding the victim aloft (Aesch. *Ag.* 232–5). Other details of Aeschylus' treatment, with masterly restraint, he omits; though in the moving picture drawn by Aeschylus of Iphigenia singing in her father's house there is perhaps a hint of the contrast exploited by Lucretius between what was and what should have been.

41 Cf. Kenney (1971) on lines 174, 258.

42 For the terminology used here cf. Platnauer (1951), 5.

3   A VERSION OF PASTORAL

Bibliography. A fair idea of older views on *Ecl.* 4 can be gained from Mayor–Warde Fowler–Conway (1907). A very useful survey of more recent views on the poem is given by Büchner (1955), 175–93 (this is a separate printing of Büchner's article on Virgil in Pauly–Wissowa). Still worth reading for its wide learning – and in spite of its 'orientalizing' interpretation – is Norden (1924). By far the best work on *Ecl.* 4 has been done by Jachmann (1952), 13–62 (there is a shortened version in Jachmann (1952*a*), 37–62). Little is added to the actual understanding of *Ecl.* 4 by Becker (1955), 328–41 or by Klingner (1967), 68–82. Of commentaries, the most useful is Conington–Nettleship (1963), though this was largely based on Heyne–Wagner (1830–1) which is still worth consulting. For a treatment of *Ecl.* 4 in the context of similar poetic techniques, see G. Williams (1968), 274–85.

1 Theocritus was born in Sicily, though later he probably lived in Cos and Alexandria. On him see also above, p. 2 n. 1.

2 Tamarisks (μυρῖκαι) are a prominent feature of the landscape at the beginning of *Idyll* 1 (line 13) and Virgil's use of this Greek word here underlines the connexion with Theocritus (though Romans, in fact, also, as often, used the Greek term as the botanical name: cf. Pliny, *N.H.* 13. 116; 24. 67). The word *arbusta* is a generic term for 'forested region'.

3 Virgil often uses the basic symbolism which equates 'writing pastoral poetry' with 'being a shepherd' (see especially *Ecl.* 10 and G. Williams (1968), 233–9). From this, various symbolic details are deduced whereby objects in the pastoral landscape or situation represent aspects of the poet's subject-matter.

4 On this pattern see Pearce (1966), 140–71, 298–320. This pattern is referred to below as the 'framed' line.

5 At least ten Sibyls were known and listed by Varro (*Res Diuinae* in Lactantius, *Inst.* 1. 6. 8–12), but for Romans the Sibyl of Cumae was supreme. From her originated the Sibylline Books which were consulted, on order of the Senate, by the *quindecimuiri* (these books were burnt in the Capitol fire of 83 B.C. and a new collection made; there was further pruning by Augustus some time after 12 B.C. – Suet. *Aug.* 31. 1). It seems, however, that the Sibyl from time to time produced oracles on consultation (like the Delphic Oracle) and it is to one of these, and not to the official Books, that Virgil refers. See Latte (1960), 160–1. A selection of the later (largely Jewish and Christian inspired) Sibylline oracles is conveniently edited with a good introduction, translation and notes by Kurfess (1951).

6 This does not mean that Virgil counted on his reader's knowing the actual oracle (the poet reveals its contents in the poem) but only the nature and authority of such oracles.

7 Cf. *Aeneid* 7. 44 *maior rerum mihi nascitur ordo* 'a grander series of events is opening before me'. The sense is that of Horace, *Odes* 3. 30. 4–5 *innumerabilis* | *annorum series et fuga temporum* 'the unnumbered series of years and the flight of ages'.

8 *ultima aetas* cannot mean 'the end of the present age' when qualified by *Cumaei carminis*, and *uenit* cannot mean 'has come and gone'. What Virgil means is a final age which is really a repeat of the first age of the world.

9 The 'Great Year' of the Stoics was just one of several theories of

cycles in the history of the universe: on one calculation the cycle lasted 291,400, on another 12,954, years; it ended with a conflagration of the world and then the process started again. For the various schemes and their variations see van der Waerden (1952), 129–55. The concept has no relevance to *Ecl.* 4 since Virgil envisages no repetition of the ages again, but only a final age which repeats the first (see previous note).

10 The idea of five ages of the world goes back to Hesiod, *Works and Days* 109ff. The ages were Golden, Silver, Bronze, Heroic, and Iron. The ancient commentator Servius here speaks of ten ages... *saecula per metalla diuisit; dixit etiam quis quo saeculo imperaret, et Solem ultimum, id est decimum, uoluit.* Censorinus, *De Die Natali* 17. 6 speaks of an Etruscan system of ten *saecula*, and cf. the story of Servius on *Ecl.* 9. 46 *sed Vulcanius aruspex in contione dixit cometen esse qui significaret exitum noni saeculi et ingressum decimi; sed quod inuitis diis secreta rerum pronuntiaret statim se esse moriturum: et nondum finita oratione in ipsa contione concidit. hoc etiam Augustus in libro secundo de memoria uitae suae complexus est.* No doubt Augustus recognized good propaganda when he saw it, but this 'oracle' belonged to July 44 B.C. The reason for regarding such systems of ages as irrelevant to *Ecl.* 4 is that Virgil goes on to use the scheme of Hesiod and Aratus. For the same reason, speculations based on supposed Pythagorean doctrines are disregarded here: for them see Carcopino (1930), 57ff. Servius on *Ecl.* 4 imagines a repetition of the ages, and, for that reason (see n. 9), his view is disregarded.

11 As often by Virgil with *magnus* and *ingens* (see Austin (1955) on *Aeneid* 4. 89).

12 This version of the legend is that of Aratus (*c.* 315–240 B.C.) in his *Phaenomena* 96–136, where he describes Justice finally leaving the earth in the Age of Bronze. In Hesiod Αἰδώς and Νέμεσις leave earth in the Age of Iron.

13 For Hesiod (*Works* 111) it had been the time of Kronos. But for Virgil's view cf. *Georg.* 2. 538 *aureus hanc uitam in terris Saturnus agebat,* and for Augustus as the founder of the new Golden Age, *Aen.* 6. 792ff.

14 Cf. e.g. *Aeneid* 7. 327 *odit et ipse pater Pluton, odere sorores | Tartareae monstrum.* See Conington (1963) ad loc.

15 That is the point which is emphasized in (8) *primum.*

16 Any such assertion about Apollo by a poet in this period would be implausible. In the *Aeneid* Apollo is mentioned more than any god except Iuppiter, but he is not an active god, with the single exception of his intervention at *Aeneid* 9. 638ff. to congratulate Ascanius and dissuade him from further fighting, but even this has a strong element of prophecy in it and was doubtless inspired by the fact that Augustus regarded Apollo as his own personal protecting deity. Apollo's function throughout the *Aeneid* is to deliver prophecies not to initiate action. See Bailey (1935), 163–72.

17 The ancient commentator Servius asserts that the Sibylline prophecy made the last age the age of the sun, but this is a mere guess and 40 B.C. is too early a date to assume an identification of Apollo with the sun in

Roman literature (see Fontenrose (1939), 439ff.). Servius' weakness is shown by his quoting Horace even on 46–7, and never referring to Catullus 64. Apollo was the favourite god of Octavian (Augustus), but again this connexion belongs to a later period (probably the battle of Actium in 31 B.C. was decisive), and anyway such a partisan connexion is alien to the general political impartiality of this poem. But one has an uneasy sense with Virgil that his ideas are not readily exhausted or explained. See further note 71 below. Norden (1924) has a most ingenious theory about the position of 1 January (when consuls entered on office) as midway between two festivals of the sun, but it relies on oriental evidence and is quite unconvincing.

18 It is worth noticing that Apollo is never mentioned by name in Delphic oracles unless some directions for the observance of his cult are needed. An outstanding example of this is the oracle given to Thera, ordering the foundation of Cyrene, quoted in a short form by Herodotus 4. 150 and a longer form by Diodorus Siculus 8. 29 ('king Phoebus Apollo sends you...Phoebus Apollo guides you'). Otherwise Zeus, Pallas Athene etc. are mentioned in the oracles as the activists. It is less important that Apollo is not named in the later Sibylline oracles (see n. 5 above).

19 Such a revelation would be the most natural to imagine for a poet from the god of poetry and prophecy.

20 See pp. 36 and 44–6, above.

21 That this is to be seen as a parenthesis is clearly shown by the force of (11) *adeo* ('what is more', cf. e.g. *Aeneid* 11. 369 where also a subordinate expansion rather than a fact of parallel weight is added) together with the fact that (15) *ille* immediately takes up the reference to the child in 8–10.

22 Literally 'this glory consisting in an age' (cf. 24 *herba ueneni*); on this genitive see L–H–S 62ff. The phrase cannot mean 'the child' ('this glory of the age') for which *inibit* would be an implausible verb, though perfectly suited to the beginning of a temporal age.

23 The form *si qua...uestigia...* is merely indefinite ('all traces that exist') and does not throw doubt on the existence of such traces.

24 Cf. e.g. Horace, *Odes* 1. 2. 29; 35. 33.

25 See p. 44, above.

26 For *deum uitam accipiet* cf. Terence, *Heaut.* 693 *deorum uitam apti sumus*.

27 The connexion with Catullus 64 will be seen to be very important to the understanding of *Ecl.* 4. This situation particularly mirrors the time when the gods regularly came among men as Catullus describes it in 64. 386 *nondum spreta pietate* and when it was not the case that (398) *iustitiamque omnes cupida de mente fugarunt* (and cf. 406). These were virtues which Apollo, guardian of law and order, especially upheld. On this aspect of Apollo, see e.g. Guthrie (1950), 183ff.

28 This is probably the meaning rather than 'a world made peaceful by the bravery of his father' because the peace implied seems to be the peace that will come particularly from cessation of civil war (cf. 13–14 and 31), and it is this that is important rather than the wars implied in 34–6. At this period wars against external enemies were actually desirable

as a means of expiating the shame of civil war: see Nisbet–Hubbard (1970) on *Odes* 1. 2. 51.

29 It is relevant here to remember that in most of the tradition about Achilles it was Apollo who, at the wedding of Peleus and Thetis, delivered the prophecy about the (as yet unconceived) hero's future: *Iliad* 24. 62–3, Aeschylus fr. 284a Mette, Plato *Republic* 383B. Catullus varied that in poem 64.

30 See note 4, above.

31 See further p. 39, above.

32 On the flora of Theocritus see e.g. Lindsell (1936), 78ff.; and for Virgil's see Sargeaunt (1920).

33 For descriptions of the Golden Age see Lovejoy and Boas (1935), 24ff., 145ff., and 156ff.

34 A re-arrangement of lines with 23 transposed to follow 20 (designed to produce four lines directed to the child, followed by four lines devoted to the traditional Golden Age) is mistaken since not only are the differing senses of *ipse* then made to follow one another immediately and (23) *fundent flores* to follow (20) *fundet acantho*, but also the clear intention of Virgil is defeated (see above, p. 39).

35 See further p. 39, above.

36 Nicander (Alexandrian poet of second century B.C.) in *Theriaca* 8ff. quotes Hesiod for the view that snakes sprang from the spilt blood of the Titans – implying an age when they did not exist. But, of course, once they do exist, they can only be killed off.

37 See note 4, above.

38 Cf. Cicero's description of 'heroic lays': *Brutus* 75 *atque utinam exstarent illa carmina quae multis saeculis ante suam aetatem in epulis esse cantitata a singulis conuiuis de clarorum uirorum laudibus in Originibus scriptum reliquit Cato.* Cf. *Tusculan Disputations* 4. 3, and Varro apud Nonium 77. 2.

39 This spontaneity of growth is clearly implied from the context, since there would be no point in mentioning corn otherwise.

40 On the so-called 'golden' line, see Norden (1926), 393ff. and Wilkinson (1963), 215–16.

41 Cf. Seneca *Epistle* 84. 3–4 *de illis non satis constat utrum sucum ex floribus ducant qui protinus mel sit, an quae collegerunt in hunc saporem mixtura quadam et proprietate spiritus sui mutent. quibusdam enim placet non faciendi mellis scientiam esse illis, sed colligendi.* Aristotle (*Hist. An.* 5. 22) and Pliny (*N.H.* 11. 30) express the common ancient belief that honey dropped as a kind of dew from heaven. Only Seneca expresses doubts. Virgil here means that the work of bees will not be needed to collect it.

42 This is analogous to (13) *sceleris uestigia nostri. fraus* is the basic untrustworthiness of behaviour which in *Georgics* 1. 502 (*Laomedonteae luimus periuria Troiae*) Virgil traces to an origin in the building of Troy when Laomedon cheated Apollo and Neptune of their agreed payment. This is, once again, a reference to the shame of civil war; citizens should trust and respect one another. (See further above, p. 52.)

43 Horace treats this as a sin, a basic transgression of God's ordinance, in

Odes 1. 3. 23–4 *si tamen impiae | non tangenda rates transiliunt uada*: see Nisbet–Hubbard (1970) ad loc.

44 Catullus 64. 1–10 – especially (4) *cum lecti iuuenes = delectos heroas*, and 338 *nascetur uobis Achilles*.

45 This idea is conveyed particularly by (40) *patietur* and (41) *robustus*.

46 Catullus 64. 38–42

rura colit nemo, mollescunt colla iuuencis,
non humilis curuis purgatur uinea rastris,
non glaebam prono conuellit uomere taurus,
non falx attenuat frondatorum arboris umbram:
squalida desertis rubigo infertur aratris.

47 See p. 36, above.

48 See note 4, above.

49 This is technically the ἀπὸ κοινοῦ position, when a word which is common to two clauses and required in each is postponed to the second of them.

50 The -*s* sounds are continued in 46–7.

51 See Fraenkel (1962), 261.

52 See G. Williams (1968), 226–8 and Bramble (1970), 26ff.

53 I have made a break in the exposition between 47 and 48 because it is convenient – the content of 46–7 belongs closely with that of 18–45. But this obscures a feature of *Eclogue* 4. It seems to be composed in units of seven lines, subdivided into four and three. So the poem opens with three lines and ends with four. The fourteen lines 4–17 are composed in units of three and four (4–7, 8–10, 11–14 and 15–17). Virgil, in the *Eclogues*, avoids any obvious arithmetical balances (for instance, *Ecl.* 1 opens with two speeches of five lines each and ends with speeches of five, fifteen and five lines respectively, but the balance is not carried further; *Eclogue* 10 opens and closes with sections of eight lines each). In *Eclogue* 4 the central prophecy occupies twenty-eight lines, divided into units of eight, eleven and nine lines each. Since the wishes of 53–7 form a unit of seven lines, the poet probably viewed 46–52 as a unit of composition in which, as it were, he joined the Parcae in their wish for a speedy approach of the Golden Age. On the numbers, see Skutsch (1969), 158.

54 See especially Fraenkel (1957), 242 n. 1.

55 The other possible meaning 'the germ of a (future) Iuppiter' is impossible in the context since the child is clearly not in itself a god and the equation of an emperor with Iuppiter is out of the question in 40 B.C.

56 See Nisbet–Hubbard (1970) ad loc. and G. Williams (1968), 161 and 441.

57 The elevation of these lines is increased by two Greek metrical features: the spondaic ending of 49, and the lengthening in arsis of (51) *terrasqué tractusque*. See Maas (1962), 59 and 76, and Norden (1926), 438, and 451f.

58 This rules out the interpretation which would take *conuexo nutantem mundo* as an adjectival description of *mundum* and *mundum* as standing in a simple series with the nouns in 51 which would all then be taken up

in (52) *omnia*. In that interpretation *nutantem* could only suggest a collapsing world.

59 Virgil was 30 when he was writing this poem.

60 Roman writers were inclined to avoid final -*s* followed immediately by initial *s*-. So, instead of writing *spiritus et quantus...*, Virgil has compressed this structure: *spiritus et (tantus) quantum (eius spiritus) sat erit...* For the avoidance of the above-mentioned clash of -*s*, see Löfstedt (1933), Chapter 5, 'Zum Gebrauch von *quis* und *qui*'.

61 On the literary form of *recusatio* see Wimmel (1960), and G. Williams (1968), 46f. and 'Index' s.v.

62 On Virgil's invention of Arcadia as an ideal pastoral region and the setting for bucolic poetry, see Snell (1953), Chapter 13, 'Arcadia: The Discovery of a Spiritual Landscape', pp. 281–309.

63 See, most conveniently, Dover (1971), xiv–l.

64 For the origin of these patterns in non-literary songs and ritual compositions see Merkelbach (1956), 97–133 (esp. 117ff.).

65 The MSS here uniformly provide *cui non risere parentes*. This gives inadequate sense since nothing is then required of the child and since it necessitates understanding (60) *risu cognoscere matrem* most implausibly as 'recognize your mother by *her* smile'. Pliny (*N.H.* 7. 72) asserts that only of Zoroaster was it recorded that he smiled on the day of his birth (and that his brain throbbed so violently as to shake off a hand placed on his head – a sign of his future wisdom). Censorinus, *De Die Natali* 11. 7 asserts that babies never smile before the fortieth day. Quintilian, *Inst. Orat.* 9. 3. 8 says '*qui non risere parentes, | nec deus hunc mensa, dea nec dignata cubili est*: ex illis enim "qui non risere", hic, quem non dignata.' Clearly his MS of Virgil read *qui*, and *parentes* is corrupt and easily emended to *parenti* (Bonnell) – the dative corresponds syntactically to *ad*+acc. in Catullus 61. 219 *dulce rideat ad patrem*. The shift from *qui* (pl.) to *hunc* (sing.) is a Greek rather than Latin syntactical feature; examples in Latin normally place the singular first (see L–H–S 432f.). But Greek syntactical usages were one means which late Republican and Augustan poets used to construct a poetic language, particularly Horace and Virgil (compare the Greek metrical features in 49ff. – see note 57, above). For Greek examples, see K–G 1. 87. On the corruption, see especially Maas (1958), 36f.

66 See particularly Homer, *Odyssey* 11. 602–3 μετ' ἀθανάτοισι θεοῖσι | τέρπεται ἐν θαλίῃς καὶ ἔχει καλλίσφυρον Ἥβην, 'among the immortal gods, he enjoys himself in banqueting and has for wife trim-ankled Hebe'. But it is even more relevant (see pp. 44f.) to remark that a picture of Herakles' bliss in heaven (feasting and Hebe) is prominent in Theocritus, *Idyll* 17. 20–33.

67 On the details see Syme (1952), chs. 15 and 16.

68 See Brunt (1962), 69–86.

69 The marriage was a purely political move, intended to conciliate Pompeius, and it failed both as politics and as a marriage. Within a year followed the birth of Julia, divorce, and a new pact with Pompeius at Puteoli.

70 That the children of both marriages turned out to be girls does not affect

the issue – prophecy cannot be corrected and, when darkly poetic, need not be withdrawn.

71 Yet it is not surprising that the poem was misunderstood from a time soon after it was composed. It was the poem's sheer difficulty that enabled Pollio's son, C. Asinius Gallus, to make the absurd claim to Asconius (Servius on *Ecl.* 4. 11) that he was the designated child. However, the possibility that Asinius Gallus was also intending a leg-pull cannot be ignored.

72 My thanks are due to Mr J. H. Simon for helpful criticism and advice.

4   *SCILICET ET TEMPVS VENIET...*

The best all-round introduction to the *Georgics* is Wilkinson (1969). See too R. D. Williams (1967), 14–22. Stimulating are the relevant chapters of Otis (1963) and Klingner (1967); particularly the latter, a most sensitive and sympathetic discussion. The commentaries I have found most useful are those of Conington–Nettleship (1963), Huxley (1963), and Richter (1957). T. E. Page (1898) is also a steady stand-by. I have assumed the reader has at least one of the English commentaries to hand.

A word about what I have and have not done in this essay. There has not been room, and it has not really been my inclination, to comment except in rare instances on Virgil's word-music and word-patterning. My concern has been within the *sense* of words; to show the poet exploiting their semantic resonances, their associations and backgrounds of meaning; to show how these are made to interact and cooperate; for hence comes the real stuff of poetry. As the piece I have chosen (the end of Book 1) is part, indeed a climactic part, of a longer poem, my analysis has necessarily involved comment, albeit allusive, on the poem, and its meaning, as a whole. The general remarks with which I begin are indispensable for my analysis.

Mr J. Griffin very kindly criticized a draft of this essay. He will notice but I hope forgive the fact that stubbornness has sometimes prevailed over wise advice. I am also grateful to the editors for their helpful comments.

References to *Georgics* Book 1 are by line number alone and to the rest of the poem by book and line number.

1 Cf. Wilkinson (1969), 1–15, 49ff. and chaps. 5–7; though I am not sure Mr Wilkinson would agree with my 'greater'; also Otis (1963), 145ff., R. D. Williams (1967), 14ff., and especially Klingner (1967), 178–84, and e.g. 194, 220–1.

2 See Wilkinson (1969), 69; a fuller discussion Klingner (1967), 222–6.

3 The idea of 'Italy' was increasingly felt and increasingly fostered for various purposes by various people: cf. Klingner (1961), 11–33; Syme (1952), 86ff., 276–93; Wilkinson (1969), 153–9.

4 Cf. Syme (1952), 450–2, and 254; Brunt (1971), 129.

5 On Varro see Wilkinson (1969), 5off. and 65–8. For Varro's views cf. *Res Rusticae* 2. 1. 6 *de antiquis illustrissimus quisque pastor erat*; or e.g. 2 *Praefatio: uiri magni nostri maiores non sine causa praeponebant*

rusticos Romanos urbanis..., 3. 1. 4 *diuina natura dedit agros, ars humana aedificauit urbes...necque solum antiquior cultura agri, sed etiam melior. itaque non sine causa maiores nostri ex urbe in agros redige-bant suos ciues, quod et in pace a rusticis Romanis alebantur et in bello ab his alleuabantur. nec sine causa terram eandem appellabant matrem et Cererem, et qui eam colerent, piam et utilem agere uitam credebant atque eos solos reliquos esse ex stirpe Saturni regis.* (The allusion to the Golden Age is in the last clause.) Cf. too Cato, *De Agri Cultura* 1. 2 *et uirum bonum quom laudabant, ita laudabant, bonum agricolam bonumque colonum.*

6 For the religion of the *Georgics* cf. Klingner (1967), 196, 213–14 etc.; also cf. his remarks in connection with *labor*: see n. 10, below.

7 *arma* was probably first applied to the farmer's tools by Virgil: cf. Wilkinson (1969), 80. Huxley (1963) on line 160 is misleading.

8 Cf. Wilkinson (1969), 128–9.

9 The poet brings alive what we know to be a common rustic idiom: see Cicero, *Orator* 81, Conington–Nettleship (1963), on l. 1; and quite possibly this idiom was founded on a more concrete sense to *laetus* (cf. *laetamen* 'manure', 'dung') – see Palmer (1954), 69f., Huxley (1963), 65.

10 The remarks of Klingner (1967) on *labor* are particularly perceptive: see e.g. 192–3, 198–201, 208–10 and 212. See too Wilkinson (1969), 54f. and 59.

11 Cf. 2. 458ff.: *O fortunatos nimium...agricolas!...extrema per illos | Iustitia excedens terris uestigia fecit*; 2. 538 *aureus hanc uitam in terris Saturnus agebat.*

12 Typhoeus was a monster often associated with the Giants; see e.g. his entry in *OCD*; and Giants and Titans were often confused or identified. See Horace, *Odes* 3. 4 for a famous example of the exploitation of the symbolic import of such monsters, with the discussion of Fraenkel (1957), 273ff.

13 Parallels might suggest that the tense is by analogy with Greek practice and not to be pressed: cf. Tränkle (1960), 73. But I think that the full implications should be given a chance; and when they are, that the tense *is* seen to be significant. Cf. my remarks below on *Cyclopum.*

14 Cf. Wirszubski (1950), 7–9; cf. too Klingner (1967), 193–4.

15 Macrobius, *Saturnalia* 5. 16. 4–5; cf. Richter (1957), on lines 461ff.

16 Virgil uses *tumesco* only at *Georgics* 1. 357, 465 and 2. 479; *tumultus* often in the *Aeneid*, but in the *Georgics* only at 1. 464.

17 *OLD* s.v. *caecus* gives useful documentation on the word.

18 We find roles reversed in the *Aeneid*: cf. e.g. *Aeneid* 7. 525f. *sed ferro ancipiti decernunt atraque late | horrescit strictis seges ensibus....*

19 Cf. very interestingly how the historical Caesar, not without precedent, seems to have associated himself with the God *Sol*: Weinstock (1971), 381–4, to which Dr Woodman refers me. (In our present passage the logic or theology of the poetic impression is not of course to be pressed too far.)

20 Cf. *OLD* s.v. *ex(s)tinguo* 1b. Cf. particularly Cicero, *De Natura Deorum* 2. 14 *Tuditano et Aquilio consulibus...P. Africanus, Sol alter, extinctus est.*

21 Cf. Plutarch, *Moralia* 267A, Pauly–Wissowa VIA 2231. 4ff. Compare above, p. 109.

22 For the currency of such an idea cf. Wilkinson (1969), 161.

23 See Fordyce (1961), 304.

24 See e.g. Plutarch, *Caesar* 69; Suetonius, *Caesar* 81; the question is well and concisely discussed by Wilkinson (1969), 204–6.

　　Particularly interesting to compare perhaps is Cicero, *De Diuinatione* 1. 97–8 (published just after Caesar's assassination but not directly referring to it) which has many parallels with Virgil – and interesting differences. But there is a great deal of conventionality in such lists: cf. Dio Cassius 41. 14, Cicero, *Catiline* 3. 18 and a quotation from Cicero's poetry in *De Diuinatione* 1. 17ff. (with Pease (1920) ad loc.), Apollonius Rhodius 4. 1280–7.

25 I shall not cite parallels for the individual portents unless it illuminates the discussion to do so. The reader has the passages in the previous note to compare, and there is further documentation in the commentaries at the relevant points.

26 Cf. L & S s.v. *obscenus*; on both see Conington–Nettleship (1963) ad loc. or, more fully, Richter (1957) on line 470.

27 Cf. L & S s.v. *signum* II A 2.

28 Our response to the suggestive power of the *words* I think is not affected, not anyway swamped, by the specifications (*globos*, *liquefacta*) imposed by the literal context of the portent.

29 Huxley (1963) ad loc. 'Cyclopum...in agros: i.e. over the region round Etna.'

30 *Theogony* 139–46 on which see M. L. West (1966), 206.

31 Cf. Cicero, *De Diuinatione* 2. 43.

32 See *OLD* s.v. 1c and f.

33 See Pliny, *Naturalis Historia* 2. 194 for the Ancients' belief in earthquakes in the Alps. (And for earthquakes as portents see Cicero, *De Diuinatione* 1. 97.)

34 For *motus* see L & S s.v. II A.

35 Cf. the use of *tremit* at 330.

36 Cf. Ovid's imitation at *Metamorphoses* 15. 792f.; but cf. also e.g. *Eclogues* 8. 86, 10. 58.

37 Cf. Otis (1963), 162.

38 Interestingly, this precise idea, that of 'weeping statues', may be from Virgil's imagination. Tibullus 2. 5. 77 and others are most likely imitations of this passage.

39 For sweat as a symptom of fear cf. Lucretius 3. 154.

40 *manare* is a neutral word drawing its colour from its context. Cf. e.g. 3. 310 *laeta magis pressis manabunt flumina mammis*, *Aeneid* 3. 175 *tum gelidus toto manabat corpore sudor*, *Aeneid* 3. 43 *non...cruor hic de stipite manat*; it therefore contains no clue of the horror to come.

41 The military-violent potential to *dirus* and *ardeo* is fully exploited by Virgil in the *Aeneid*. It is instructive to look at his use of the words there (via Merguet (1912) or Wetmore (1911)). *dirus* is also a more or less technical term for – 'dire' – portents: see *OLD* s.v. 1.

42 *fulgura* for the more obvious *fulmina*, as *cecidere* shows.

43 Cf. Nisbet–Hubbard (1970), 376f. as well as the passages cited in note 24.

44 See Scullard (1970), 166; Charlesworth (1952), 24f.

45 See the passages quoted in Conington–Nettleship (1963) on line 490.

46 See Conington–Nettleship (1963) on line 492.

47 Cf. Wilkinson (1969), 200–1.

48 Cf. the fine note of Richter (1957) on lines 493ff.; cf. too Huxley (1963) on line 497.

49 See Klingner (1967), 192–3.

50 Huxley (1963) on line 175 is instructive.

51 Cf. Huxley (1963) on line 498. I think Romulus and Vesta are to be considered apart, not just as examples of the aforementioned general categories. The exact sense and origin of *Indigetes* is disputed: see Richter (1957) on lines 498f., Latte (1960), 43–5.

52 And perhaps if we think back to the famous account of Jupiter's purpose at 121ff., questions now occur to us – ambiguities or confusions in it not wholly resolved. Indeed some may be apparent from my allusions to the account at pp. 48–9, which aimed truthfully to represent an initial response. 121ff. should be closely re-examined. Was Jupiter rather *over*-diligent in providing conditions to sharpen men's wits? How do we react now, for example, to 130 *praedarique lupos iussit* (cf. p. 57)?

53 For *euerto* itself of ploughing cf. *OLD* s.v. 2.

54 See *OLD* s.v. for the various nuances of *abduco*; on *squalent* cf. R. D. Williams (1967), 18.

55 Cf. Varro, *Res Rusticae* 2 *Praefatio* 3, describing the despicable migration from the countryside: *nunc intra murum fere patres familiae correpserunt relictis falce et aratro....*

56 Thus Conington–Nettleship (1963) ad loc.; contrast Huxley (1963). Huxley is wrong but it is as well he makes us look at the word again. The point *is* that the context imposes this sense; indeed in general we could say that the sickle is as *rigidus* as the sword. The fact that Virgil chose to use an unobvious word for the notion of straightness supports my contention that he was after another effect too.

57 Cf. the description of Latinus at *Aeneid* 7. 600 (with Conington–Nettleship (1963) ad loc.) and of Aeolus at *Aeneid* 1. 53f. quoted below.

58 Cf. Otis (1963), 227–35; Pöschl (1962), 13ff., especially 19.

59 A weakness of Klingner (1967): e.g. p. 220.

60 Cf. 4. 560f. *Caesar dum magnus ad altum | fulminat Euphraten bello uictorque uolentis | per populos dat iura....* Interesting vocabulary.

5

OF MICE AND MEN

1 Ellwood-Smith (1931).

2 Fraenkel (1957), 143.

3 Horace is quoted from Klingner (1950). This essay draws without specific acknowledgement on the standard commentaries, notably Kiessling–Heinze (1957). There is nothing about the fable in Seel (1972), 13–93, 'Bemerkungen zu Horaz *sat*. 2, 6'.

4 Sturtevant (1921), 306 and Nilsson (1952), 132–5 and 209.

5 E.g. Jocelyn (1967), 472, s.v. polyptoton. The commentators are followed by Witke (1970), 72n., but the case for the mock heroic style is supported by Marouzeau (1946), 321, 325, and L–H–S 707–8.

6 Babrius 108 Perry (Loeb); Phaedrus, *Fabulae Nouae* 9 (OCT).

7 Brink (1971) on Horace, *A.P.* 249.

8 D. West (1973), 40–4.

9 *Praelambere* occurs only here and is a mousy perversion of *praegustare*. Another interpretation is that the Town Mouse cannot resist taking a little nibble for himself, but Rudd (1966), 305 n. 4 well argues that the parallel cited refers to slaves picking at the leavings *after* a meal and that any such suggestion is contrary to the ethopoeia of the fable.

10 'VIS non interrogantis modo est ut VIN; sed orantis, hortantis, flagitantis, jubentis' (Bentley (1728) ad loc.).

11 So it appears from this satire; from line 3 beginning a prayer with *auctius*; from line 32, beginning a military metaphor mock-heroically applied; from line 100 beginning the parody of an epic formula. Strong punctuation at the bucolic diaeresis is very much more common in Horace's *Satires* than in other hexameter verse (Nilsson (1952), 136–8 and table XIX), but work remains to be done on the effects of it (see Marouzeau (1946), 306; Perret (1956), 153; R. D. Williams (1960) on *Aeneid* 5. 815). For instance in *Satires* 2. 1 it twice begins direct speech (5, 17, cf. 2. 6. 34) and often introduces an emphatic utterance: exclamations (42, 60); rhetorical question (52); epigram (32); the second half of an antithesis (83).

12 So D. West (1967), 29–39. Scholars are not amused, e.g. McGann (1969), 41–2, and Foster (1972), 303–6.

13 1. 3. 33, 12. 36, 28. 16; 2. 13. 19; 3. 22. 3, 27. 61; 4. 9. 50.

14 Ebeling (1963).

15 Compare *ergo iter inceptum peragunt* (Virgil, *Aeneid* 6. 284). For this and other Virgilian comparisons see Cèbe (1966), 304 n. 6.

16 As in *Satires* 1. 5. 20.

17 For colour contrasts in Horace see D. West (1973), 37–9; in Virgil, Norden (1926), cites a dozen examples from *Aeneid* 6 in his note on lines 9–10. See also above, p. 90.

18 Brink (1965), 7–8.

19 Compare the material in Mette (1961).

20 MacQueen (1967), 126–7. The religious symbolism seems to be not proven. Henryson certainly attributes biblical language to the mice, but that does not justify the deduction that the mice symbolize those of whom the bible speaks. Henryson is quoted from the Harleian MS edited by Gregory Smith (1905).

21 See MacQueen (1967), 200–7 on Henryson's sources.

6 *CVI NON DICTVS HYLAS PVER?*

1 Apollonius 1. 1207ff., Theocritus 13, Propertius 1. 20, Valerius Flaccus 3. 521ff.

2 For a comparison of Valerius 3. 521ff. with the account of Apollonius see Garson (1963), 260ff.

3 For Nicander fr. 48 Schneider see Antoninus Liberalis, *Metamorphoseon Synagoge* 26, from which it appears that he dealt with the story in the second book of his *Heteroiumena*. Propertius may have known the account, for Nicander seems to have mentioned the river Ascanius (absent from Apollonius and Theocritus), as well as turning Hylas into an echo (cf. Schol. Apollonius 1. 1234). For Euphorion see fr. 76 Powell.

4 See Skutsch (1963), 238–9, employing the criterion of pentameter endings to establish order of composition within the *Monobiblos*.

5 See *Eclogues* 6. 43–4 and *Georgics* 3. 6.

6 Like the majority of critics, I believe the thirteenth *Idyll* of Theocritus to be a polemical reworking of lines 1207ff. of the first book of Apollonius' *Argonautica*. See, e.g., the commentaries of Gow (1952) and Dover (1971); cf. Gow (1938).

7 Compare Apollonius 1. 1243ff. (and the bull simile at 1265ff.) with Theocritus 13. 62f.

8 Auerbach (1953), Chapter 1.

9 That is, Gaius Cornelius Gallus, born around 69 B.C., committed suicide in 26, after incurring the displeasure of Augustus. Unfortunately only one line of his poetry survives.

10 *nomine*, line 5, is to be translated 'name', not 'fame' as Butler–Barber (1933).

11 See also Virgil, *Georgics* 4. 517ff. 'solus Hyperboreas *glacies* Tanaimque *niualem* | aruaque Riphaeis numquam uiduata *pruinis* | lustrabat'.

12 Strabo 9. 436. For further examples of such word-play see, e.g., Nisbet–Hubbard (1970) on Horace, *Odes* 1. 21. 6, and note lines 33–4 of Propertius 1. 20 where *Pege* (πηγή, 'spring') is glossed by *domus . . . umida*.

13 Fr. 3. 22 Powell αὐτὸς δ' ἐς Νύμφας ᾤχετ' ἐφυδριάδας.

14 As, for instance, Postgate (1926) in his translation of lines 41–2, 'and now bent in artless wonder over the beauteous waves and prolonged his truancy with their mirrored charms', or Enk (1946) on line 42, 'itineris errorem vel moram longiorem reddit, adridentibus imaginibus suis captus'.

8   *EXEGI MONVMENTVM*

The most recent full discussion of this poem is that of Pöschl (1970), 248–62; earlier there was Fraenkel (1957), 302–7. Individual aspects of the ode are treated by Korzeniewski (1968 and 1972) and Hulton (1972). I have also consulted a large number of Horatian commentaries, although references to them in the notes are severely restricted. I think it only fair to say that I had completed a final draft of this essay before I saw the extremely thorough work of Suerbaum (1968), especially 325–9.

It is a pleasure to acknowledge friendly criticism I have received on various points from Mr R. G. G. Coleman, Mr A. G. Lee and Professor D. A. West.

1 G. Williams (1968 and 1969), Nisbet–Hubbard (1970) and Cairns (1972) are especially concerned with the categories into which Horace's lyric poems fall.

2 Cf. Kranz (1961), and Curtius (1953), 515. With reference to Horace cf. Fraenkel (1957), 362–3.

3 This is also the conclusion of Paratore (1959), 181–2.

4 For place of origin cf., e.g., *CLE* 1318. 2 *uixi Lucrinis*, 856. 1 *Tibur mihi patria*. For details of career cf., e.g., 372. 1 *natus sum summa in pauperie, merui post classicus miles*, and see especially how Trimalchio demands that on his tombstone there be inscribed the motto *ex paruo creuit* (Petronius, *Cena* 71. 12): this is very close to Horace's *ex humili potens*. Further examples in Korzeniewski (1968), 33–4, (1972), 386.

5 Pasquali (1920), 320–4, saw that this ode is an epitaph poem but his discussion is only of the most generalized nature; Korzeniewski (1968 and 1972) pointed out just how many details Horace's ode shares with epitaphs proper. Neither scholar, however, seems to have appreciated fully the metaphorical terms in which Horace is talking.

6 E.g. *CLE* 1103. 5–6 *dicite qui legitis solito de more sepulto:* | *pro meritis, Pylades, sit tibi terra leuis*. Also *IG* 4. 800; Korzeniewski (1968), 34, (1972), 387.

7 Cf. Kiessling–Heinze (1964) ad loc., Korzeniewski (1968), 32, (1972), 384.

8 E.g. Sappho 55 and 193 Lobel–Page; Plato, *Symposium* 209D; cf. Curtius (1953), 476.

9 E.g. *CIL* I². 1319 *haec est domus aeterna . . . hoc est monumentum nostrum*, *IG* 12. 9. 285. Further examples in Korzeniewski (1968), 32, (1972), 385, and also Lattimore (1942), 167 n. 78, whose work is a rich mine for those interested in epitaph poetry.

10 E.g. *CLE* 1278 *quodque meam retinet uocem data littera saxo,* | *uoce tua uiuet quisque leges titulos, CIL* 8. 7156 *hic ego qui taceo uersibus mea uita demonstro*.

11 *Anthologia Palatina* 7. 715 = lines 2535–40 Gow–Page: 'Far from the land of Italy do I lie. . . but the name of Leonidas has not been forgotten; the Muses' gifts proclaim it till the end of time.' Two other poems are similar in theme but not strictly epitaphs: 7. 12 'The fine work of your poetry, Erinna, cries out that you are not dead but join in the Muses' dance'; 7. 713 = lines 560–7 Gow–Page: 'Erinna has written few verses and her songs have few themes, but she has been assigned this brief epic by the Muses. Therefore is she remembered and is not confined by the shadowy wing of black night.'

12 Ennius, *Varia* 17–18 Vahlen. See again Pasquali (1920), 320–4.

13 No poet before Horace has used the metaphor of a tombstone to describe his poetry, and the only certain example I have found after Horace is the fourth-century A.D. writer Themistius (*Orationes* 4. 59d ἡρία τῶν ψυχῶν τὰς βίβλους, 'books are the tombs of the spirit'). Horace's vocabulary is of course quite different from such expressions as *litterarum monumenta* (Cicero, *De Inuentione* 1. 1, *De Officiis* 1. 156 etc.) or *annalium monumenta* (*Pro Sestio* 102, Livy, 7. 21. 6 etc.), where *monumenta* has its commonest meaning of simply 'monuments'. For *monumentum* used without qualification of literary productions cf. Catullus 95. 9, Cicero, *Ad Atticum* 12. 18. 1, *Ad Familiares* 5. 12. 1. For less sceptical remarks than mine on the word *monumentum* see Suerbaum (1968), 327–8.

14 Cf. De Witt (1939), 129, who rightly sees a 'pointed interpretation' of the opening of this ode. Hulton (1972), 501–2, even observes that for true Epicureans poets were people *in quibus nulla solida utilitas omnisque puerilis est delectatio* (Cicero, *De Finibus* 1. 72).

15 For a *sphragis*-poem ending with a prayer see the 'seal' of Posidippus in Lloyd-Jones (1963), 80–1, 92–3, 96.

16 The ascending tricolon is (*a*) *aere perennius*, (*b*) *regalique...altius*, (*c*) *quod...temporum*. For a definition of ascending tricolon see above, p. 5 and n. 5.

17 G. Williams (1969), 150, following Kiessling–Heinze (1964) ad loc., goes so far as to translate *situs* here as 'grave'.

18 The usual parallel is Martial 8. 3. 5–7 'et cum *rupta situ* Messalae saxa iacebunt | altaque cum Licini marmora puluis erunt, | me tamen ora legent'.

19 Simonides 531 Page. In line 4 I have adopted an emendation by M. L. West (1967), 133. The exact meaning of Simonides' verb ἀμαυρώσει is doubtful (cf. Lloyd-Jones (1965), 243n.) but is used frequently of time (cf. Pfeiffer (1949) on Callimachus, *Iambus* 12. 67, Borthwick (1971), 431 n. 2). On the question of whether Simonides' ἐντάφιον is metaphorical or not compare M. L. West (1970), 210–11, and Page (1971), 317–18.

20 For a survey of scholarly opinion cf. Pöschl (1970), 251–3, who himself strongly favours 'decay'. Korzeniewski (1968), 31–2, strongly favours 'site'.

21 This is also the view of Plessis (1924) ad loc.: 'Ici, malgré la plupart des commentateurs, n'écartons pas l'idée de ruine: la dégradation est justement un témoignage d'antiquité; et ne négligeons pas la suite des idées: grammaticalement, *situ pyramidum* ne dépend que de *altius*; mais, dans la pensée du poète, il dépend aussi de *perennius.* ...*situ* doit donc, de toute manière, faire allusion à la fois à la longue stabilité des pyramides et à leur commencement de décrépitude.'

22 Highbarger (1935), 251. This is the usual tradition, cf., e.g., Macleane (1853) ad loc., 'What follows seems to be imitated from Pindar.' To his credit Pöschl (1970), 253–4, notices the differences between Horace and Pindar but does not even begin to consider their implications and does not go into any detail.

23 The motif is at least as old as Aristotle, *Physics* 8. 3 (253b). Some, but by no means all, of its occurrences are listed by Smith (1971) on Tibullus 1. 4. 18, a passage which is an instance of the image's commonest function, illustrating the way a lover gradually wears down the loved one. For the image used to illustrate mortality or immortality *after* Horace cf. Ovid, *Ex Ponto* 4. 10. 1–7, Sulpicius Lupercus, *PLM* 4. 107. 7.

24 Propertius 2. 25. 15–17 *sed tamen obsistam. teritur robigine mucro* | *ferreus et paruo saepe liquore silex:* | *at nullo dominae teritur sub limine amor...*; Ovid, *Ex Ponto* 1. 1. 67ff. *non igitur mirum, si mens mea tabida facta* | *de niue manantis more liquescit aquae.* | *...aequorei scopulos ut cauat unda salis,* | *roditur ut scabra positum robigine ferrum.*

25 Columella, *De Re Rustica* 7. 5. 12 *aeris robigine*, Pliny, *Natural History*

7. 64 *aes etiam ac ferrum robigo protinus corripit*, 34. 99 *aera extersa robiginem celerius trahunt quam neglecta* (Pliny here also tells us that bronze was used on *monumenta* to make them more durable).

26 Compare also *Amores* 1. 10. 61–2 *gemmae frangentur et aurum;* | *carmina quam tribuent fama perennis erit.*

27 Catullus 68. 149–52 *hoc tibi, quod potui, confectum carmine munus* | *pro multis, Alli, redditur officiis,* | *ne uestrum scabra tangat robigine nomen* | *haec atque illa dies atque alia atque alia*; Ovid, *Tristia* 5. 12. 21–2 *adde quod ingenium longa rubigine laesum* | *torpet et est multo quam fuit ante minus.*

28 Tacitus, *Dialogus* 22. 5 *nullum sit uerbum uelut rubigine infectum*. Compare also Quintilian 10. 1. 30; and Curtius (1953), 411.

29 For words being scattered on the wind cf. Nisbet–Hubbard (1970) on *Odes* 1. 26. 2. It is possible that we are meant to understand *altius* (line 2) metaphorically too. *altus* is a familiar term for describing the kind of poetry, with elevated themes, which Horace believes many of his *Odes* to be. He might be declaring a belief in the seriousness of his poetry; it is not simply a collection of *nugae*. Such a belief would sound natural in a poem of this type, although on other occasions of course Horace can look upon his poetry as light and even trivial: for this apparent paradox see Hulton (1972).

30 Lines 1–14 thus form a climax, followed by a concluding prayer. For a different, rather eccentric, view, cf. Collinge (1961), 69–70, who sees these lines as a three-part *anti*-climax, and the final prayer as a return to the 'opening bravado' of lines 1–5.

31 Laberius, *Prologue* 124 Ribbeck. For further exs. of this idea cf. Suerbaum (1968), 326, adding *CIL* 6. 9604.

32 This notion is thus not exclusively 'the conceit of a later age', as Hulton (1972), 499, says.

33 The reading of line 312 here adopted is that of Munro (1873). The line has caused a great deal of discussion, e.g. D. A. West (1965).

34 But Lucretius 5. 306–37 is quoted by none of the Horatian commentators I have seen, nor by Merrill (1905). It is, however, quoted by Suerbaum (1968), 328.

35 An idea which became quite common, e.g. Florus 1. 6. 11, Lucian, *Charon* 23, Ausonius, *Epigrams* 35. 9–10, Rutilius Namatianus, *De Reditu* 1. 409–14.

36 For a discussion of Lucretius' metaphor see D. West (1969), 2–3.

37 For poets' claims to originality see Nisbet–Hubbard (1970) on *Odes* 1. 26. 10.

38 So too Huber (1970), 126 n. 3.

39 See Nisbet–Hubbard (1970) ad loc., with further references.

40 A reading of *Exegi monumentum* should make us sceptical of the remark that 'The mature poet of the *Odes* was in the habit of producing unambiguous constructions' (Fraenkel (1957), 251 n. 6). On pp. 304–5 Fraenkel discusses the repeated *qua*-clauses and unhesitatingly takes them with *dicar*; more realistic, it seems to me, is the comment of Quinn (1960), 40: 'It is most unlikely that Horace was unaware of the perils of an ambiguously related relative clause, or inadvertently committed

one in a poem written with such obvious care for so prominent a place in the collection.'

41 For a brief survey of this debate see Pöschl (1970), 257–9, who himself favours spinning.

42 See Nisbet–Hubbard (1970) ad loc.

43 The best parallel is Virgil, *Georgics* 3. 10–11 'primus ego in patriam... | Aonio rediens *deducam* uertice Musas'. Cf. also Horace, *Epistles* 2. 1. 156 'Graecia capta ferum uictorem cepit', Greece taking Italy captive. In Horace's ode I take the word *modos* to mean 'music', or 'rhythms', or more generally 'poetry', as at *Odes* 2. 1. 40 *quaere modos leuiore plectro*, 2. 9. 9–10 *urges flebilibus modis | Mysten ademptum*, 2. 12. 3–4 *mollibus | aptari citharae modis*, 3. 3. 72 *magna modis tenuare paruis*, 3. 9. 10 *dulcis docta modos*, 4. 6. 43–4 *reddidi carmen docilis modorum | uatis Horati*, *Epistles* 1. 3. 12–13 *fidibusne Latinis | Thebanos aptare modos studet*. I do not think that Horace here uses the word = 'metres' (as he does on some occasions, e.g. *Epistles* 1. 19. 27) since his *metres* could in no sense be called 'Italian'; but this is not to deny that Horace's debt to the Greek lyric poets was above all a metrical debt: see above, p. 126 and nn. 50–1. A rather different interpretation is given by G. Williams (1969), 151.

44 On Callimachean influence in general cf. above, p. 2 and n. 1. For Callimachus and Horace cf. Wehrli (1944), Wilkinson (1968), 118ff., Brink (1963), 288 (index), and Newman (1967), 303ff.

45 Virgil, *Eclogues* 6. 5 *deductum dicere carmen*, Propertius 1. 16. 41 *at tibi saepe nouo deduxi carmina uersu*, Horace, *Epistles* 2. 1. 225 *tenui deducta poemata filo*. Further instances in Pöschl (1970), 258.

46 Propertius 3. 1. 8 *exactus tenui pumice versus eat*, Horace, *Epistles* 2. 1. 71–2 *sed emendata uideri | pulchraque et exactis minimum distantia miror*, Ovid, *Metamorphoses* 15. 871 *iamque opus exegi*.

47 There is a further Callimachean feature in the final stanza of *Odes* 2. 16, that of rejecting the common crowd. See Callimachus, *Epigrams* 28. 4 Pfeiffer, Nisbet–Hubbard (1970) on *Odes* 1. 1. 32.

48 See Mette (1961), 138 'Wahl des Bios und Wahl der Gattung fallen für Horaz in eins. Gattung und Bios sind aufeinander zu stilisiert.'

49 The paradox between *potens* and *humilis* (or *tenuis*) is only superficial: see Hulton (1972), 499, 'In the last analysis we are confronted...by simply another example of the well-known Horatian "dualism" or "ambivalence".'

50 Of *Odes* 1–3 71·5% are written in the two Aeolian metres, the Sapphic stanza (26 poems) and the Alcaic stanza (37 poems). A glance at the statistics in Raven (1965), Appendix B, will show that in composing lyric poetry in Aeolian metres Horace had virtually no rival. No one, so far as we know, had written Latin Alcaics before, and there were no Latin Sapphics before Horace with the exceptions of Catullus 11 and 51. But scholars have usually decided (e.g. Williams (1969), 151) that Catullus' two poems hardly impair the justice of Horace's claim. Even so, when he came to write *Epistles* 1. 19, Horace narrowed his claim to exclude any originality as far as the Sapphic stanza was concerned (lines 32–3).

51 So too Wilkinson (1968), 13, 'His pride at having introduced Aeolian lyric to Italy is very likely due, not to the phrases or ideas, nor even to the small amount of spirit, which he derived from Alcaeus and Sappho, but to his success at mastering and adapting their metres.' It is quite wrong to say that 'Horace is not primarily interested in metre as such', as does Newman (1967), 343.

52 The opposite phrase is *ponere superbiam*, as at *Odes* 3. 10. 9; for *ponere* and *sumere* as opposites cf. *Odes* 3. 2. 19.

53 Cf. Versnel (1970), 57.

54 For the contemporary popularity of the *triumphator* motif see Galinsky (1969), who discusses Propertius 3. 1 at pp. 88–9.

55 G. Williams (1969), 152 and (1968), 153.

56 Cf. Solmsen (1948), especially 106. Also Flach (1967), 97ff.

57 Seneca, *Epigrams* 27 and 28; Jerome, *Epistles* 108. 33 *exegi monumentum aere perennius quod nulla destruere possit uetustas*; for possible influences upon Shakespeare see Leishman (1961), 27–91; Ronsard, *A sa Muse* in Laumonier (1914), 2. 152; Herrick, *Pillar of Fame* and stanzas 5 and 6 of *His Poetrie his Pillar*; Klopstock, *An Freund und Feind*, last three stanzas, in Schleiden (1954), 110; for Derzhavin and Pushkin see Bayley (1971), 302ff. I am very grateful to Cesca Thompson for the reference to Klopstock and to Professor J. Gwyn Griffiths for the references to Derzhavin and Pushkin.

58 Correspondences of language are conveniently set out in parallel tables by Bauer (1962), 17–18, but he regrettably uses Ovid in an attempt to disparage Horace.

59 It is interesting to note that Shakespeare (*Sonnet* 55), in his allusion to the Ovidian passage, tried to strengthen this weakness but in so doing fell into loose writing elsewhere in his couplet: 'Nor Mars his sword nor war's quick fire shall burn | The living record of your memory.'

60 For the teeth of time see Simonides 75 Diehl; Shakespeare, *Measure for Measure* 5. 1; Phineas Fletcher, *Purple Island* 1. 15 in Boas (1909), 2. 15; W. B. Yeats, *The New Faces*. For the teeth of death cf. Lucretius 1. 852; Seneca, *Hercules Furens* 555. For other personifications of time and age cf. Leishman (1961), 134–42.

61 Day Lewis (1947), 74.

62 Nisbet–Hubbard (1970), on *Odes* 1. 26, introductory note.

9 EPILOGUE

1 Full discussion of these theories and controversies will be found in Wellek and Warren (1963). More briefly, from a historical point of view, Watson (1962). Bateson (1972) contains much common sense on method in literary criticism. For a brilliant and sensitive analysis of what makes a poem, one cannot do better than refer to Press (1955).

2 Excellent discussions of the relationship between classical scholarship and modern literary criticism are given by Segal (1968) and Wilkinson (1972).

3 Gardner (1959), 17–18. Eliot (1957), 103ff., is an example of the anti-historical approach.

4 Page (1895), 164; Klingner (1956), 77. The attitude is also found in Nisbet–Hubbard (1970), as is pointed out by G. Williams (1972), 2–3.
5 Henry (1873), 150.
6 Eliot (1957), 113.
7 Frye (1957), 65–6.
8 E.g. *Rhetorica ad Herennium* 4. 67; Seneca, *Controuersiae* 3 *praef.* 7; Seneca, *Epistulae* 59. 4–5; Quintilian 6. 3. 48, 8. 3. 44–7, 83–6, 9. 2. 64–6.
9 Empson (1965), xii–xiii; Nisbet–Hubbard (1970), xxii.

Abbreviations and Bibliography

Note. Standard works of reference and titles of periodicals are abbreviated as follows under list A. Scholarly discussions and commentaries are listed under B and throughout the book are referred to by author's name, date, and page number only. E.g. 'Brink (1965), 7–8' is a reference to pages 7–8 of Brink, C. O. (1965). *On Reading a Horatian Satire.* Sydney.

A. ABBREVIATIONS

AJP   *American Journal of Philology*
CIL   *Corpus Inscriptionum Latinarum*, Berlin, 1862–
CLE   *Carmina Latina Epigraphica*, Leipzig, 1895–1926
CM   *Classica et Mediaevalia*
CP   *Classical Philology*
CQ   *Classical Quarterly*
CR   *Classical Review*
Daremberg–Saglio
      Daremberg, C.–Saglio, E. *Dictionnaire des Antiquités Grecques et Romaines*, Paris, 1897–1919
GR   *Greece and Rome*
GRBS   *Greek, Roman and Byzantine Studies*
Gymn.   *Gymnasium*
H   *Hermes*
HSCP   *Harvard Studies in Classical Philology*
IG   *Inscriptiones Graecae*, Berlin, 1873–1939
JHS   *Journal of Hellenic Studies*
JRS   *Journal of Roman Studies*
K–G   Kühner, R.–Gerth, B. *Ausführliche Grammatik der griechischen Sprache.* II. *Satzlehre*, 3rd edn., Hanover–Leipzig, 1898–1904
L–H–S   Leumann, M.–Hofmann, J. B.–Szantyr, A. *Lateinische Grammatik.* II. *Syntax und Stilistik*, Munich, 1965
L & S   Lewis, C. T. and Short, C. *Latin Dictionary*, Oxford, 1897
MH   *Museum Helveticum*
Mnem.   *Mnemosyne*
OCD   *Oxford Classical Dictionary*, 2nd edn., Oxford, 1970
OCT   Oxford Classical Texts
OLD   *Oxford Latin Dictionary*, Oxford, 1968–
PCA   *Proceedings of the Classical Association*
PCPS   *Proceedings of the Cambridge Philological Society*
PLM   *Poetae Latini Minores*, ed. Baehrens, Leipzig, 1879–86
PMLA   *Publications of the Modern Language Association of America*
Pauly–Wissowa
      Paulys Real-Encyclopädie der classischen Altertumswissenschaft, ed. G. Wissowa et al., Stuttgart, 1893–

Philol.	*Philologus*
REL	*Revue des Études Latines*
RM	*Rheinisches Museum*
TAPA	*Transactions of the American Philological Association*
TLL	*Thesaurus Linguae Latinae*, Leipzig, 1900–
WS	*Wiener Studien*

Walde–Hofmann
> Walde, A.–Hofmann, J. B. *Lateinisches Etymologisches Wörterbuch*, repr. Heidelberg, 1965

B. BIBLIOGRAPHY

Auerbach, E. (1953). *Mimesis. The Representation of Reality in Western Literature.* Eng. trans. by W. R. Trask. Princeton

Austin, R. G. (1955). *P. Vergili Maronis Aeneidos Liber Quartus.* Oxford
  (1964). *P. Vergili Maronis Aeneidos Liber Secundus.* Oxford

Bailey, C. (1935). *Religion in Virgil.* Oxford
  (1947). *T. Lucreti Cari De Rerum Natura Libri Sex.* Oxford

Baker, R. J. (1970). 'Catullus and Friend in carm. XXXI', *Mnem.* 23. 33–41

Bateson, F. W. (1972). *The Scholar-critic.* London

Bauer, D. F. (1962). 'The function of Pygmalion in the *Metamorphoses* of Ovid', *TAPA* 93. 1–21

Bayley, J. (1971). *Pushkin.* Cambridge

Becker, C. (1955). 'Virgils Eklogenbuch', *H* 83. 314–49

Bell, A. J. (1923). *The Latin Dual and Poetic Diction.* London

Bentley, R. (1728). *Q. Horatius Flaccus.* 3rd edn. Amsterdam

Boas, F. S. (1909). *Giles and Phineas Fletcher. Poetical Works.* Vol. 2. Oxford

Borthwick, E. K. (1971). 'Emendations and interpretations in the Greek Anthology' *CQ* 21. 426–36

Bramble, J. C. (1970). 'Structure and Ambiguity in Catullus LXIV', *PCPS* 16. 22–41

Brink, C. O. (1963). *Horace on Poetry.* Vol. 1 *Prolegomena.* Cambridge
  (1965). *On Reading a Horatian Satire.* Sydney
  (1971). *Horace on Poetry.* Vol. 2 *The Ars Poetica.* Cambridge

Brunt, P. A. (1962). 'The Army and the Land in the Roman Revolution', *JRS* 52. 69–86
  (1971). *Italian Manpower 225 B.C.–A.D. 14.* Oxford

Büchner, K. (1955). *P. Vergilius Maro: der Dichter der Römer.* Stuttgart

Butler, H. E.–Barber, E. A. (1933). *The Elegies of Propertius.* Oxford

Cairns, F. (1969). 'Catullus I', *Mnem.* 22. 153–8
  (1972). *Generic Composition in Greek and Roman Poetry.* Edinburgh

Camps, W. A. (1967). *Propertius. Elegies Book II.* Cambridge

Carcopino, J. (1930). *Virgile et le mystère de la IVe églogue.* Paris

Cèbe, J.-P. (1966). *La caricature et la parodie.* Bibliothèque des écoles françaises d'Athènes et de Rome 206. Paris

Chapman, R. W. (1920). *The Portrait of a Scholar.* London

Charlesworth, M. P. (1952). 'The Avenging of Caesar' in *Cambridge Ancient History.* Vol. 10. repr. Cambridge

Clausen, W. V. (1964). 'Callimachus and Latin poetry', *GRBS* 5. 181–96

Bibliography

Collinge, N. E. (1961). *The Structure of Horace's Odes*. Oxford

Conington, J.–Nettleship, H. (1963). *The Works of Virgil*. repr. Hildesheim

Curtius, E. R. (1953). *European Literature and the Latin Middle Ages*. Eng. trans. by W. R. Trask. London

Day Lewis, C. (1947). *The Poetic Image*. London

Denniston, J. D. (1952). *Greek Prose Style*. Oxford

De Witt, N. W. (1939). 'Epicurean doctrine in Horace', *CP* 34. 127–34

Dissen, L. (1835). *Albi Tibulli Carmina*. Göttingen

Dover, K. J. (1971). *Theocritus: Select Poems*. London

Duckworth, G. E. (1969). *Vergil and Classical Hexameter Poetry*. Ann Arbor

Ebeling, H. (1963). *Lexicon Homericum*. repr. Hildesheim

Eliot, T. S. (1957). *On Poetry and Poets*. London

Ellwood-Smith, M. (1931). 'Aesop, a decayed celebrity', *PMLA* 46. 225–36

Empson, W. (1965). *Seven Types of Ambiguity*. 3rd edn. Harmondsworth

Enk, P. J. (1946). *Sex. Propertii Elegiarum Liber I*. Leiden

Ernout, A.–Robin, L. (1962). *Lucrèce De Rerum Natura*. 2nd edn. Paris

Fisher, J. M. (1969). 'Three textual points in Tibullus I i', *H* 97. 378–80
    (1970). 'The Structure of Tibullus' first elegy', *Latomus* 29. 766–73

Flach, D. (1967). *Das literarische Verhältnis von Horaz und Properz*. Giessen

Fontenrose, J. E. (1939). 'Apollo and Sol in the Latin Poets of the First Century B.C.', *TAPA* 70. 439–55

Fordyce, C. J. (1961). *Catullus*. Oxford

Foster, J. (1971). 'Horace, *Epistles* 1. 3. 25ff.', *Mnem.* 25. 303–6

Fowler, A. (1970). *Triumphal Forms. Structural Patterns in Elizabethan Poetry*. Cambridge

Fraenkel, E. (1950). *Aeschylus. Agamemnon*. Oxford
    (1957). *Horace*. Oxford
    (1962). Review of Fordyce (1961), *Gnomon* 34. 253–63

Friedländer, P. (1941). 'Pattern of Sound and Atomistic Theory in Lucretius', *AJP* 62. 16–34
    (1969). *Studien zur antiken Literatur und Kunst*. Berlin

Frye, N. (1957). *Anatomy of Criticism*. Princeton

Galinsky, K. (1969). 'The triumph theme in the Augustan elegy', *WS* 82. 75–107

Gardner, H. (1959). *The Business of Criticism*. Oxford

Garson, R. W. (1963). 'The Hylas Episode in Valerius Flaccus' Argonautica', *CQ* 13. 260–7

Giussani, C. (1921). *T. Lucreti Cari De Rerum Natura Libri Sex*. Vol. 2. 2nd edn. Turin

Gow, A. S. F. (1938). 'The Thirteenth *Idyll* of Theocritus', *CQ* 32. 10–17
    (1952). *Theocritus*. Cambridge

Gregory Smith, G. (1905). *The Poems of Robert Henryson*. Scottish Text Society 55. Edinburgh

Guthrie, W. K. C. (1950). *The Greeks and their Gods*. London

Hanslik, R. (1956). 'Tibull I i', *WS* 69. 297–303

Headlam W.–Knox, A. D. (1922). *Herodas. The Mimes and Fragments*. Cambridge

Henry, J. (1873). *Aeneidea*. Vol. 1. London–Edinburgh

Heyne, C. G.–Wagner, G. P. E. (1830–1). *P. Virgilius Maro*. 4th edn. Leipzig

Highbarger, E. L. (1935). 'The Pindaric Style of Horace', *TAPA* 66. 222–55

Huber, G. (1970). *Wortwiederholung in den Oden des Horaz.* Zürich

Hulton, A. O. (1972). '*Exegi monumentum.* Horace on his Poetry', *Latomus* 31. 497–502

Huxley, H. H. (1963). *Virgil. Georgics I and IV.* London

Jachmann, G. (1952). 'Das Vierte Ekloge Vergils', Annali della Scuola Normale Superiore di Pisa 21. 13–62

(1952a). 'Das Vierte Ekloge Vergils', Arbeitsgemeinschaft für Forschung des Landes Nordrhein-Westfalen 2. 37–62. Düsseldorf

Jocelyn, H. D. (1967). *The Tragedies of Ennius.* Cambridge

Kenney, E. J. (1970). 'Doctus Lucretius', *Mnem.* 23. 366–92

(1971). *Lucretius. De Rerum Natura Book III.* Cambridge

Kiessling, A.–Heinze, R. (1957). *Q. Horatius Flaccus. Satiren.* 6th edn. Zürich–Berlin

(1964). *Q. Horatius Flaccus. Oden und Epoden.* 11th edn. Zürich–Berlin

Klingner, F. (1950). *Q. Horati Flacci Opera.* 2nd edn. Leipzig

(1956). *Catulls Peleus-Epos.* Munich

(1961). *Römische Geisteswelt.* 4th edn. Hamburg–Munich

(1967). *Virgil.* Stuttgart

Korzeniewski, D. (1968). 'Monumentum regali situ pyramidum altius', *Mnem.* 21. 29–34

(1972). 'Exegi monumentum. Hor. carm. 3, 30 und die Topik der Grabgedichte', *Gymn.* 79. 380–8

Kranz, W. (1961). 'Sphragis, Ichform und Namensiegel als Eingangs- und Schlußmotiv antiker Dichtung', *RM* 104. 97–124.

Kroll, W. (1924). *Studien zum Verständnis der römischen Literatur.* Stuttgart

(1968). *C. Valerius Catullus.* 5th edn. Stuttgart

Kurfess, A. (1951). *Sibyllinische Weissagungen.* Tusculum

Lachmann, C. (1882). *In T. Lucreti Cari De Rerum Natura Libros Commentarius.* 4th edn. Berlin

Latham, R. E. (1951). *Lucretius on the Nature of the Universe.* Harmondsworth

Latte, K. (1960). *Römische Religionsgeschichte.* Munich

Lattimore, R. (1942). *Themes in Greek and Roman Epitaphs.* Illinois Studies in Language and Literature 28, Nos. 1–2. Urbana

Laumonier, P. (1914). *Pierre de Ronsard. Œuvres Complètes.* Vol. 2. Paris

Leich, G. (1910). *De Horatii in Saturis sermone ludibundo.* Weimar

Leishman, J. B. (1961). *Themes and Variations in Shakespeare's Sonnets.* London

Lindsell, A. (1936). 'Was Theocritus a Botanist?', *GR* 6. 78–93

Lloyd-Jones, H. (1963). 'The Seal of Posidippus', *JHS* 83. 75–99

(1965). 'A problem in the Tebtunis *Inachus*-fragment', *CR* 15. 241–3

Löfstedt, E. (1933). *Syntactica.* Vol. 2. Lund

Lovejoy, A. O. and Boas, G. (1935). *Primitivism and Related Ideas in Antiquity.* Baltimore

Maas, P. (1958). *Textual Criticism.* Oxford

(1962). *Greek Metre.* Oxford

McGann, M. J. (1969). *Studies in Horace's First Book of Epistles.* Collection Latomus 100. Brussels

MacLeane, A. J. (1853). *Q. Horatii Flacci Opera Omnia.* London

MacQueen, J. (1967). *Robert Henryson.* Oxford

Marouzeau, J. (1946). *Traité de Stylistique Latine*. Collection d'études latines 12. 2nd edn. Paris

Mayor, J. B.–Warde Fowler, W.–Conway, R. S. (1907). *Virgil's Messianic Eclogue*. London

Merguet, H. (1912). *Lexicon ʒu Vergilius*. Leipzig

Merkelbach, R. (1956). 'Der Wettgesang der Hirten', *RM* 99. 97–133

Merrill, W. A. (1905). *On the Influence of Lucretius upon Horace*. University of California Publications in Classical Philology 1. Berkeley

Mette, H. J. (1961). '"genus tenue" und "mensa tenuis" bei Horaz', *MH* 18. 136–9

Moore, J. L. (1891). 'Servius on the Tropes and Figures of Vergil', *AJP* 12. 267–92

Moritz, L. A. (1968). 'Some "central" thoughts on Horace's *Odes*', *CQ* 18. 116–31

Munro, H. A. J. (1873). *T. Lucreti Cari De Rerum Natura*. 3rd edn. Cambridge.

Newman, J. K. (1967). *Augustus and the New Poetry*. Collection Latomus 88. Brussels

Nilsson, N.-O. (1952). *Metrische Stildifferenʒen in den Satiren des Horaʒ*. Studia Latina Holmiensia 1. Uppsala

Nisbet, R. G. M.–Hubbard, M. (1970). *A Commentary on Horace: Odes 1*. Oxford

Norden, E. (1924). *Die Geburt des Kindes*. Leipzig

(1926). *Vergil. Aeneis VI*. 3rd edn. Leipzig

Ogilvie, R. M. (1965). *A Commentary on Livy Books 1–5*. Oxford

Otis, B. (1963). *Virgil. A Study in Civilized Poetry*. Oxford

Page, D. L. (1971). 'Poetry and Prose: Simonides, *P.M.G.* 531, Ibycus 298', *CR* 21. 317–18

Page, T. E. (1895). *Q. Horatii Flacci Carminum Libri IV. Epodon Liber*. 2nd edn. London

(1898). *P. Vergili Maronis Bucolica et Georgica*. London

Palmer, L. R. (1954). *The Latin Language*. London

Paratore, E. (1959). 'L'evoluzione della "sphragís" in Ovidio', Atti del Convegno Internazionale Ovidiano 1. 173–203. Rome

Pasquali, G. (1920). *Oraʒio lirico*. Florence

Pearce, T. E. V. (1966). 'The Enclosing Word-Order in the Latin Hexameter', *CQ* 16. 140–71, 298–320.

Pease, A. S. (1920–3). *M. Tulli Ciceronis De Divinatione*. Illinois Studies in Language and Literature 6 and 8. Urbana

(1935). *P. Vergili Maronis Aeneidos Liber Quartus*. Cambridge, Mass.

Perret, J. (1956). 'Ponctuation bucolique et structure verbale du quatrième pied', *REL* 34. 146–58

Pfeiffer, R. (1949). *Callimachus*. Vol. 1. Oxford

Platnauer, M. (1951). *Latin Elegiac Verse*. Cambridge

Plessis, F. (1924). *Q. Horati Flacci Carmina. Odes, Épodes et Chant Séculaire*. Paris

Pöschl, V. (1962). *The Art of Vergil*. Eng. trans. by G. Seligson. Ann Arbor

(1970). *Horaʒische Lyrik*. Heidelberg

Postgate, J. P. (1922). *Selections from Tibullus*. 2nd edn. London

(1924). *Tibulli aliorumque carminum libri tres*. 2nd edn. Oxford

(1926). *Select Elegies of Propertius*. 2nd edn. London
Press, J. (1955). *The Fire and the Fountain*. Oxford
Quinn, K. (1960). 'Syntactical ambiguity in Horace and Virgil', *AUMLA* 14. 36–46 (1970). *Catullus. The Poems*. London
Raven, D. S. (1965). *Latin Metre*. London
Reitzenstein, R. (1912). 'Noch einmal Tibulls erste Elegie', *H* 47. 60–116
Richter, W. (1957). *Vergil. Georgica*. Munich
Rudd, N. (1964). 'The style and the man', *Phoenix* 18. 216–31
    (1966). *The Satires of Horace*. Cambridge
Sallmann, K. (1972). 'Epische Szenen bei Lukrez', *CM* 29. 75–91
Sargeaunt, J. (1920). *Trees, Shrubs and Plants of Virgil*. Oxford
Schleiden, K. A. (1954). *F. G. Klopstock. Werke in einem Band*. Munich
Scullard, H. H. (1970). *From the Gracchi to Nero*. 3rd edn. London
Seel, O. (1972). *Verschlüsselte Gegenwart*. Stuttgart
Segal, C. (1968). 'Ancient Texts and Modern Criticism', *Arethusa* 1. 1–25
Skutsch, O. (1963). 'The Structure of the Propertian *Monobiblos*', *CP* 58. 238–9
    (1969). 'Symmetry and Sense in the *Eclogues*', *HSCP* 73. 153–69
Smith, K. F. (1971). *The Elegies of Albius Tibullus*. Repr. Darmstadt
Snell, B. (1953). *The Discovery of the Mind*. Eng. trans. by T. G. Rosenmeyer. Oxford
Solmsen, F. (1948). 'Propertius and Horace', *CP* 43. 105–9
    (1961). 'Propertius in his literary relations with Tibullus and Virgil', *Philol.* 105. 273–89
Spengel, L. (1856). *Rhetores Graeci*. Leipzig
Stanford, W. B. (1939). *Ambiguity in Greek Literature*. Oxford
Sturtevant, E. H. (1921). 'Word-ends and Pauses in the Hexameter', *AJP* 42. 289–308
Suerbaum, W. (1968). *Untersuchungen zur Selbstdarstellung älterer römischer Dichter*. Hildesheim
Syme, R. (1952). *The Roman Revolution*. 2nd edn. Oxford
Timpanaro, S. (1970). 'Alcuni casi controversi di tradizione indiretta', *Maia* 22 (n.s. 4). 351–9
Tränkle, H. (1960). *Die Sprachkunst des Properz*. Hermes Einzelschriften 15. Wiesbaden
van der Waerden, B. L. (1952). 'Das Große Jahr und die ewige Wiederkehr', *H* 80. 129–55
Versnel, H. (1970). *Triumphus*. Leiden
Watson, G. (1962). *The Literary Critics*. Harmondsworth
Wehrli, F. (1944). 'Horaz und Kallimachos', *MH* 1. 69–76
Weinstock, S. (1971). *Divus Julius*. Oxford
Wellek, R. and Warren, A. (1963). *Theory of Literature*. 3rd edn. Harmondsworth
West, D. (1967). *Reading Horace*. Edinburgh
    (1969). *The Imagery and Poetry of Lucretius*. Edinburgh
    (1973). 'Horace's Poetic Technique in the *Odes*' in Costa, C. D. N. (ed.). *Horace*. London
West, D. A. (1965). 'Lucretius 5, 312 and 5, 30', *H* 93. 496–502
West, M. L. (1966). *Hesiod. Theogony*. Oxford
    (1967). 'Prose in Simonides', *CR* 17. 133
    (1970). 'Melica', *CQ* 20. 205–15

Wetmore, M. N. (1911). *Index Verborum Vergilianus*. New Haven
Wigodsky, M. (1972). *Vergil and Early Latin Poetry*. Hermes Einzelschriften 24.
    Wiesbaden
Wilkinson, L. P. (1963). *Golden Latin Artistry*. Cambridge
  (1968). *Horace and his Lyric Poetry*. 2nd edn. Cambridge
  (1969). *The Georgics of Virgil*. Cambridge
  (1972). 'Ancient Literature and Modern Literary Criticism', *PCA* 69. 13–26
Willcock, M. M. (1964). 'Mythological Paradeigma in the *Iliad*', *CQ* 14. 141–54
Williams, G. (1968). *Tradition and Originality in Roman Poetry*. Oxford
  (1969). *The Third Book of Horace's 'Odes'*. Oxford
  (1972). *Horace*. Greece and Rome New Surveys in the Classics 6. Oxford
Williams, R. D. (1960). *P. Vergili Maronis Aeneidos Liber Quintus*. Oxford
  (1967). *Virgil*. Greece and Rome New Surveys in the Classics 1. Oxford
Wimmel, W. (1960). *Kallimachos in Rom*. Hermes Einzelschriften 16. Wiesbaden
Wirszubski, C. (1950). *Libertas as a Political Idea at Rome*. Cambridge
Witke, C. (1970). *Latin Satire*. Leiden
  (1972). 'Verbal Art in Catullus 31', *AJP* 93. 239–51

SELECT INDEXES

A. LITERARY INDEX

(*Note.* Heavy type indicates where the definition of a literary term may be found.)

B. INDEX LOCORUM